I can't take any more CRAP!

Best wishes

Robert MacGregor

I can't take any more CRAP!

Robert Macgregor

with cartoons by
Martin Wallace

Troubador Publishing
9 De Montfort Mews,
Leicester LE1 7FW, UK
Tel: (+44) 116 2555 9311
Email: books@troubador.co.uk
Web: www.troubador.co.uk

ISBN 10: 1-905886-11-X
ISBN 13: 978-1-905886-11-1

Cover illustration: Martin Wallace

Typesetting: Troubador Publishing Ltd, Leicester, UK
Printed in the UK by the Cromwell Press Ltd, Trowbridge, Wilts, UK

t² is an imprint of Troubador Publishing Ltd

For Jane,
without whom, nothing.

Contents

Contents

Introduction

Whatever gave you the idea that those grumpy old whingers on TV, no matter how charming, have a monopoly on the skips-full of crap which life seems intent on dumping on our heads?

Whatever age and whatever of the many sexes we belong to, there is stuff that drives us to distraction every day, and we watch, powerless again, while some new idiocy is jammed up our arses, or when we come across yet another phenomenon which seems to have no purpose other than to annoy or hurt us. The red mist rises, our hands jerk into fists, our faces contort into paroxysms of fury and our blood pressure rises to the level our GPs warned us about.

Most of the population over the age of two either does its nut every day or wishes it could. Grumpy? Grumpy does not even come close. Grumpy indicates a mild level of annoyance and irritation. This is about stuff which turns mild-mannered me into a murderous sore with a bare head. I am incandescently up to here about a shed-full of stuff. Is this book a rant? Of course it's a rant. In parts, it's a Super-Size rant. Mega-rant. It is designed to remind you how irritated you are, as if you really need reminding, by the life-garbage which lands on us every day. I want to hear you say, "Yes, YES, that pisses me off too", and I want you to be in a bad mood each time you put the book down, and go looking for a dog to bite.

The things I raise in this book range from those which merely irritate us, to those which do no more than drive us mad, to life-sapping soul-vampires, and they are deeply rooted, every one of them. They won't go away or dissolve with time, and the list grows daily, even in a world over-stuffed with every possible kind of intrusiveness where one would not think there would be room for them. Is this confined to stuff which drives me nuts; a personal profile of *my* disgust and dismay? Not entirely. Once I had had the idea, I talked to dozens of friends and acquaintances and two things happened. First, they agreed with the list I had put together. Then, they added to it. So this compendium is an otherwise unscientifically personal poll of stuff which, I am completely certain, hacks off a very large percentage of the populace.

But they do not all inspire similar level of annoyance. So I have invented a rating system for those I am about to list. Well, it's hardly a rating system the way it panned out. More a piss-take on ratings of all kinds. And I may not stick to that either. Depends. I may piss myself off with this rating business. The little sub-headings for each item represent the CRAP SCALE reading I have assigned to them.

Let's get something clear: There is nothing politically correct about this book. I will be at pains to avoid breaking any laws, but that's as far as my tolerance goes. I know for certain that you will find quite a lot of it with which you utterly disagree and even find offensive. Bad luck.

One other thing: I have come to the conclusion that some writers have special short-cuts on their keyboards, foul language for the quick production of. They can't produce a paragraph without using shit, fuck, cunt or bollocks, repeatedly. Fine. That's the way a great many people speak and it is common (very common) especially on TV. Example: "The thick of it", wonderful political satire and funny enough without the use of bad language, would leave the actors saying almost nothing if "fuck" were excised from the script. It's not that I object, not that I am a prude and, unless I can do some reincarnation and grow a couple of tits, not Mary Whitehouse either. It's just that I am bored to sobs with it. So, in this book, you won't find many, if any, needless fucks or other genitally- or scatalogically-inspired words. But I also recognised that I stood little chance of getting this book published without a minimum quota. So. Let's get most of this over and done with in one hit. If you come across any of these later, they will be in context, and essential to the plot, so don't write to me, please. Here they are:

fuck shit cunt bollocks fuck shit cunt bollocks fuck shit cunt bollocks
shit cunt bollocks fuck shit cunt bollocks fuck shit cunt bollocks fuck

Will that do? Good.

Introduction

P.S. I promised the minimum of lavatory humour, didn't I, so how do I explain the very title of this book?

Some years ago, Alan Coren wrots a book called *Golfing for cats*. It had nothing to do with golf or cats, but, he explained, those two words in the title went a long way towards attracting the attention of potential buyers and readers, because everyone loves either cats or golf. Same principle at work here; put "shit" or "crap" in the title, and in the anything-goes third millennium, it works. Sorry about that.

ABSURDITIES
Eleven out of ten on the New Crap Scale

The apparent increase in our standard of living stands in direct proportion to the absurd things which are there to make us pay for being better off.

- The manufacturers of motor cars make them capable of eye-watering speed, while the Government imposes "safety-cameras" to stop them going fast
- Digital clocks, watches and timers are "designed" for one-touch setting, while the last touch they ever feel is a hand throwing them out of the window because they don't work
- Teachers are absolutely not allowed to punish children by hitting them, on pain of prosecution, while children are allowed to kick teachers half to death, with impunity
- Somethings in City firms are paid chokingly huge bonuses for doing almost nothing, while people who do real work in real jobs can just about manage on sweatingly low incomes
- Television and radio give us hundreds of channels in what they describe as expansion of choice, while the number of programmes we actually want to watch or hear approaches zero
- Governments pour millions into education-education-education while the standards of literacy and numeracy drop steadily and growing numbers of first-year university students are found to be functionally illiterate
- The NHS expands like a balloon while Parkinson's Law of Disease makes it certain that the number of sick people grows

to fill any increase in NHS capacity, and does so even faster than the balloon can expand

- More and more people use more and more trains, while the train service steadily becomes less and less reliable, less and less comfortable, less and less pleasant as an experience
- Successful small-to-medium sized businesses do not feel that they have succeeded, really, until they have been bought out by huge conglomerates thereby becoming Big Businesses which then proceed to go spectacularly bust
- We are all being bored to sobs by politics, and turnouts at elections go steadily downwards, while more and more newspaper space and broadcast time are devoted to the inanities of politicians
- The *technical* ability to communicate with people anywhere and any time has reached unimagined heights, while the *actual* ability of people to speak to, and understand, one another is plummeting
- We have the ability to write letters and documents directly onto computer screens, and send them anywhere in the world without having to print them onto paper, while the increase in the use of paper has ballooned by an exponential factor.

And on, and on, and on. In a third-millennium-world where everyone is busting a gut to be more structured, more rational, more organised, more scientific and more logical, we seem to descending into disarray, chaos, irrationality, disorganisation, religio-superstition and illogicality. What clever old *homines sapientes* we are.

AIRPORTS

Three nervous breakdowns, terminal at five

No-one saw it coming. Not one of the designers of these ever bigger passenger aeroplanes appear to have given any serious thought as to how those millions of passengers were going to get onto them and off them again. I swear, those who thought about it at all took their inspiration from the cattle-yards in Chicago. As long as the passenger-cattle can be herded, processed and kept in order, *that's* all that matters.

And now, a Super Airbus is being made. It's called the A380. Air*bus?* It will hold 600 people or more. It is eight stories tall at the tail. It is, wingtip to wingtip, the distance from Bristol to Reading, or something. It is a flying block of flats, a whole flying suburb, not a *bus* of any kind. It frightens the living juice out of me. It's just not natural. And I was a pilot, once. I *love* 'planes.

But talk to the airlines and airports people about the awfulness of airports and air-travel and they say …

"For God's sake, we are now able to go from here to there in no time flat, so for the convenience of that, what's a few hours of abject misery? What does it matter if the flight takes two hours, but you have to check in three hours before it leaves, and spend most of that time standing in a queue which barely moves while slack-faced check-in staff treat you and several hundred like you with indifference? Why *should* you be upset if, after finally making it to the departure lounge, you are forced to sit (if you can find a seat) with your cheek much, *much* too close by the jowl of the fat and sweating flooze-mother whose uncontrollable children are running amok? Why should you be so damned ungrateful for the fact that the public address system keeps telling you *"whermm flerrrm sperm merm aherm geherrrrmm merm blerm?* Be grateful that it is telling you *anything.* We are doing our best, and we, the poor airport staff are in a constant state of suppressed hysterics at the thought of some crazed suicidal sub-human somewhere in this part of the cattle pen just aching in several senses of that word, to detonate the penis-bomb which our endless searches have failed to locate.

"And, yes, goddammit, we have to put on this endless charade of security checks to make you feel better, in the certain knowledge that if a crazed subhuman etc., etc., is determined enough to blow himself up and you/us with him, there is very little if anything we could do to stop him. Air travel is torture, but mercifully over fairly quickly. So stop moaning."

Robert MacGregor

To travel hopefully is better than arriving, as someone clumsily put it (I paraphrase)? Possibly, but if travelling by air involves, as it always does, the skull-crushing tedium and spine-twisting discomfort of airport check-in and check-out processes (see? *processes*, as in abattoir, or factory) then leave it out. Me? I go to France, by ferry, with my car, when I take a rare holiday on The Continent. But I did have to make a trip to the USA recently. By air. When I came back I killed three people in the car-park, set fire to a hospital and kicked anyone who came near me. Not guilty on the grounds of diminished responsibility; temporary insanity brought on by Terminal Four at Heathrow.

APHIDS
Ten cans of spray and nine effings

OK, God, what are they for? Food for ladybirds, huh? That's it? Meanwhile they cause me and thousands of others endless frustration and hassle and many, many pounds in spray stuff to keep them away. Good job, God.

ARCHERS, THE
Five million episodes, same plot, repeated at nauseam

I weigh thirteen stone bone dry, but the second I hear the mind-sapping tum-te-*tum*-te-tum-te-tum of that signature tune, I can levitate across a large room and hit the "off" button in three nanoseconds. I have to. If I hear any more than two seconds worth of this pap, my brain starts to melt.

What *is* it about this serial, which has been on the air since Marconi invented radio, that I cannot abide? Everything. Simpering, bellowing, sobbing but unbelievable characters, with shoe-horned agri-messages and plots so thick you couldn't stir them with a spade. How does this turgid load of cobblers manage to sustain any audience at all, never mind

4

the fixated thousands who continue to tune in daily? And then, as if a double daily dose of this aural castor oil is not enough, the BBC allows an "omnibus" version on a Sunday, lasting for hours. But if I don't listen to the Archoles, how do I know that the plots are, the people are, the messages are., etc., etc? Because every time I go anywhere, some brain-dead dough-head is talking about them as if they were really happening. Conversation in pubs or at dinner parties or wherever people gather are opened these days with "do you believe what Doris/Morris/Horace is up to now…?" I have frequently suggested that it was time they got a (real) life, but in a split second I can't see through the indignant spittle that has been sprayed at me.

You like the Archers? Never mind, keep taking the tablets. You'll be better soon.

AUSTRALIANS IN THE UK
Five tubes, no, three on the Rolf-Germaine scale

Fairly low rating, only because they redeem themselves, partially, by being a *completely* different kikapoo stew back home. In Britain, they drive me to distraction. They are brash, loud, arrogant, cocky know-alls, and they are *everywhere*. Big Australian bankers, TV people, medics, dentists. All ending every flat-accented phrase they utter with that infuriating upward inflection at the end? Until you want to deck them? They never stop telling us how wonderful things are in Australia where they have better weather, government, food, buildings, sportsmen, (yes, and women, *please*). In which case *what the hell are they doing here?* What they are doing here, of course, is trying to absorb a little history and culture, both of which are in short supply back home and where seriously clever-dick Aussies know that they have to come to Europe (Yerip) in order to rub off the rough edges and make something of themselves. As raucously as possible. And to make money. Loadsa money.

All of which is odd, really. Back in Aus, they are relaxed, courteous, funny, helpful, hospitable and delightful overall. They don't boast while they show off Australia's good stuff, and there's plenty of it.

They seldom talk about whingeing Poms except, of course, in the meeja led by "news"papers where the personnel are encouraged and paid to be objectionable, but that's the rule-proving exception and no different from anywhere else in the world.

Schizo. I think that the Aussies invented it.

BANGALORE
Four, but please to hold the line while I am trying for five

Global economy, yeah? English as the international language, yeah? Down with racism and snide remarks about our brothers across the seas, yeah? Give me a break.

Call-centres? I am not going there, because there is absolutely *nothing* I can add to the torrent of totally justified and aggravated bile which others have already poured on them and are still pouring. But call-centres in *Bangalore?* – open season on them as far as I am concerned, because they are enough to make me gird loins, brave airports and fly out there with mass GBH in mind.

The main reason for having people who can deal with customer complaints and problems is that customers have complaints and problems – or they want to buy something. For the most part, this is a very sensitive collection of human activities, where the clearest possible communication would seem to be a *sine qua non*, would it not? Essential to have people on the end of a phone who can communicate clearly with English-speaking customers, would you not agree? *In English.* In English which does not require us to say, every few seconds, "What? *What?* Sorry, could you say that again … please?"

Some months ago, while I was in the USA researching something or other I happened upon a TV documentary about call-centres in India, and about the "colleges" where local people *desperate* for jobs are trained to become call-centre operatives. It was cringe-making. That the students were keen and desperately anxious to pass muster was not in doubt. And they all seemed like very decent and hard-working people, mostly achingly young. What *was* in doubt though, was the superficiality of the training given to these poor blokes and bloke-esses, not one of

7

whom (obviously) had *ever* set foot in Britain nor was ever likely to. The alpha and omega of the courses boiled down to the fact that Indlish is the official language of India, and everyone with any education at all can speak it, after their fashion. Very useful when it comes to dealing with one's fellow country-people. Lingua franca, common heritage from the days of the Raj, all that. But listen to a conversation between someone in Chorlton-cum-Hardy and someone in Bangalore (or worse, take part in such a conversation) and it sounds like something out of an experiment in linguistic lunacy.

So, no, I am sorry, but as a consumer, customer, passenger, client, I hate having to struggle through a series of fractured sentences with people who are doing their best but whose best is very often not good enough. Call centres in India should be there to deal with the customers of Indian companies, period.

Why is this Bangalore Babel happening? Because our wonderful British Corporations have found a way to save money. They need to, of course, so they can stuff even more cash down the fat necks of their top people and "keep the shareholders happy". I wonder how happy the shareholders will be when, in due course, customers like me simply take their custom somewhere else, in droves, having had enough?

Now, having been very rude about India, may I redress the balance just a bit? Whatever problems we may have in dealing with call centres in Simla and similar, the people of India have one huge saving grace. Because Near-English is spoken by a great many people in India, Pakistan and Bangladesh, we British are allowed a peek, but only a peek, into the cultures and psyches of the people of that great subcontinent though a shared language. So, through that more-or-less common means of communication, and centuries of interaction we understand one another, just a bit. Contrast that with the Chinese, who are, and will remain, impenetrable, un-penetrated, inscrutable, incomprehensible and rather frightening. Can you imagine what life would be like if we had to deal with call centres in Shanghai or Hangshai? What? Oh, no. They are already training the people and building the sheds? Won't be long, then, before we are all saying "come back Bangalore, all is forgiven."

8

BANKS

Four unavoidable mistakes, but with compound interest

Are you surprised? Of *course* not. Of all the grudge-purchases I have to make, buying services from banks tops the list. Well, no, buying insurance policies does, actually. But banks are a very close second.

Can we do without them? In theory, of course we can, and some do, but in practice have you ever tried to obtain credit, or conduct almost any other transaction where the application form always asks "how long you have been with your present bank?" Do you understand why they ask this question? Neither do I. With every high-street bank anxiously and unctuously vying for your custom, promising everything but (or even including – I haven't checked recently) baths in asses' milk and virgins of any sex a go-go, how do you explain to Really Big Card plc that you have only been with your *"present"* bank for four and a half minutes, because they offered you a free penis/breast enlargement? And you may as well forget any dealings on a credit basis altogether if you tell them that the spare-room mattress does you very nicely, thank you, and you don't use a bank at all. So for that, among other, reasons stemming from our thrusting, progressive and technologically wa-hoo world, it seems we *have* to have bank accounts. Just as we have to grudge-buy fuel if we want to go anywhere in our cars.

I feel terribly sorry for the powerless and faceless bank personnel who have to apply to head-office in Helensburgh, Hammersmith or Harrogate for permission to take a leak, never mind authorise a loan. I loathe the stunning brass face with which these organisations pay their senior executives the kind of money in salaries, bonuses, share options and who knows what engorged expense accounts, which the rest of us could only hope to win in a lottery jackpot.

The reasoning behind their who-cares attitude is interesting. Public relations consultants (now *there's* a group who deserve all the abuse I can throw at them – see "Relations, Public") will have told their banking clients that their image is absolutely rock-bottom, down there with lawyers, politicians and estate agents and nothing they do could *possibly* make it either worse or better. "So, what the hell", they say," do what you like and stick up as many fingers as you like at the poor public, because they all have to have bank accounts, so they have to do business with you". But what about competition between banks? Pish and phooey. Given the stranglehold they have on us, the accounts they lose today will be balanced out by those they gain tomorrow, and so on round the high street. This isn't competition – it is thinly-veiled collusion endorsed by successive governments and does not even carry a health warning. And have you clocked the billions of pounds they are making in profits? *No* company, no matter how much their gaggingly overpaid managers whine about the bulk of their investors being your pension, funds should be making this much. A pox on all of them.

BASIL BRUSH
Four idiots and eight speakers (very loud)

No, not the TV puppet. Basil Brush is our family name for those mentally deficient and aurally damaged cretins who drive about in crappy small cars fitted with refrigerator-sized bass-box loudspeakers, with the windows open, and BOOM-BOOM issuing into the street. You get the Basil Brush connection now? Good.

The cretins in question are usually male, always spotty whatever their age; they are always wearing grimy t-shirts, wrap-around sunglasses whatever the weather or the state of the light; baseball-caps back-to-front and facial expressions somewhere between a sneer and constipation, and they tend to spit a lot. Female versions? Yes, occasionally, some of them slightly better turned out, slightly easier on the eye, but equally brain- and ear-damaged.

When I can, and frustratingly the situation does not arise very often, I pull up alongside the throbbing prick-mobile, wind down my window and give them Stockhausen or Bartok at full pelt. Or Harrison Birtwhistle. Nothing tuneful. No Mozart or Brahms. I keep a couple of truly horrible classical CD's in my car, reserved specifically and

exclusively for blasting the Basils. I am no more likely to listen to any of the above than you are. But when I do get the chance, the expression on the faces of the Basils is worth the wait.

BBC, THE

Retune to channel fourteen or ninety-seven, or ...

In a chequered career, I have stumbled in and out of the broadcasting world, and I mean world, including Britain, the USA, Canada and too many places elsewhere. There was a time, when I lived abroad, that I strutted about telling everyone that BBC radio and TV was the best in the world. Not any more. The overall standard of BBC broadcasting output has dropped every year, each year by a little more, until we now have no more than a quivering rump of quality in the form of bits of Radio Four, bits of the Overseas Service, bits of an occasional evening on BBC 2 – and everything else is a mighty turn-off, except for some sports coverage. The BBC has been working the British Culture Secretary from behind recently in this Year Of Charter Renewal, having her explain that the BBC's real task is to produce as much more garbage, in the form of "entertainment" as possible, as fast as possible. And to increase the licence tax (that's what it is; forget any of the euphemisms which are used to disguise it). The BBC will get away with it of course – again. The Octopus Empire Rules.

But here's the thing: many of the people who make the programmes are clever, hard-working, inventive, dedicated and thoroughly decent and some of them make good stuff, but they work for an organisation which raises arrogance and dog-in-the-manger nastiness to an art form, while lowering standards as fast as their huge salaries permit them. Examples: They squat on dozens and dozens of radio frequencies which they either do not use at all, or where they duplicate, triplicate and quadruplicate exactly the same programming output, and no-one is able to do anything about it. They receive almost three billion Pounds – count them, three *billion* – every year in TV licence tax (and growing). Writing and saying "three billion" is too easy. So, just to remind you, that is £3,000,000,000 which means about £54 per year for each man woman and child in Britain. Everyone barring a handful of the really elderly has to pay the licence tax, just for having a TV set in the front room, *on pain of prison*, and the BBC scurries about chasing maximum audiences as though their very existence depended on it. Hang on. That's just it, isn't it? This is literally true. Perhaps the brain-washed-and-then-blow-damaged politicians who are responsible for renewing the BBC charter every ten years or so, and who have to decide on the amount of licence tax we have to pay are being driven completely barking by accountants who insist on "value for money" – and value in this case means more, which means less.

While all this is reviewing was going on, and while the management of the BBC was showing everyone how prudent it is, and how cleverly it spends all that public money by sacking staff to cut costs, the Director General was given (gave himself?) a pay rise from his miserable £580,000 per year to £620,000, (mu-u-u-uch better) with others in senior management getting similar rises. The rationale, presented by the BBC Chairman Michael Grade, clearly outraged that anyone should question this, was that the BBC "lives in a marketplace and has to pay its top people what they would otherwise be able to command in the commercial sector". Such balls. If the Director general and the entire top echelon of the BBC – together with every single overpaid presenter such as Jonathan Woss and Chris "Gay" Moyles as well – were to resign en masse, there would be dozens, scores of equally competent and talented people gagging to take their places, and the BBC audiences would not be drastically affected. Repeat after me, Mr. Grade: no-one, not a single soul on Earth is worth £620,000 per year.

The so-called public service BBC insist, in a country where there is commercial broadcasting (which *does* have to maximise audiences or die) that it should be allowed to do the same thing – drag in ever greater audience numbers. Quality is an occasional by-product. Where that tyrannical old bastard John Reith laid down that the BBC should Inform, Entertain and Enlighten (and that was fair enough at the time) the "entertain" bit of that equation has taken on a dominance which he never intended. At a guess, the total output of the BBC is, these days, eighty-five percent entertainment. No wonder that challenging, interesting and controversial programming, with a few exceptions noteworthy by their sheer exception to the rule, is pushed down, dumbed down and (almost) out.

The BBC, without having to ask a by-your-leave of anyone, can create new radio and TV channels whenever they like, deliberately in order to compete with and actually destroy, if they possibly can, any other services which commercial (free) TV and radio would like to try their hand at. Commercial radio and TV entrepreneurs, by contrast, have to jump through the most strangulatory hoops put in their path by legislation and an extremely arrogant and capricious regulator if they want to start up a new terrestrial service. Fair? Not.

What's to be done? Simple enough. Let's not have any nonsense about privatising the *whole* of the BBC. Instead, force the BBC to relinquish BBC One TV and all the other TV channels it operates except for BBC 2. The same for all of its radio services except Radio Four and the Overseas Service. Create an open bid for the rest of the services which the BBC is forced to sell, and let public service broadcasting in the form of one national TV channel and two national radio channels remain, their heads held high as they produce the kind of quality which only properly funded, properly British, properly public service broadcasting can manage. You don't like the idea of Radio One, Two etc., etc., and most of TV being commercial? That's fine. Don't listen to them. Don't watch them. You know where the off- and retune-buttons are on your remote controls and radio sets, don't you?

BEER, ENGLISH (OR IS IT BRITISH?)
Three pints and an Indi-gestion

I swore a mighty oath the day I left university: I would never, ever again drink a drop of the God-awful dish-water that masquerades as beer in this country. I know, I know, I ought to be calling it "ale" as the real-ale anoraks do, to make a distinction between this stuff and what other people all over the world drink, including lagers, pilsners, etc., etc. For the moment, for beer read ale and vice versa.

What happened at Uni? I was the archetypically fund-free student, but social interaction between students simply does not happen without gallons of alcohol, and it has to be the cheapest. Therefore, pints of cheap wallop, which comes out of the beer-tap in a dirty yellow-brown warm stream – and if that sounds familiar, then deal with it. And not for nothing is it called "bitter".

At least six pints of this stuff would be bought in rounds for half a dozen or so friends (their eyes roaming the pub for anything even vaguely female, the beer being consumed in order to get up enough courage in order, possibly, to get it up later; the daily victory of optimism over yesterday's failure). Stomachs were bags of acid, mouths were shrivelled, and everything in between was a channel of bile.

And then came the predictable end-of-evening stagger to the nearby Indian, to gobble down a prawn curry. Why always a *prawn* curry? I can't remember, but I have no doubt that it had something to do with the fact that prawns are roughly identifiable and not even a curry house can produce prawn-shaped prawns from, well, whatever

14

they produce shapeless chunks of "lamb" or "chicken" from – and that prawn curry was as cheap as the beer.

I don't know how I lived through it all. It was hell back there, I tell you. But nothing on Earth will ever persuade me to allow British Warm to pass my lips again. I know that I will not have made a friend of you if you are a drinker of British beer. You love the stuff. You have spent a lifetime getting used it. Getting your suffering insides used to it. Have you made a will?

BELLS, CHURCH, GREEK, CHIMING
Four clappers and βοηκ αc, possibly

When I am able to listen to them during the day or even the early-ish evening, what could be more delightful? *Bing bong plang plang bong.* Lovely. But when this continues twenty fours out of every twenty four, I turn into Quasimodo. As do any light sleepers who need the nearest they can to dead silence in order to get a decent night's.

For the most part, church authorities in most places understand this, and they muffle or turn off the bells after 11.00 p.m., and start them bonging again at 7.00 a.m. They even do this in parts of France, where, on virtually all other matters, they simply do not give *merde* about you or anyone else. But in Greece, oh misery oh bags under the eyes. In the interests of research into the relative qualities of beach sand in the Aegean, or that's what I told my editor, I spent a week not long ago on the Greekly gorgeous island of Skopelos, and aside from the nightly assault on my shins by starved and very bold cats at harbour-side restaurants, I loved it. Except that I needed to go to bed for a week when I returned, as I did so in a state of near terminal exhaustion.

When we arrived in Greece, I threw open the shutters of the charming little town-house top-floor bedroom, and the view over the pretty roofs of the town was stunning in the evening sun. "Look, darling," I chirruped, "there's a pretty little church just over ... *BOINNNGGGG ... CLANNNNGGG ... WHANNNNG ...* there.

Oh, and ... *BONG BONG* ... and it appears to be chiming the hour. That's *BONG BONG BONG BONG BONG* ... nice. Then it clanged and bonged the half-hour. And every hour and half-hour after that unto eternity. The sound carried unobstructed and un-muffled directly into the bedroom, from the bells no more than fifty yards away.

Sleep was just, but only just, possible between midnight and 2.00 a.m., as we were able to doze fitfully through the single bongs of midnight-thirty, 1.00 a.m., and one-thirty. After that, the mounting cadences and frequency left us staring at the ceiling, our every nerve quivering in apprehension of the forthcoming *CLANGS*.

We tried drinking a lot of wine with dinner to knock ourselves out, but how much *retsina* can a non-Greek digestion handle? The only sleep we managed for any length of time was on the beach, during the day. Where I developed a grilled midriff from exposing it to the sun for a long, long time, comatose from exhaustion.

We asked residents how they lived through this. What bells? they wanted to know. I gave up.

BOMBERS, SUICIDE
Five hundred pounds of semtex and twenty virgins

Who understands these people? And I don't want anyone to get offended, please

Go to war, run at the enemy with your weapon pointed in the right direction, shouting *geronimo* or *allahu akbar* or whatever is your pleasure, die for your country or cause because you are on the receiving end of an enemy as indignant as you are, and you have my respect.

Tie a belt of high explosive round your body, walk into a crowded place and blow yourself and others to pieces, and you do not. Put parcels full of high explosive on buses and trains, leave them there and escape, and you are a coward. Do cowards have a passport to Valhalla or Paradise? Not in my book. And why does *any* version of God welcome murdering cowards of any description into His Heaven anyway? Because, as Christians would have it, Jesus pre-atoned for their sins. Pardon me if I deliver myself of a derisory snort.

As to the martyrdom stuff which poor demented young people are being sold, involving twenty-two virgins: what use is even one virgin when you have blown your penis to Pentonville and your testicles to Tooting, with the rest of you in bits across a large parking lot? Oh, I get it. Faith means that your God restores your body, genitalia and all, in Heaven. So virtual-you gets to enjoy twenty-two virtual virgins with your virtual wedding tackle. Good.

I have to confess that I never enjoyed *anything* with *any* virgin, but at least on the one occasion when I regrettably and unintentionally deflowered a young woman, it was for real, however little we both enjoyed it. And while I am thinking about this, what is the paradise-prize for those few *women* who turn themselves into bombs? Twenty-two male virtual-virgins? How exhausting. But of course in the Islamic culture, women are there to receive sex, not to give it. Male virgins are out. So what do female suicide bombers believe they have coming to them aside from a terminally loud noise and a final bright light? As for the idea that committing suicide (however nobly you think you have done so) gets you a fast-track to The Perfumed Garden, well. It this is such a brilliant thing, then why does half the Islamic world not commit suicide, immediately? Isn't the way to Paradise more likely to be signposted "be a good Muslim, and live the way of peace, just as Mohammed did"?

I think that those poor demented young people (male or female) who become suicide bombers are being sold a bill of goods by people who do not really understand the wise teachings of the Koran, and maybe at least some of the sobbing wives, children, mothers and fathers who are left behind in the real world to cope with the aftermath of their exploded loved-ones think so too. That's all I am saying.

I happen to believe that the idea of a life after death, whichever religion promotes it, is at best not proven and at worst a cruel fairy-story. Having said that, I fully understand that the idea of a place where one can meet one's departed loved ones and ancestors gives comfort to those who believe it, but I can't get *my* head around it. No offence intended to anyone or any faith, OK?

Let me clarify something; I have a great deal of sympathy for people whose lives have been crushed under the boot of The Empire. And which empire would that be? Well, any empire will do, but in the context of this item, let's nominate the American Empire, intent, as it is, on re-working the world in its own image. No-one can fight the US colonial military machine on equal terms in our bright new millennium, so those who feel the need to kick against the USDA or its allies tend to resort to guerrilla attacks, and that is not hard to understand. So, ambush soldiers with roadside bombs or AK47 crossfire, and that's war. (Soldiers ought to have enough information and equipment to defend themselves – that's what soldiering is about. I am always desperately sorry for the fasmilies of soldiers killed on active service, but being in harm's way comes with the territory, don't you think?)

But attack entirely innocent civilians, whether you die in the attempt or not, and you deserve everyone's condemnation. And just in case anyone thinks I am being one-sided about this, I also despise any uniformed army which gives itself the right to kill innocent civilians – and that includes the Israelis, the Sri Lankans, Indonesians, Burmese, Zimbabweans, Russians ... and ... you fill in the rest.

BT
Three but see pages nine, six, eight and twelve

Oh, dear. A privatised all-but-monopoly, and it acts that way. I desperately wanted Broadband in my area. I happen to live and work in a relatively out-of-the-way place, as writers tend to do. But this is not Outer Pimple at the far end of the Hebrides. Does not matter – I had to wait until BT decided when *it* was going to allow the local exchange to be converted for Broadband use. Everywhere else (Ireland, France, Kygrykakigystan) Broadband was available to everyone ages ago. But when it arrived in my area, BT could barely manage to provide me with the lowest speed broadband on the planet, despite the fact that I pay the same as everyone else whose service is up to eight times faster. Haven't got the technology to get you a decent speed, squire. So, live with it.

Something goes wrong with your phone line? A BT engineer will be along to sort it out. When? When he's ready. You don't like that? Bite me.

And the bills, the bills. Bad enough that the quarterly line-rental is cash-sappingly high and keeps going up, but then ... The total on page three? – refer to page five. Page five? – refer to pages seven and eight except for special services, refer to page six.

For special services, refer to page two. For explanation of page two, take a train to Leeds, walk to the BT Offices and torture someone.

OK, you have had enough, so you get a contract with some other cheap-rate call-provider and you don't have to pay BT for calls. Good. Unless you are willing to chance your arm with yet another fringe supplier, you *still* have to pay the BT line rental but your cheap-call provider gives you cheap calls to everything except mobiles, national rate calls such as 0870, calls to your mother except on Friday morning at 03.00 hrs, provided it is the second Friday in the month, the wind is in the East and you have not eaten carrots. *Then,* they are free. Meanwhile, if you dial 1334584467755890 before making a call, and provided it is after 18.05 hrs and before 06.27 hrs, or during weekends provided they are no less than three days on either side of Septuagesima Sunday, those calls are also free. So, in desperation, you go back to BT – but PAY YOUR BILL *NOW,* or we will cut things off you.

BUSINESS, BIG
Off the scale, with a bonus

You have already had the benefit of my mini-rant somewhere else about the payments made to Big Business People, so let's move on from there.

If bigger is always better in business, why does stuff like Big Enron and Big Arthur Andersen happen? Stuff like Big Shell having to confess that they are running out of places where they can suck oil out of the ground. Stuff like Big BT and Big Banks (we are still only with "B", please note). Stuff like huge motor manufacturers going tits-up after having to try to beg the Chinese – the *Chinese*! – for cash to bail them out, and the tits went north anyway. Stuff like The Big Dome, Big Railtrack, Big Swissair, Big TransWorld Airlines, massive banks all over Japan – all stuffed. Why, if bigger is better, is the NHS permanently unwell, the MOD permanently under attack, the Home Office on its way to the asylum, the Metropolitan Police under arrest, and all of the so-called main political parties (all of them large organisations) always losing votes?

The theory is that big organisations can benefit from "economies of scale" which is econo-speak for doing the same thing with fewer people, and sometimes doing a *lot* less with even fewer, so money can be saved, and profits can be bigger. None of them seem to have come across the eggs-in-one-basket phenomenon, so when things go wrong, they go *completely* wrong, leaving hundreds of desperate ex-employees, busted pension funds and dismal, deserted buildings. *Completely* wrong? No, not completely. The executives who rode the company into the dust always manage to leave with handsome severance packages, don't they? And with the comforting certainty that, the way things work in Britain, nothing succeeds like failure. Provided the old-boy connections are still in place and the departing bigwigs have not actually been caught doinking the Chairman's girlfriend, off they go to the next Big Company, ready willing and able to make a bullocks of that too.

BUZZ-BIKES
One brainless child at 2,000 decibels

On this, I could cheerfully kill. Given the overall levels of noise pollution in every village, town and city, anything that adds to the problem ought to be stamped on, hard and often. And in the case of these infuriating wheeled insects, they ought to be kicked over, beaten to a wreck and

taken to the dump. Complete with the idiot children who ride them.

I don't have a problem-in-principle with small-engined motorbikes which give young people a degree of freedom, but I have a *massive* problem with the manufacturers and sometimes the purchasers who piss about with the exhaust systems to the point where they make that god-awful howling scream. Why do they scream? Because the 50cc engines, which only work if revved up to fifty-thousand rpm, *will* make the most colossal row if they are barely- or un-silenced.

Things are bad enough in the UK. But have you had the miserable experience of staying overnight in a *centre-ville* hotel in France, Spain or Portugal? Or even, for that matter, out in the countryside but close to a road? It is part of the modern Continental culture that the daytime is for sleeping and working, and the night is for eating and rushing about. So out come the barely-pubescent with their bikes, and they ride them aimlessly in all directions at all hours. *Yeeeeeeow yeeeeeeow yeeeeeeow yeeeeeow bzzzzzzzzzzzzzzzzzzzzz* **yeeeeow.** All accompanied by endless demonstrations of the Doppler effect as the sound builds, climaxes and recedes only to be duplicated seconds later by the next one.

I have promised myself that the next time I come up behind one of these screeching menaces in my car, I will open the door and side-swipe it into the scenery. Like swatting a mosquito. One less, maybe.

CALLERS, COLD-
Three, five if I happen to be at home

I don't get too many door-steppers or cold-callers where I live. It's at the end of a long lane, and you really, *really* have to want, badly, to cold call on me. Just getting here is a schlep. But telephone cold-callers? Despite being registered with the BT "call preference" service? Oh, yes, and too often. My wife, not usually the most patient of souls, keeps reminding me that the telesales people are only doing their job. Only doing their job? These days, they use a predictive dialling system which calls endless numbers in succession until some poor jerk answers the phone within four or five rings.

And if you happen to be, say, having the first truly imperial bowel movement you have been able to manage for several days, you haul up your trousers to about knee-height, hobble to the phone and find that the calling-machine has rung off just as you get there.

I have a new trick. Which I pass on, with pleasure. If I pick up the phone, and someone from a telesales company asks for me or my wife, I say "Just hold a minute please, I'll get him/her". I then put the handset down next to the phone, without ringing off, and I go away. For about half an hour. That ties up their line, and possibly, just possibly, gets a red flag against my number.

CARDS, GREETING
Three or so, here we go

Greeting cards are full of crap

Composed by morons, worse than rap.
Why do we buy these ghastly rhymes?
The authors are committing crimes.
A sad indictment of our times,
They're far from witty or sublime.
They're even worse than pantomime.
Worse, even, than this rhyme of mine.

CARDS, ID, OBJECTIONS TO
Two eyes and a nose-job

What's so wrong with ID cards? Why do groups such as Liberty get their tripes in such a mince about this issue? I do not agree with the Blair and Whoever-Is-The-Home-Secretary-Today approach to this business, where they are trying to frighten us into believing that the best way to beat terrorists is to force people to carry ID cards. And then have to resort to a range of negative stuff which is damned hard to sell. No wonder so many people just don't get it, and when they do, they don't like it. It all sounds too police-state-like and big brother-ish in the 1984 sense. You can't sell that to people.

But have you tried recently to open a bank account, consult a lawyer, get a mortgage, or do anything involving a Government department? If so, you will know that you have to produce a wad of documentation to prove that you are who you claim to be, and that can involve passports, utility bills, driving licences, birth certificates etc. Before too long they will doubtless demand a urine, hair and blood sample, your inside-leg measurement and a doctor's certificate as to the state of your genitalia, digestion and mental acuity.

For a while, I lived in a country where, as a semi-permanent resident I *had* to equip myself with an ID card. No choice. But it was free. It contained, in one small booklet, about two inches by three and about the thickness of a … of a … not very thick, absolutely everything that anyone would need to know about me. Not what they *wanted* to know – just what they *needed* to know. There was *no* biometric trollocks about eyeballs and fingerprints.

It was designed with one thing in mind – help Citizen Joe and Joanne to satisfy bureaucrats and others that they were dealing with the right person. Period. And the country in question was up to its oxters in terrorists, insurgents and worse. ID cards were not issued in order to terrify terrorists, who can replicate anything they like, anyway. What self-respecting terrorist would be put off by having to equip himself with an ID card, no matter how sophisticated? And while on that subject, those demented Islamic fundamentalist murderers who killed people on the London tubes and bus were *British* citizens. Their ID cards would have been perfect in every way, no matter how intricate. And, by the way: the current British Government informs us that ID cards *might* become compulsory by 2010 or something, by which time Al Qu'aida and its British-recruited British lunatics will have had years to blow up pretty much anything they like. So much for ID cards as counter-terrorist items.

And let's drop the pretence, shall we, that we are terrified about an ID card central register which will give the Government a complete picture of who we are and everything about us. They know everything, already. There may not be a central register (although I happen to believe that there is one; it's just that no-one is telling) but the Government has instant access to a dozen or so sources anyway, which, put together, add up to you, me and our relatives in every detail, in colour. I don't understand the fuss. What I *do* understand is that this or any other Government has no moral right to force us to pay for ID cards. They should be compulsory, and free.

CATS, FAT
Five Jags, several brandies, and have a cigar, Sir John

I've touched on this before, and will doubtless do it again – like a scab I can't help picking.

There are some things in life's rich economic soup which can be

explained. However twisted and insane, there is a sort of logic to some of
the stuff which goes on in the business world. But when it comes to the
salaries, bonuses and perks given to Chief Executive Officers, Chairmen,
and other predators high in the corporate food chain, I am lost. My dear
old dad used to say, "How many chairs can you sit on at a time? How
many meals can you eat at a time?" He barely hid his blushing
embarrassment at the insistence of his Board of Directors on paying him
loadsa money, and tried to keep it under some kind of control. He could
not bear the thought of his receiving payment greater than some of his
employees, by a multiple which would choke a snake. He was no
socialist, believe me, but fat-cattery was simply not within his ability.

In contrast, look about you. Look, and rage at the amounts being
gulped down by the people who run our large businesses. And public

services. And football clubs. (I should have included this under "football" [see later] but now that it is on my mind, let me state that I have a lot of problems accepting that groups of people gathered together for the purpose of playing a game with an inflated sheep's bladder can be businesses, but such they have become.)

The reasons given for this *unspeakable* corporate hoggery is always the same: the apologists say that these outrageous amounts have to be paid because that is the only way to attract the absolutely top people who are needed to run our big businesses (sometimes into the ground). No, they don't say the last part of that, but when one looks at the number of fat-cats who have waddled their way out of utter disasters, gasping as they wheel barrow-loads of severance pay to the bank, it is painfully clear that there is no demonstrable connection between the amount of money paid to these monstrous moggies and the talent they bring to business.

It is completely out of hand, and much as I detest the idea of having to legislate this practice out of existence because I am fed up with the amount of legislation overall, I will, as soon as I become President, pass an Act which says that anyone can be paid anything at all, but all income to individuals will be taxed at 95% once the total package exceeds, say £100,000 per annum. Make that 99%. May as well bring some of that money back into the Treasury to pay for hospitals, schools, Olympic bids, don't you think? Do you suppose that this will cause fat-cat Chief Executives to resign en masse and leave the country in order to go looking for pussy-bix somewhere else? And if that happens, are we so poorly off in Britain that there will be no-one left to step into their sweaty shoes? You know and I know that this is a non-scenario. And you can set that to music.

CELEBRITY
Sky ten, Channel 4 nine – on pain of penalties

I detest the cult of celebrity which drives our public culture in Britain today. But if people want to make cults of themselves, that's their business, I say. I just wish they were forced to keep themselves to themselves. But then they would no longer be celebs of course. Vicious circular problem. Pity.

Look, if I do suddenly get rich and famous, I will become an instant hypocrite and bask in the public recognition. I *long* to be a celebrity. I am *outrageously* intelligent, witty, clever, articulate, good looking, easy-going, modest and did I mention clever? In contrast to almost all of those who currently enjoy celeb status, with their gutter-manners, mumbling Chimp-speak utterances, awful wives/husbands/currently-but-briefly-significant-others and kitch-for-brains, I could steal the show. Really I could. Straight onto the "A" list, whatever that is. But I can relax, and so can you. It ain't going to happen. I haven't actually got what it takes, whatever *that* is.

Human nature always has and always will throw up a fairly large handful of people who, for whatever reason, stand out from the crowd. Most of them erupt like unwelcome boils on the body public but some, of a totally different stripe, give us a good deal of second-hand pleasure because they have achieved something stunning, something we could never even dream about, something that takes colossal amounts of dedication, sacrifice, triumph over adversity, personal courage and superhuman strength of intellect, character or muscle – or all of the above.

Steve Redgrave, Kelly Holmes, Ellen MacArthur, Stephen Hawking, Ranulph Fiennes, Salman Rushdie, Jacqueline Du Pre. The celebrity past or present of any of those, I salute. They deserve their celebrity, sort of.

But – soap-opera "stars"? The purveyors of popular music of any kind? Film and TV actors who speak most prettily the lines written by others, but who have not a glimmer of character or personality of their own? Football players and managers, hawking, gobbing, swearing, flaunting the kind of wealth that ought to be illegal in the hands of such people? Clearly mad conductors of large orchestras, with even madder prima donnas and male leads? Business tyros, for the sake of mercy – Branson, Gates, Trump, Sugar? And politicians. Of all the people who deserve celebrity the least, these are the leaders of the celebrity cult-pack.

The self-satisfied mugs and voices of those who have achieved celebrity status assault us *wherever* we go, without the slightest chance of avoiding them unless we chuck it all in and go to a desert island. And even *there*, I just *know* it, David Beckham will appear in the surf one day with his latest stupid haircut (why he would want to draw attention to his *head*, of all things, I can't begin to imagine). They leer at us from newspapers and magazines, shout silently but insistently, fifty times life-size from billboards, strut all over the TV, mouth off on radio. No escape.

CHAVS
Free, nah, fawer, narmean?

There is a certain amount of debate as to the derivation of this word among those who really ought to get a life. Some say "Chatham Average" whatever the hell that is supposed to mean, because it originated in Chatham dockyards. Why? No idea. The most recently accepted derivation is the Gypsy word "chavvo" meaning "lad" or "bloke". Either way, I don't care. It just works as a wordette so perfectly to sum up the slobbering glottal yobs who mooch about in a crouch in every village, town and city in the land, their pubes and clefts exposed above filthy jeans where the crotch never makes it above the knee. Tins of something alcoholic clutched in claws which never see soap and water, never mind a nailbrush. Streams of drunken, shouted foul language spewing from snouted faces past drooping and fetid rollup-cigarettes, in between gobs of spittle fired in any direction they like. T-shirts designed (designed?) to shock, with *"masturbation is not a crime"* (oh, but in *your hands*, it is, mate, it is) emblazoned across pigeon chests, or stretched to splitting-point over mounds of hairy flaunted flab. Then there are the motorised versions – see boom boxes earlier on.

It's a British thing, this chav-ness. I don't know why. I suspect that it is part of the General Decline In Absolutely Everything In Britain. Go

to any European city, and their chav-equivalents are seldom seen and nameless. They are there, of course, usually associated in some way with football. But Britain is the world chav capital. Well done!

CHEESE, GOAT
Four peeooeys and a phwaw.

I suppose it was inevitable, all those thousands of years ago, that some schmuck would figure how to make cheese out of goats' milk. Worse, before he did that, he had to milk a goat. How it was possible, even for unwashable Neolithics, to get close enough even to think about milking this reeking ill-tempered beast is testament to mankind's eternal quest for the hard way to do things.

With the solitary exception of Feta, which is a mystery, goats-milk cheese reeks the way I imagine the armpit of an Albanian heavy-duty weight-lifter does. No matter what you do to, or with, it, goat-cheese stinks. It tastes the way it stinks too. Less Feta, than fetid.

Some years ago, I visited a cousin who lives high on the hog in Geneva, and you don't get much higher or hoggier than that. As a special treat, he took me to a restaurant perched on a small mountain overlooking the lake – a view of paradise. We ate some succulent lamb, garlicked just so, with heavenly veg, after a light fish something or other.

Then, announced my cousin, we were in for the house speciality, and with a flick of his elegant wrist he summoned a waiter who pushed across one of those domed trolleys which usually hide wonderful frenchified puds. When it hove to alongside our table, the waiter rolled back the dome, and my eyes rolled back in my head. It contained nothing but goat-milk cheeses, and the air vibrated with a stunning cloud of goat-gas, pent up for several hours under that dome and now released for the kill.

Insects for miles around fell to earth. Local airline flights were diverted. The wallpaper started to curl. My nose went into spasm, as did my throat, then I ... I don't remember anything more for a bit. When I came round, a few moments later, it was to see my cousin smiling the smile of perfect anticipation, his nose a-twitch with pleasure. I had to watch him eat his way through pounds of this excruciatingly awful stench. I have never fully recovered. But he's fine. Good of you to ask.

CIRCUSES INVOLVING ANIMAL "ACTS"
Four rings going on five pathetic seals

Do they still do circuses with animals? I only ask because I gave up going to the circus decades ago, when I realised how deeply I loathed the fact that twentieth-century mankind was taking exactly the same amount of pleasure out of animal-degradation as his eighteenth-century and earlier ancestors did out of bear-baiting, cock-fighting and similar bloody entertainments.

Also, I gave up pulling the wings off flies when I was about four, having received the most colossal clout about the ear from my outraged mother. Then another from my incensed father, when he learned that I had done something, anything, to cause my mother displeasure. Since then, I have had more respect for animals than for people, and using wild animals as entertainment puts us not only on a par with the above-mentioned baiters and cockers, but right down there with the blood-loving Romans.

I am reasonably comfortable with a circus which confines itself to clowns making arses of themselves and the audience, and to using domesticated four-legs like poodles to do cute tricks. But when it comes to elephants being made to sit up and beg, to lions and tigers perching on kiddie-stools, and more of the same with seals, then I get quite hot under the collar. I would hardly call myself an animal rights supporter, and most emphatically I am not a supporter of the evil filth who terrorise people in the name of animal rights, but if a circus with wild animal acts were to come anywhere near my neck of the woods, I would become an *instant* activist. On with the balaclava, stink-bombs tucked up the jumper, and off to cause maximum disruption. I would get into the ring by disguising myself as a clown, of course. No-one would give me a second thought.

CLEANERS, VACUUM
Three sucks and four bags full

What am I doing, doing vacuuming anyway? You may well ask. Fact is, it comes with the territory, because we have a deal. I do not paint things. Ever. I make a mess everywhere, so my wife will not allow it. So in return I shove a roaring vacuum cleaner about when asked to do so. Least I can do.

But oh, how I loathe the things. They come in two varieties. One is a crouching pig which has its sucking snout attached to a long trunk, and this makes it utterly impossible for the operator to move it anywhere without the pig crashing into an item of furniture. And the trunk never goes where you want it to go. These floor-hugging thugs are always of the split-bag type, meaning that the dust goes into paper bags which split as soon as you take them out, and the dust goes right

back onto the floor where it started.

The other is a priapic upright howling Dalek which always comes with seventeen filters in case the house-person is allergic to, well, to dust of course. Which was *everywhere* until the "cleaner" started to suck it up, and somehow, the allergy never strikes until the vacuum-cleaner gets involved. No, I don't understand either. The multiplicity of filters means that the motor, already big enough to power a truck, labours, moans and howls with the effort of sucking air through dozens of air-proof barrages. And increasingly, these upright things are bag-less, which means that the plastic container where the dust is finally pleased to have reached its destination has to be emptied every few yards or the machine's lights start to blink and/or a siren sounds and it stops, to suck no more. The upright types are too heavy to be lifted over such things as fringes on rugs, or the occasional nameless splodge of something which, if sucked into the works, causes instant thrombosis in both the machine and the operator.

And here's the worst bit. Whether they are crouching pigs or motorised indoor lawnmowers, all vacuum cleaners have to be plugged into the mains, and that means a length of cable which is (a) never long enough to get to the end of the room (b) always wrapping itself around table and human legs (c) always falling off the silly little flanges on which it is supposed to stay put until next time (d) carefully measured by some sadist at the factory so that the plug always dangles irritatingly and never tucks neatly away when you are done with it (e) always lies like a thin dead snake exactly where you want to push the cleaner. How come all these clever vacuum-boffins have not yet come up with a battery-driven model powerful enough to do a proper job? Yes, yes, I know there are some battery-driven models, but they are so wimpish that they could not suck the pollen off a pansy.

To make one powerful enough to do a proper job, the batteries would have to be too big? Too heavy? Not enough battery power available to drive the roaring motor? I don't believe this. If it is possible for manufacturers of pretty damned heavy power tools (some of which have to generate huge amounts of torque in order to drill holes in concrete) to make battery-driven models, surely it is also possible for something that has to do nothing but suck, because the motive power is provided by you and me, to be powered by rechargeable batteries?

But you will have to excuse me now. I have been summoned to vacuum the lawn.

CLOCKS, FORWARD AND BACK, PUTTING
Four o'clock or maybe three, or was it six?

Spring back, Fall sideways. Autumn upwards Spring downwards. Whatever. No matter how hard I try when the Day of Clock Madness rolls around again, I end up wondering where breakfast went and why there's no hot water. There's no hot water because I forgot to change the timer which controls the immersion heater, didn't I? And if I remembered, I changed it the wrong way.

I realise that there are other idiot cultures where people have elected to change from *this* kind of time to *that* kind of time, and I am not straying into Einsteinian mind-boggle here. But in bonkers Britain, we have BST and GMT, and I don't know of any other civilised place on earth where this, or its equivalent, happens *for so little reason*. Yes, it happens in America, and the French are at it as well (but then they would be, wouldn't they?). There is a dim memory from something I read that it all started in The War when we did stuff with double summer time, lightly whipped, with a hint of nutmeg, to confuse Nazi parachutists (*"OK, Heinie, synchronise watches, on my mark, eleven hundred hours … no, wait, that's yesterday, or was it tomorrow? What? It's noon in Norwich and midnight in Manchester? How can we be expected to conquer a degenerate race like the British when they don't even know what the swine time is?"*)

But, leaving parachutists dangling, what exactly do we gain with this back and forth nonsense twice a year? Longer summer evenings, they say. No, wrong, the summer evenings grow lighter or darker, earlier or later, with daily variations because the Earth's rotation causes the sun to set and rise slightly earlier or later. If you put the time forward by an hour in March, that is balanced out at the other end of the day with darker mornings. You can't have it both ways. There is some hannocks bruited about that longer evenings make it safer for kiddiewinkles to walk back from school (even though ninety percent of them are taken there and back in large 4X4's) but as to getting there – well, that's different, isn't it? Or is there something I *really* do not understand?

And then there's the tartan toshocks about Scots farmers who need the time-change so that they can feed or milk or prod or whatever else they do to their cows in time to get back into their wee crofts and watch the soup-opera on JOCK-TV because, you see, cows are *terrible* at telling the time no matter *how* many clocks you put in the barn, so they insist on being attended to according to where the sun is in the sky. So, if this theory is right, everyone south of Berwick-on-Tweed has to do the clock-dance, to keep those north of the Tweed happy.

And now, as if things are not bad enough, some seriously synapse-challenged member of the House of Lords, still living in 1942 with not enough to do, is suggesting that we conduct an experiment to bring back *double* summer time, so that the mad clock dance gets even madder. Take your partners ...

Two steps forward, to and fro,
Double your clocks and away we go.

And ... do-si-do your cowshed,
Watch where you put your feet.
All together now, backwards,
Lunacy complete

But don't let's fret, those of us who live down south. The European Union will issue a directive before too long, and that will be that. We will all be on the same time, all the time, from Gdansk to Galway. About time too.

COMMERCIALS
One or two and have one free

I have to be a bit careful, here. I earned some of my living, once upon a time, writing scripts for radio and TV commercials before I went temporarily insane. But I'm better now. I appreciate and respect some of the purveyors of commercial broadcasting, only because they give us something other than the arrogant BBC, which lives in a world where it believes that advertising does not exist, or if it does, it should not be touched, and if it *has* to be touched, one should wash one's mind out *immediately*.

But, dearie me, some commercial radio and TV does try my

patience. And I wonder what's going through the loosely-connected minds of the unisex advertising agency bimbettes *and* the brand-managers in their client companies when they come up with the rubbish they do. I have to make special mention here of TV advertisements for cars, to which I award the All-comers Farting Cuckoo Cup and Gong.

I've always believed that the purpose of advertising is to turn the consumer towards the brand of goods or the service being advertised (that is the literal meaning of "advertise", by the way) and that far too many advertising people actually *enjoy* swimming in the pools of nonsense they "create" when they start on airy-fairy rubbish which they justify as "creating long-term brand-awareness". Bullshit, as I say. The real and proper purpose of advertising is to get people to *do* something involving the exchange of cash, and to do it as soon as possible. Anything else is a waste of the advertisers' money.

Actually, I have to salute the advertising industry. They have been able to con cosmic amounts of money out of businesspeople who ought to know better, by covering anyone within a fifty-metre radius in truly epic jargon, backed up, they would have us believe, by research foc-us groups, concept testing, trial exposure and whole lot of other research-cobblers besides. And then, having produced a sensationally bad commercial at a cost of shed-loads of money, they *have* to milk that commercial until it begs for mercy, and so do we. A million pounds a throw is not unusual for producing a TV ad these days. So we cry out in pain at the umpteenth time we have to see the awful thing. Radio is not much better at it, either. Far too many commercial radio people only know three words. Repetition, Repetition, Repetition. Bored, bored, bored.

But whether it's TV or radio, it gets so bad that I take a deliberate policy decision when I'm thinking about buying something. If one of the advertising campaigns has irritated me to screaming point with its inane and repeated-ad-nauseam commercials, I strike that product off my list. At least I feel that I am getting a tiny little bit of my own back.

Robert MacGregor

CORRUPTION, BRITISH, GENTEEL
Two knights, a peer and a gong

We don't do lot of obvious high-level brown-envelope backhanders in Britain. Oh, it *happens*, and too much, but *obvious* British corruption takes a different form from the kind one knows about in Italy or Russia, the 'States or everywhere in the Middle East, Africa and the rest of the Americas.

Here's the starting point: we are regulated in this country to an extent which ought to have us out on the street baying for blood. But that would be bad form and altogether too emotionally European, so we mutter into our warm pints of beer and go home for a nice cup of tea. And who does the regulating? Why, a massed phalanx of quangos and Government agencies and departments, bestriding the land from Anglesea to Anglia, Kintyre to Kent. Do you know how many quangos are currently leaping about the British towns, cities and countryside? Go on, have a guess. No? Five hundred and twenty nine. That was yesterday. Today? A whole lot more. Plenty of room for Prime Ministerial and other patronage to reward the great and the good for being great and good, and being *especially* great and very, *very* good by supporting the Prime Minister's political party. These quangos have to be manned and womanned, and you would not *believe* the eye-gouging and scratching that goes on when the chair of a quango is up for grabs. And it is worth fighting for, because with the post comes a shocking amount of power and the near-certainty of a knighthood if the new appointee is a mere citizen, and a peerage if the new chairman/person is already booted and spurred.

Do you have any idea how far people in Britain will go to get themselves a title via appointment to a quango or similar? There are hordes of them, *herds* of them gagging for it, ready to do anything to change their lives from grubbing about in the commonery to being addressed as Sir, Dame, Lord or Lady, with all the forelock-tugging that goes with it – as I will be explaining when we get to "H" for "Honours". And more about quangos under "Q".

But that's just a part of our ever-so-British, ever-so-subtle form of corruption. Not much actual cash changes hands under the table, as I have intimated (or so I like to believe and I could be horribly wrong) but the right person in the right place at the right time has his/her life changed by the acquisition of a title and a path to power which can lead to that cash. However, in a strange reversal of that normal flow, money *does* come into it, where the chairman of a body is directly in the gift of a Minister, Prime or other, and where the wannabe chairperson (oh, bugger it, chairman), already as rich as Croesus, has slid a large wad of cash in the general direction of the political party either currently in power or thought to be close to it. So, if you are already someone rich, and you want a title, you pay. If you are a bit short, financially speaking, and you manage to parlay yourself into a quango chair somewhere, you get paid, then you get a title anyway. Good, eh?

This whole wretched business bedevils Britain as effectively as a large leg-iron clamped to the national leg. Is that it? Does British genteel corruption end there? No, no. There is the "sound fellow" principle at work as well, which goes like this: two or more chaps (of any sex) will meet at Eton, Sandhurst, Oxbridge, or any one of the many seedbeds of English-British special-needs under-development. They make a pact. If one of them is ever asked about any of the others (in a job-interview or quango-appointment situation for example), the response, however expressed, is "sound fellow". Even if the fellow in question is as thick as a yard of planks, is clearly known to be fond of a little light S&M on the side and is doinking his dog. If Sir Forstup Bottomley is asked about his old Etonian chum "Biggie" Dickson-Tongueue, he has to say the right things, because he depends on the vice being versa-ed at some future date. How do you think it would otherwise be possible for so many abject top-person failures to bounce from one chair to another, leaving trails of financial and political disaster in their wakes? It's the British way.

CURRENCY, FOREIGN
Four kopecs and a centavo, but we do not give change

Of course, if we had the sense we were born with, I would not be able to say anything much about this, because all of us in Europe would be dealing in Euros and that, mercifully, would be that. But I really do think that the name "Euro" is crap – it not only sounds more than vaguely like a medical condition not entirely un-associated with the passing of water, but is pronounced differently according to where it is in use. Yew-ro. Oi-ro. Eh-oo-ro. Ay-you-ro. And more. Just wait until the Turks get their throats around it. Why could the Europrats not have done the obvious thing and called it, oh, I don't know, ask some "creative" in the advertising world, especially those who have to think up names for cars. They would have some up with *something* appropriate, Europe-wide, short and *pronounced the same way* everywhere. What are you telling me? Euro *was* thought up by an ad agency? Oh, well.

But we remain fiercely, proudly British, don't we? And we cling to the Pound like people tipped off a jetty, holding onto floating bits and pieces, in the name of sovereignty or some such dead idea. Then, by the million, we clamber aboard CattleTruck Air and fly to every part of Europe, where we boil our brains trying to deal with how-many Euros to the Pound today, Doris? And if that is not bad enough, and if we are of the adventurous kind, how many dollars, how many baht, roubles, yen, pesos, lira, dinars, krone, rupees and ringgit?

Can't be helped. I have to travel a fair amount, and I have a drawer full of very odd looking coins worth absolutely nothing put together. Also some notes, more of the same.

I don't really like the idea of any more Americanisation. But it would be *ever* so convenient if we could have one international currency. The dollar will do. I know you don't like that, and nor do I, but as the dollar is the international currency in all but name, what the hell? In fact, going to the USA itself is a pleasure in this context – it is a very large country but there is just one currency to deal with, from one end to the far distant other. I suppose, when we do come to our senses in Britain one day, I will be able to say more or less the same thing about European travel and I will not have to pay a silly amount of money to change my pounds into Euros and back again, thus stuffing even more profit down the necks of the bankers.

"DAYS", VALENTINE'S AND OTHER
Ten stupid cards and eight bankruptcies

And all the other "Cash-days" before and after. Mothers'. Fathers'. Uncles'. Aunts'. Neighbours'. Any others which the thrice-cursed rapacious reptilian retail industry invents. Doomsday. Boomsday, now on the drawing board, to celebrate the day the second lot of London bombs did *not* go off, just like Guy Fawkes Day. All accompanied by cards, chocolates, flowers, presents. I am working on Bah Humbug Day, which is the fourth Sunday after Curmudgeon Day, and a month before Spleen Sunday.

But, really. Haven't you had enough of this commercialised nonsense? Haven't you got at least a fraction of common sense, enough to call a skidding halt to this pocket-plundering banditry and to stop buying stuff to "celebrate" days which have little real meaning in any religion or history and have been invented by fat marketing people? (Americans, probably, although I could not be certain).

So you want to mark the day for someone you care about. Fine, noble. Write them a letter, with your tongue sticking out of the side of your mouth. A *proper* letter, using a pen and paper, *and* an envelope *and* a stamp. Give them something of yourself and your time, rather than taking the easy way out with e-mails, a trip to a card-sharp's card shop, and a sigh of relief. Can't be arsed? Then don't bother at all, because obviously the sentiment is as hollow as that stupid coffee mug you bought them.

What about Christmas and Easter? Go ahead. Do what you have to do, in the knowledge that these festivals have at least *some* legitimacy in religion or tradition. And I might just allow you Mothering Sunday because that too has some pedigree. But that's it. Stop wasting money. Just say "no".

Robert MacGregor

DEODORANTS, LAVATORY

Yugh, bleah, two and if I can get another breath, three ...

Depending on the virulence of the flora in the gut, I am told, the odour of human excreta ranges from slightly unpleasant to downright evil. I don't want to go into too much biological detail here, but it seems that some members of my family have extremely active flora, and the results are, see above. So either the rest of the family puts up with farmyard odour-odium until the air returns to breathability, or some form of toilet deodoriser has to be used. We have tried everything. Stuff that is squirted from an aerosol, or sits on a shelf looking sullen, or crouches in the lavatory pan to be doused with water which is supposed to release its vapours. The aromas and essences they disgorge range from boiled sweets to rotting pine, and each one is worse than the one before. Gagging, cloying, ridiculously long-lasting clouds of the stuff seep from the lavatory through closed doors and windows and leave the rest of the house stinking of wilted flowers long past their compost-by date.

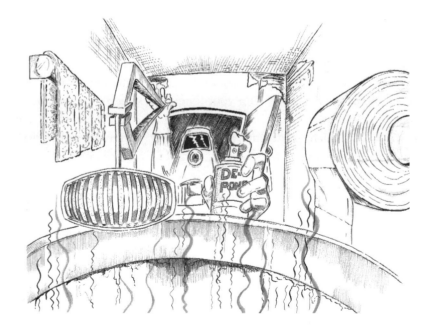

Walk along a supermarket shelf, read the names on the aerosol cans, and you know that the makers of this stuff are taking the, um, urine out of us. How anyone could believe that these ghastly affronts to the olfactory system are better than the odours they are supposed to eliminate, I don't know. We have even tried a brand whose research boffins *seemed* to have understood the problem, so they came up with an odour-destroyer which, they claim, is itself odourless. Cleans the air without polluting it. Utter smellocks. It emphatically *does* have its own aroma, which is somewhere between a hospital disinfectant and another kind of hospital disinfectant. Peeeeeyoooo.

And then there's the match-trick. After completing one's business, strike a match, allow it to burn for a few seconds, blow it out and … ah, Jaysus. Railway station lav's. Latrines at army boot-camp. The loos in clubs for very old men. Boarding school. Oh, yes, boarding school. Remember, and your eyes will water.

I am thinking of turning back the clock and building a small outhouse at the end of the garden. Complete with old newspapers torn into strips. Or little boxes of Bronco anus-sandpaper. Remember that? And just fresh air blowing through the open window (no glass).

DESIGNERS
Three mistakes, very cleverly drawn, and two ballsups

OK – stuff *has* to be designed, however roughly. Nothing man-made simply arrives fully formed out of the air. But there are times when I have wondered if the designers ever actually *use* the stuff they have designed. An example: Not long ago, I borrowed a large, and I mean *very* large American mobile home with which to make a lightning tour of parts of the US South West. I had talked a Mobile Home Rental Company out of one of its vehicles and we set off, partner reluctantly in tow or more correctly somewhere about two city blocks back in the bowels of the motoring mammoth given with endearing naïveté into my charge.

Eventually, after adventures with surly Navaho teenagers and vehicle electrics which caused small but entertaining fires in unreachable places we reached the Proper American South West in and around Monument Valley. The lumbering motor-home lurched onto the rutted road for barely ten yards before every cupboard snapped open, and vomited every cup, plate, knife, fork, spoon, can, bottle, jar and packet onto the floor in a cascade which took half a day to clean up. The cupboards had been designed for a vehicle which never leaves the flat tar road – despite lots of reassurances from the rental company that this particular rolling home was designed for use "anywheres". When I called them, I got the usual. "Garsh, we never had anyone complain about this ba-fore."

Stacking chairs which cause almost instant backache. Corkscrews which don't. Flatpack furniture. Computers where the plugs are at the back, against the wall, invisible and unreachable. TV remotes and mobile phones where the operating buttons are made exclusively for very small children's fingers. Almost all car dashboards and instruments. Lawnmowers which clog up with grass if the grass being mowed is more than 2mm long, having been "tested" exclusively on the already immaculate and bone-dry greensward of Castle Hoverfly in Homeshire. Computer keyboards which assume that everyone can touch-type, so the keys are too close together and thius is the sory of thinhg that happennns allthe tinme wnewhn I am tyring to type too fasy by the hunt yann pecx methogs, thr onlu ome I knoe. Thirteen amp plugs, wiring thereof. All toilet roll holders. Clingwrap, which clings to itself (which you do not require it to do) and absolutely not to plastic, out of which most fridge-type containers are made. On and on. Designed? Not really.

DIETS

Three GI's, two Atkins, nine fat-frees, but I can't get no …

You don't try diets. Diets try you.

Because I have spent most of a lifetime sucking in my stomach in order to deflate the spare tyre which my body stupidly insists I need in case … I have no idea why, I have driven all members of my family close to fratricide, patricide and husbandicide with first this miracle diet, then that. Why have I had this problem for so long? My mother is to blame, of course. From the moment she tore the tit out of my mouth and started me on solids, she fed me everything in sight and most of it was porridge, potato, bread, sugar, and more porridge. My little body created fat cells all over the place, the better to store spare tyres, extra comfy arse-pillows, fat ears.

But since then, I have turned myself yellow by OD-ing on carrots. I have made myself drunk and sick by eating nothing but grapes and drinking nothing but wine for a week. Bananas ditto, but without the comfort of getting drunk. I have eaten raw food including liver and other organs until I howled at the moon. I have communed with Hay, Atkins, and several other American (it's always American) diet-shamans to no avail.

Until I discovered something amazing. I really ought to write a book about it, call myself Wilbur O'Tool Deforested the Third, get it published in the USA, and make a fortune. Trouble is, it would be a very short book, because it would carry only one simple message. *EAT LESS FOOD, YOU FLABBY JACKASS*. That's *it*. I realised that every fad-diet that ever existed is intended to make you do exactly that, viz., eat less, because the diet is so God-awful that you just don't want to eat much of what is suggested. But we are all greedy for instant and constant gratification using any orifice that happens to be handy, and where food and mouths are concerned, we are capable of eating a horse and all its hay at a sitting. Then we decide we must loose weight, but we need some sort of crutch to lean on so that we feel suffering in the dietary cause. Hence all the diet books. We can't simply stop eating, just like that. We have to be bullied, pushed and shoved, by some idiot who has invented the latest stupid diet-fad. The books and fads help us, we think, to identify the cause of our over-eating and, miraculously, offer a cure. The fact that the *real* cause was our greed in the first place is not to be admitted. It had to be somebody's *fault*. (It was. Ours.)

I checked with the medical profession; anyone who thinks that their fatness is caused by glands malfunctioning or some other mysterious bodily dysfunction is delusional. Obesity can cause glands to pack up, not vice-versa.

I hate being hungry (the smallest hunger pang will sleep-walk me to the kitchen in search of, well, anything, really). So, having decided that I would say goodbye forever to diets, but anxious to lose some midriff pounds I did not need, I laid in a store of dried fruit, nuts and similar, and I nibble/graze small bits at a time. Overall, I am eating a lot less. My spare tyre is deflating, fast. I do not feel hungry between meals. All without reading any daft, boring, dangerous and expensive diet books. And without eating/drinking sawdust or wallpaper paste got up as "diet-foods". As I walk past any one of a dozen flab-laden two-arse three-belly four-chin flubs as they waddle down the street with their thighs fighting each other for which goes first, I mutter, very softly "Eat less food, you flabby jackass". Much as I would like to scream it into their ears.

DOGSHIT
Ten turds and a skid

I love dogs, but dogshit is a load of crap. There isn't another substance like it. It contains *adhesotricrapulate caninostenchine*, so that it sticks to anything, *anything,* not just blankets, like nothing else on Earth and stinks massively worse when smeared by your stepping into it, than it did in a pile. Strange, that. It doesn't permit of complete removal either. No matter how assiduously you try to clean those bedogshat shoes, there's always a square millimetre or three of the stuff clinging to a lace or tread somewhere, so the miasma lingers on. Now, look. As I said, I love dogs. Most dogs. Alright, some dogs. British dogs are mostly OK, whereas French dogs are all insouciantly enthusiastic pavement-shitter-critters, actively encouraged by their owners to cover as much of France as possible with their excreta. This is especially so in Paris, especially in the path of the visiting *salauds Anglais*, as revenge for our having had the cheek to rescue their grandparents and then their parents from the

Germans once each, within thirty years.

But far too many British dogs' owners also conspire to cover the country in doggypoop with essential help from their mutts. And they do so without fear of getting caught even where it's illegal. Have you ever seen a Dogshit Warden leap out from behind a tree to give a Notice of Impending Prosecution to the be-Gucci-ed prat with a poodle straining at the lead on one end, while straining at the other to coil one down? No. Now I know that one is supposed to carry little plastic bags, doggy bowel product for the picking up of. With a deft twist of the wrist you turn the bag inside out and then … you are supposed to reach down and grab the pile of still-hot, steaming turds, stop to barf into the gutter at the sheer horror of having actually *done* that, and then *carry it around.* Yaaaaargh!

DRIVERS, BIMBETTE
650cc at 100 mph

Because I am determined not to stuff money down the neck of any police force or other authority, I tend to drive on motorways, double-carriageways and anywhere else for that matter at the speed of the traffic around me, and with a very wary eye out for flashing jam-sandwiches and what some arse has been pleased to call "safety cameras".

With heart-stopping regularity, I find myself being overtaken as I pootle along at 71 mph, by a ten-year-old Metro or Fiesta going so fast that I wonder if I have inadvertently stopped. At the wheel, you can almost bet on it, is a *very* young girl, throttling the steering wheel and stamping on the throttle, with the engine howling in agony as she red-lines it, pushing the poor thing to its limits and beyond. I suppose that modern engines are built to take this kind of high-rev punishment, as are the other moving parts, so the chances of meltdown and puffs of blue smoke are relatively slim, unfortunately. When the bimbette-racers *do* strand themselves and their terminally exhausted little cars by Motorway-side, no discomfort is more richly deserved. But here's a thing:

If a blow-out or a bearing-seizure were to happen, most of them would have not the *slightest* clue as to how to control the vehicle, and the most likely scenario in that event would be that their crippled car would jump over the crash barrier onto its roof and into the oncoming lane, possibly into my path. The driver would have let go her stranglehold on the steering wheel in order to wave her hands about in panicked incompetence, and/or cover her face, and that would be that. Straight into the scenery. Or into me.

But why do I single out girls ? Isn't it true that young men of about the same age would be just as incompetent and just as likely to cause motoring mayhem? Actually, no. For whatever reason, even the youngest of men seem to have a minimum of hard-wired ability to handle mechanical upset with *some* degree of competence, and can wrestle the most recalcitrant of wounded motors into a semblance of a safe landing. By no means always, but more often than their female counterparts.

Some weeks ago, I was overtaken by a Fiat Poopo or something, doing ninety at least. The driver, not a day over eighteen at a guess, had a cigarette dangling from her pouting mouth, a mobile phone clapped to her ear, and a pile of baggage visibly teetering this way and that on the passenger-seat. A few miles further along, I saw her again. Her car was upside down in the shrubbery, and a very different shape from what it had once been. The bimbette driver was sitting by the roadside, being swabbed down by a paramedic.

I stopped to enquire. Blow-out at high speed. Very high speed. Set a new world record for the number of times a vehicle can roll. Miraculous escape. Q.E.D.

EATING HABITS, JAPANESE
Four, gorge rising to five

I love sushi and sashimi. Heavenly food and *s-o-o-o-o* healthy.

I can't get Japanese food anywhere near the place where I have chosen to live, so when I go to London I get off the train and go with a surprising turn of speed straight to a sushi place having arranged a second mortgage, using my mobile, en route. By Hirohito, the stuff is so bruddy expensive. But wonderful. I leave, an hour later, and spend a lot of time horizontal from the waist up, through excessive bowing to everyone. My eyes go just slightly slanty, and I bump into the people because I have had an irresistible urge to put on my spectacles. Which I usually wear only for reading. I say "Ah, soh" a lot for the rest of the day. *That* is how much sashimi I have eaten.

But straight sushi and sashimi is where I draw the line. I will eat any amount of raw fish provided it comes from a fish-shaped fish and not some weird thing with tentacles all over the place and googly eyes. Yergh.

The Japanese draw no lines. I went to a proper Japanese restaurant once, in Japan. I looked forward to mountains of sushi, piles of tempura, rice by the cubic metre and great swishing buckets of sake. I got all that, but one of my dining companions mysteriously stopped in a corner of the restaurant en route to the place on the floor where we crouched, lolled and squatted to eat. At a table, yes, but three inches off the floor. Back-ache Central. I watched as he and a waiter had an animated discussion involving a lot of pointing and bowing. A little while later, as I was getting ready to go into super-power-eat mode, the waiter appeared with a fish on a plate and placed it reverently before the man who had ordered it. The fish had been cleaned of scales and

any bits of the sea. It was, however, *still very much alive,* and my companion proceeded to cut slivers off the twitching flanks of this poor creature and slurp them enthusiastically. "Great dericacy", he announced. "*Verrrrry* rare. *Verrrrrrrry* poisonous if not prepared correctry". "*Mnnnhhhh*", I said. "*Yuuurg*". I found myself hoping on that fish's behalf for revenge, and that it had been prepared verry *in*correctry.

I also hoped that my savage dining companion would find himself stranded on a desert island and that a large toothy animal would find it pleasant to eat bits ripped off his living arse.

Then I suddenly remembered a subsequent engagement and had to dash. Via the toiret. I was not invited to dinner again. Thankfurry.

As to the dog-eating Koreans. Well, we eat stuff I am sure that Koreans find equally revolting and sub-human. No, we don't. We just don't.

ECONOMISTS

Seven, but only when there are not eight, or ten

Economists take the all-comers trophy awarded annually to the group of people who say the most and do the least, get almost everything wrong, frighten everyone into desperation – and still occupy positions of high standing and respect. Trophy awarded by whom? By me, of course. Close second? Educationalists. See below. Economists get respect from others who simply do not have the faintest idea what they are on about. But because they, the economists, use very long words, lots of PowerPoint graphs accompanied by worried frowns and expressions of deep sincerity, the recipients of their verbal garbage pretend to be impressed, because failure to do so would make them look like prats. After all, the econo-monkeys are being paid very large amounts of money by the very people who have to try to decipher what the hell they are talking about.

They have the most astonishing amounts of power and influence, do these economists. They only have to whisper, on the basis of series of numbers constructed in the dead of night in the presence of eye of toad, skin of newt and a very dodgy cat, that "the economy", whatever *that* is, is headed for a recession, and it instantly becomes a self-fulfilling prophesy as everyone dives for cover. Because that's all they *ever* predict, have you noticed? Even when all the signs point towards consumer happiness, booming production, good levels of retail spending, and optimism shines all round, the economists will start saying, "Yebbit, yebbit", and produce some more graphs to warn everyone that it can't last, it's a false dawn, it's bound to end in tears. People become economists because they are no bloody good at anything. We just don't need them.

EDUCATIONALISTS

Four inspections, three new Ministers and all change

As I have intimated above, if you see any word ending in "-ist", run for the hills. You *know* that it means trouble. And if you happen upon an *educationalist*, you have a public duty to beat them into the ground and cover them over with a large mound of farmyard stuff, which you should always keep handy.

Somewhere near the core of the British problem which gives rise to aggressive yobbism, greed, obesity, ignorance, political arrogance and all the rest of the ills that are setting this poor country apart from the rest of the world and rapidly turning us into a joke, lies the mess that is the British system of education. Why is it getting nowhere? Because we have allowed a tribe of "educationalists" to thrive, and we have given each of them a long stick to poke into the pot whenever the mood takes them. And each time they do it, they make an even bigger mess than existed before they got involved.

The result? Every struggling plant at primary, secondary and tertiary education level in Britain is pulled up by the roots to see if it is still growing, and this happens twice a week and three times at Michaelmas. Is not done by qualified and dedicated teachers or lecturers, of course. It is done by educationalists – a class of poltroons which includes Ofsted, other advisors to the Department of Farting About With Schools, and a phalanx of theorisers who have never set foot in a classroom in their lives. Or if they ever *did*, they very smartly set foot *outside* again, having had the liquid scared out of them, and having failed to teach anyone anything. And politicians of course. Politicians love pissing about with education. Such fun.

My sons managed to get through school quite well, considering. Considering that by the time they got to sixth form, the rules and reg's for A-levels had been so thoroughly nollocksed that none of us knew whether it was A2, AS, plain A, A for 'orses, eh, wot? or what the hell was going on. I tried to explain the system at the time to a French relative of mine. She had to stuff her elegant Hermes scarf into her mouth to stop herself from laughing, and then she had to go and have a lie down and a lot of cognac in order to recover. She giggled helplessly when I told her about the way in which the examination boards had, not many years ago, comprehensively (sorry about that awful pun) screwed up the marking of papers, juggling and struggling, with people being fired, then re-employed, then fired again. Then, some days later, she called me to receive an explanation concerning university tuition fees, student loans, and similar. She also wanted to know exactly what the Labour Government was trying to do with its most recent Education Bill. My answering machine told her that I had emigrated to Kazakhstan.

And they are at it again. Let's scrap the A levels altogether because they are all getting too easy, and have a baccalaureate instead. Let's turn every form of tertiary educational establishment into a "university" because it sounds more … more … y'know, more equal, and then make sure that fifty percent – *fifty percent* – of all school leavers go to a "University", whether they are fitted for formal tertiary education or not. Let's have teachers' assistants at primary schools. No, let's not. Yes, let's. No. Yes. No. And definitely let's make sure that local education authorities employ great herds of IT people so that they can design, and then change every third day, systems for recording absolutely everything all the time. Uses up invaluable teacher-time? Uses up head-teacher patience *and* time? Screws up secretarial time and causes the secretaries to have nervous breakdowns? So what? The educationalists and the swarms of civil servants their advice has caused to be recruited say, "What's that by comparison with all that lovely information we are gathering about everything? What do we do with all that information? Improve educational methods. What's that? You want to know *exactly* how we gather and use all this? Sorry – the Data Protection Act does not allow us to tell you". Dear God.

ENDOSCOPY
Five blurps, and, oh, sorry

I have had what the medical profession calls a grumbling ulcer for a very long time. Grumbling? Mine does better than that. It can complain loudly. Very un-British, my ulcer. I blame it on my mother. Why shouldn't I? From time to time, the complaints became so loud that it caused me to double up in discomfort and say quite a lot of rude words, sometimes in public, which tended to alarm people. These days I go to

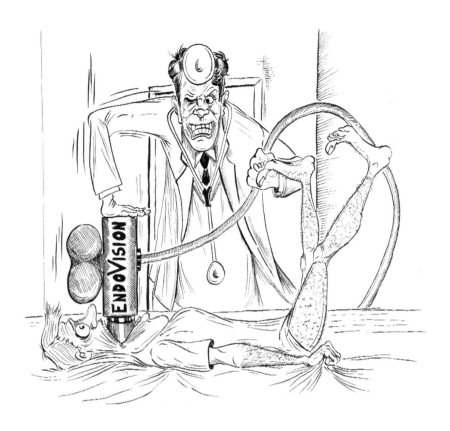

my GP who gives me some capsules to swallow, and that seems to quieten the damned thing down. But it was not that long ago that the GP would look pensive, and arrange for me to go to the hospital "so that we can have a good look at what's going on down there".

Having a look *down there* involves a procedure which subjects one to a series of indignities second only to proctoscopy. What's proctoscopy? Having a large tube shoved up your fundament, that's what, so that the medical world can have a look at "what's going on *up* there". A thought: you would think that an *end*oscope would be the right description for what goes up your *end*, would you not? But there's a big difference between endoscopy (down the throat) and proctoscopy (up the other thing) aside from the abovementioned obvious. The anus does not have a gag-reflex. Well, mine doesn't; I can't speak for you. My throat most emphatically and noisily does. I warn the endoscope operator every time. "I have a very fast gag-reflex, and if you try to push anything into my throat, I will barf instantly." "Yes, yes", they say, "swallow this pill which will relax you. Everything will be OK." BHAAAAAARGH. *HHHHAAAAARK.*

So they give up, and inject me with a mild anaesthetic, which puts me into a state of semi-coma for about an hour. During which time I am still uncomfortably aware that a three-quarter-inch garden hose with an entire television studio clamped onto the end is being pushed down my gullet and into my stomach. I do hope the people on the other end of the hose enjoy the experience.

EVIDENCE, THAT, THERE IS NO
Three, possibly more, but many studies have shown ...

You know, you just absolutely *know*, as soon as some Government official, or some other know-all allows these words to escape from his carefully marbled mouth, that the exact opposite of what he is claiming is almost certainly true.

There was no evidence to suggest that poor innocent Dr Kelly did anything other than take his own life. There is no legal evidence to suggest that the Government, *ahem*, shall we say, dissembled over Iraq and WMD. There is no evidence to suggest that asylum seekers are coming into England and then disappearing. There is no evidence to suggest that hospitals were to blame for the uniquely British phenomenon of MRSA.

And so drearily on and on. It is the classic arse-cover, the ultimate blame-shifter, the complete alibi. What it means is simply this: "We know what's going on. We know exactly who, why and where. But we are damned if we are going to let you pin it on us".

"There is no evidence..." Watch for it. Be immediately suspicious. Someone is trying to hide something.

EXAMINATIONS, WRITTEN, SCHOOL, ETC.
One side only and ten memory pills

I could have mentioned this under "educationalists" but what the hell.

I have listened to every expert I could find on this subject, because I want to confirm that I am not being obtuse or (predictably) just bloody-minded again. What I got was akin to Churchill's view of democracy: an awful system, but better than anything else we have developed so far. Which *did* make me bloody-minded, because those who dictate the shape and direction of education are taking the least line of resistance, and refusing to allow any intelligent new thoughts on the question of testing pupils and students to penetrate their hide-bound heads. Educationalists are tinkering with every other aspect of education, but devoting not even a minute to this terrible problem of exams.

Can there be any doubt that asking people to go into an exam hall and rely almost entirely on their memories to get them through, is a system very obviously in need of replacement? Passing or, even more important, doing well in an exam depends on mental regurgitation, and all too often, the examinees with the better-connected memory synapses will come out with the better results. Furthermore, it is all done against the clock so that already pressure-cooker levels of stress are increased to bursting-point. The playing field, in testing how much a student has absorbed, understood and can apply, is far from level. Exams are not tests of intelligence, nor of initiative, nor of understanding. They are tests of memory. And that is just plain wrong.

I know that some sixth-form colleges and universities have mended their ways to some extent, and allocate a (minor) percentage of the total marks achieved to course-work done during the year, but this does not go anything like far enough. And now I hear the unmistakably Antipodean voice of the bruce in charge of the QCA (Qualifications and Curriculum Authority, another of our wondrous quangos) telling us that course-work is a Bad Thing, and that exams are the only true path to testing the extent of a student's knowledge. It seems that too many parents, or so he will have us believe, are actually writing essays and dissertations for their sons and daughters, and the sons and daughters are submitting them as their own work. Really? It would take a singularly dumb and uncaring teacher or tutor to fail to spot this and throw it out. A student would only have to try this stunt once, and the lesson would be rammed home big-time. So, Bruce, nonsense.

I have never forgotten an incident in my final year at university. One of my class-mates was a brilliant student, full of insights and original thoughts, but as highly strung as Cummon-Tim and his tennis racquet. Nervous energy erupted from him like a hissing cloud in perpetual motion, and his pumpkin-sized head wobbled on his shoulders with the sheer weight of knowledge it contained. He was a running cert for a First Class with oak leaf clusters and knobs on, and he barrelled into the examination room on the first day, about three feet off the ground. He could not wait to get started. While the rest of us sat there trying to understand the questions so that we could make a start somewhere, our super-brain friend was scribbling away from the off, at several hundred miles per hour.

He left about twenty minutes before the end, shunting out the door with a fixed grin. He never re-appeared and failed to take any subsequent papers. When the results were announced, we were told that he had filled umpteen pages of exam-pad with ... his name, written over and over and over again. Nothing else. He had blown every mental gasket.

I wondered, years later, whether this had been a one-off. So I asked around. Not at all. Every year, dozens of students (often the brightest ones) simply explode with stress brought on by the knowledge that they have to demonstrate their intellect by writing three or four essays within a three hour time limit, and that they have to rely on having memorised great screeds of stuff. Hold on, I hear a voice at the back. "Surely a major part of the exam process is designed precisely to subject the examinees to stress, because that is what they will find in the cruel, cruel world?" Don't buy that. If part of the education system is designed to include stress-management, there are plenty of ways to do that without resorting to exam-room torture.

EXCESS, EATING AND DRINKING, MOSTLY
Two, three at Christmas

Low crap-scale setting, which tells you that I don't dislike every kind of excess, all the time. But for the most part, I am talking here about eating and drinking, although I could, by the time I get to the end of this item have strayed into sex, politics, sport and several social gaffe-making areas besides.

The worst of all excess is the drinking kind, especially as practised by Saturday-night herberts and herbettes who inhabit a decency-free zone which they take with them wherever they go. Enough has been written and said about binge drinking to give me a hangover, so let's not go there, but British yoof are the werl' champyuns, narmean? And as if the bingers were not perfectly capable of taking in prodigious amounts of booze all by themselves, the booze-making and marketing companies, bless their little hearts, are employing under-dressed hostesses in clubs to swish about the place offering the latest alcozonk in the form of short sharp shocks to the already-befuddled. I am all in favour of alcohol, and of getting comfortably pickled thank you very much from time to time, but seeing the revolting young retching up their rings is more than anyone needs to put up with.

And then it's Christmas. When we all take leave of our senses. When we eat and drink a quantity of comestibles sufficient to gag a buffalo. When we spend utterly unjustifiable amounts of money we do not have, so that we can add to the already swollen profits and bonuses of the supermarket and other retail companies, their executives and shareholders. Why do they do this? Dogs and genitalia, licking of, because they can, and thanks to imbecile credit-card companies, so can we. Spend, that is.

It does not stop there, of course. I am not talking about the sheer awfulness of, for example, the "banker" who recently spent £30,000 in a night-club, buying drinks for everyone because he had been paid "an insane bonus" (he ought to be put down, and not particularly humanely either). Excess permeates every aspect of our lives, from 4X4's that never see a hill or a cowpat, to teenage brand-buffoons who pay excessive amounts of money for wearing names across their tits, to grossly fat salaries paid to grossly fat fat-cats, to three-course meals for already over-weight, middle-aged men and women when two courses will do. *One* will do. Everything to do with the fashion industry, which would implode in a shower of flapping wrists and sequins were it not for the nauseating excess of the too-rich women who prop it up. People at Oxbridge Colleges who, at May Balls (in June) eat a swan, stuffed with a turkey stuffed with a goat stuffed with a wombat. I think. No, they really do. Tastes like hell on Earth, I am told. But *traditional* hell on Earth, so OK. Yah.

Excess in choice, where supermarket shelves have to make space for four hundred breakfast cereals, and counting. Excess in legislation where law-factories in every capital city churn out more and more. I have to stop now. It's all too much.

EXERCISE, FOR ITS OWN SAKE
Four circuits, six rep's and a long grunt

Just a minute; I have to go and lie down to gather enough energy to write about this.

We evolved, we humans, from a species which had to walk miles to find water and plants, or run miles and *miles* chasing supper on the hoof, or getting the hell out of it with a sabre-toothed mammoth breathing down our hairy necks. So exercise was an integral part of the eating/living experience. Not any more. Now (see "Diets" above) we have become an eat-and-do-nothing animal, so exercise has to be a deliberate act of self-imposition, in order to avoid growing an extra arse or several chins. Of course I am not overlooking strenuous sport in this mix of modern life-components; most sport does at least have the benefit of purpose, with a winning post or a higher score. And I do not include stuff like snooker and darts here. They are games, not sports, requiring no more exertion than Monopoly or chess. In terms of exercise, sex, solo or accompanied, is more of a sport than those.

But you have to do something to burn off calories, and walking to the car does not cut it. You have to do something that calls for straining and panting and going red in the face, causing your heart to thud and your lungs to squeal. You either do this by running or jogging to nowhere and back, or if you are pretentious and rich enough, by joining a gym-club, where you heave, pull, lift, squeeze, stretch and run on the spot on a treadmill, which elevates pointlessness to an art-form. And when you are done, off you go to the shower, where there are always two or three gathered together in the name of peacockery, flexing their abs and various 'ceps and posing – and paying an inordinate amount of attention to your modest schlong, while their outrageously large knobs clang back and forth between their knees. Unless, of course, they are not circumcised, when they spend a great deal of shower-time involving a lot of soap and enough foreskin-cleaning to raise questions if not other things.

No, sorry. For me, there has to be a point to taking exercise. Taking the dog for a long brisk walk (while walking quite briskly myself). A hike in a place I have not seen before, which involves going up and down hills to get the cardiovascular system moving. (But see "Hills", later.) But don't tell me about getting fit by running marathons and the like. The cemeteries of the world are full of the bodies of running fanatics who did one mile too many.

"FARMS", WIND
Three hundred feet and several sore eyes

That's the *last* time I use the word "farm" in connection with these monstrous excrescences. The makers and promoters of these eyesores have scored a major PR coup by coupling the rural, pretty, natural, warm, cuddly, countrified, green image of a farm with what is nothing less than a power-station, and it is time we called foul on that. They deliberately use "farm" to soften the image of what is a modern menace, a blot on every landscape, an intrusive industry come to the countryside.

Renewable energy? Personally, I wish I had some, and I am totally devoted to the idea. Anything which decreases the amount of fossil fuel we burn for energy-production has my support. But not at any price – and here's the problem: wind-turbine power-stations are hopelessly inefficient when it comes to producing electricity in any meaningful quantity, and as things stand, it actually *costs* all of us to subsidise these machines.

It takes a particularly perverse mind to say that these terrible towers with their whirling guillotine blades and their low-frequency headache-making roars, are *acceptable* as visual additions to the tops of the gently rolling hills where they are positioned. And they *have* to be positioned there, because the tops of hills offer the best chance of catching the wind – and that's also where they catch your eye. Furthermore, they are always painted white, apparently to make them as visible as possible for miles around in a deliberately provocative gesture designed to stick two turbines up at the country-loving public. People who live in rural areas and say that wind-turbines (which are usually well over 300 feet high) are "quite attractive, really" have clearly lost touch with reality and with the countryside in which they are lucky enough to live. The people who say this sort of thing, are, in my experience, almost always imports from Birmingham or London and have no real feeling for the countryside at all. And the same goes for city-slickers who visit the countryside and express the view that these things are "actually, very, er, dramatic, yah". These dough-heads are incapable of realising, it seems, that the potentially devastating effect on tourism or even on the simple local pleasure of roaming hardly bears thinking about, because these power-stations render large tracts of the countryside unapproachable. They frighten people, and if you have ever stood within 200 yards of a turbine, it is not hard to understand why.

So – why do these things find favour with anyone at all? The answer is the usual one: money. For every turbine a landowner permits on his land, he receives a fat bundle per year, and as well as that, a further bundle per substation, whether the turbines are turning or not. And what a price the rest of us have to pay in landscapes ruined, paths made inaccessible, and in subsidies dumped on our electricity bills.

Here's an inescapable fact: Sooner rather than later we will have to stop setting fire to fossils in order to provide ourselves with energy sources. Not only because the fossils are becoming harder to dig or suck up, but because we have to do something about carbon dioxide and the greenhouse effect. Fine. So – renewable energy sources. Good. And that includes wind power stations. Good-ish.

But if those who support the proliferation of wind power station turbines all over the countryside told the truth and said, "yes, they are horrible, unsightly and frightening, but they are the price we all have to pay for sustainable energy," then we *might* all be prepared to bite the bullet and live with it. But when they start trying to tell us that "they are, no, really, you know, quite attractive, actually," then they are slap bang in the same stupid category as those who hunt foxes with hounds and tell us that they do it as a service to the countryside.

A footnote: which organisation, do you suppose, gives its energetic (sic!) support to wind-turbine power-station energy? Friends of the Earth! No, I don't understand either.

Robert MacGregor

FASHION

Five thousand pounds and a swish and a swatch

I get very hot under the collar about parasites, sometimes literally if I am attacked by the ones that go "zzzzing" and then bite me. I am not keen on mosquitoes, midges, things that crawl under your skin in tropical places, and I am *very* unhappy about the human variety which includes lawyers, tax collectors, politicians, educationalists, economists, more lawyers, economists and actuaries. And most accountants. And estate agents. And lawyers.

But the tribe I despise most of all is the Fashion Monkeys. I fail to understand what drives the human species to follow fads designed by singularly cynical minds, whose object in life appears to be to take the maximum possible amount of piss out of the gullible, at maximum possible cost to them. How otherwise relatively intelligent people can get their minds so comprehensively addled that they believe they have to wear whatever the latest insanity might be, is beyond me. "Well, no", says a journo acquaintance of mine who reports on fashion shows all over Europe, "it is useful to have the Fashion Houses set trends, so that the public's insatiable appetite for new clothing and other things is at least directed and channelled, or otherwise there would be chaos on the high streets". Eh? Lost me there. But chaos sounds good.

How in the name of anyone can the things that one sees sashaying down catwalks, hip-before-tit, with one outrageous confection piled on other impossible doodads have anything to do with what Mrs Doris Morris wants to buy in the high street? Or even for that matter, Doris' grand-daughter? When do these ghastly fripperies actually get worn in public by ordinary people? Or do fashion shows these days actually have lives of their own, more about entertainment than about setting trends, with the terrible things worn by razor-thin moddles thrown instantly into the bin as soon as the show is over? Who on earth would want to be seen dead wearing some of the stuff "designed" by the self-important twerps who mince about making fun of people for a living?

And what unfathomable mystery is at work each year to make it possible for designers who would, for a hairpin, scratch one another's eyes out, magically to produce "this season's" colour/s, skirt lengths, hat shapes, sleeve sizes and so on? How do they *all* seem to know, in what is supposed to be a fiercely competitive business, that this year aubergine is out and avocado is in? And then, each in their closely guarded shows, stick to that generally accepted line? Very fishy. *Very.*

I have no problem with the creation of variety and choice, but, thinking about it from an evolutionary point of view, what is fashion *for*? Does it answer some deep-seated need in our crocodilian brain-remnant to wear a uniform so that we can look like all other croc's? Or the same principle for dung-beetles, vipers, slugs and spiders? It is a rich socio-anthropological vein for some bored denizen of academe to tackle.

FESTIVALS, ROCK, IN MY BACK YARD
Hundreds of tons of garbage, several almost human

Rock festivals are wonderful if you happen to be eighteen and footloose. Great music, great fun all round. Or so I am told. One of my sons went to Glastonbury recently. His tent floated away, and he discovered things about mud. He came back with earache, a streaming cold, and a mild case of food poisoning. But he loved it! Great!

Aside from the harmless young who make up most of those who attend rock festivals, they attract some seriously awful people. Most of the festival-goers are just young guys and gels out there to have their ears damaged, their livers pickled in alcohol and their sex organs reduced to smoking ruin, while ingesting e-coli. Super. Harmless to anyone else. But these events always attract a substantial number of the world's *drittsekken* (lovely Norwegian word meaning shit-bags) whose lack of morals, cretinous behaviour and aggression are world-class, and they give these festivals the stinking name they so richly deserve with anyone who has to live within a ten-mile radius thereof.

And, of course, there is the matter of the percussion. Not the music as such – much of it is great stuff – but it seems that it cannot be properly appreciated by those attending unless the sound, and in particular the bass noise, is amplified to the point of screaming torture. Problem: bass sounds can be carried by ground-waves through the earth, for miles, so that they can be felt through the feet and into the guts even when they can't be heard. Ask any elephant. And if one happens to be involuntarily close enough to hear them as well, Hell on Earth is not an exaggeration.

I have had the miserable experience of being both close enough to have had my hearing damaged, and to have to cope with drunken, doped-up turd-bags in my backyard. Literally, in one case. You would not believe what these slimes get up to. We have a little old Norman church tucked away down a lane not far from the site of a recent festival. The porch and lych-gate were ankle-deep in faeces by two days into the event, and some grave-stones bore the unmistakeable signs of urine squirted there by sub-human event-goers. A large family of deeply filthy children sat in a circle on our village green while the parents of, possibly, some of them, did it doggy-style on the grass in full view of everyone. When asked by an outraged village resident to desist (I paraphrase; you can imagine what was actually said) the doggy-on-top withdrew an empurpled organ and waved it about, while asking the aforementioned resident "if she would like some". The police were called.

By the time Plod arrived, the performance was over, the performers long gone in their crappy van, and the Police said, "Nah, sorry, nothing we can do, Madam, unless we actually catch them in the act".

A waste-of-spaced-out young woman lurched down the road, high as a house on every chemical she could lay her hands on. (Rock festivals are drug hypermarkets.) An enraged bee stung her on the arm. Even the local bees were pissed off with these people. She shrieked, and her spectacles fell into the road as she staggered and fell. A passing car reduced them to powder. A resident, seeing all this, rushed out to help, took the slattern inside, treated the bee-sting, and even took her back to the camp-site. Two weeks later, the Samaritan received a summons from the slattern's lawyer, demanding compensation for her broken spectacles, and claiming molestation. *Molestation?* It would have taken a sex-starved, blind lunatic who had also lost his sense of smell to want to get within ten feet of her. The Samaritan tore up the letter after a calming pint or two of scotch, and heard nothing more. You wonder why I think what I do about lawyers?

You suspect that these anecdotes are atypical? Don't. Similar things happen wherever a rock-festival is staged. They are magnets for humanity's detritus.

So, absolutely *not* in my back yard, sunshine. Try Dartmoor, or Salisbury plain, preferably at the sharp end of the Army's firing ranges.

FIREWORKS
Take a pair of sparkling eyes to watch the rockets

We have had several centuries to evolve a fascination with things that explode, especially, but perversely, those which can blow us all to pieces. Fine. But once we had also established that some of the exploding stuff made interesting sights and sounds at the same time, there was no stopping us. Just as we have persisted in using a highly dangerous gas for heating and cooking (See under "G" for Gas) so we have learned a delight in setting fire to packages of gunpowder (the very name would be a clue as to its viciousness) in order to help our various little celebrations go off with a bang, wheeeee or whooooosh.

I am not going start in again on the fatuousness of the British 5th November stunnocks, because I will never understand why we celebrate a failure and the hanging, drawing and quartering which followed, by successfully doing on a slightly smaller scale, what the unfortunate Mr. Fawkes failed to do. Surely we could by now have come up with a non-violent ceremony involving, I don't know, eating a cake shaped like a barrel or Big Ben.

Instead, we actively encourage imbecile parents and their either innocent or deliberately vicious offspring to fire rockets over which they have no control, and/or throw miniature sticks of dynamite about the place. Every year, people leave firework parties with fewer body parts than they arrived with. Dogs go ape, cattle give birth prematurely, sozzled revellers report UFO's, and the fire services are busier at that time of year than any other – putting out fires caused by people deliberately setting fire to highly explosive stuff which obligingly explodes and sets fire to other stuff.

I love firework displays which are professionally organised and controlled, with the explosions set off at a considerable distance from me. Magnificent. Spectacular. But allowing any Sebastian, Kevin or Tracey to go to their nearest friendly shop and buy these things for the purpose of setting them off in their own back gardens is outrageous. I have watched, frightened waterless, as a small child was allowed to light a large rocket, its stick stuck into a wobbling bottle, with the inevitable consequence. The bottle fell over at the exact moment of lift-off. The fire brigade got to the scene quite fast, all things considered. The rocket, on its way to setting fire to a nearby thatched roof, had bulletted its way past one of the neighbour's children and missed her by no more than a couple of feet. "Oopth", said the child who had lit the blue fuse. Yeth, quite.

FISHING

Four maggots, and five painful piles

Here I go again – offending people by the thousand. Fishing of one kind or another is the most popular "sport" in Britain. Or is it the most popular pastime? Can't be. That's got to be the other.

But "sport"? No more a sport than shooting defenceless birds out of the sky, or any of the other so-called sports which include fox hunting, hare-coursing, stag-stalking and so on. But fishing is a national obsession. Strangely-clad men (it is mostly men) sit on the banks of a sludgy canal or river or a lifeless looking pond, fishing rods hanging limply in front of them, like … like … well, I don't have to paint you a picture, do I? They are sitting on unbelievably uncomfortable little stools. Fishermen must suffer more from piles than any other group of humans. They crouch under great bulbous umbrellas, because, inevitably, it is raining. They have spent a fortune on huge amounts of gear and kit, which they have sweatingly humped from a distant car park to their spot on the water.

Some of the paraphernalia consists of pots of the most gorge-risingly writhing maggots – which they have to *handle* and thread onto hooks. Yeeeeurgh! Fisher-people are almost always alone. Perhaps the maggot thing explains why. They sit there for hour upon endless hour, in the hope of catching something which yields seldom more than one mouthful of muddy bones. Are they escapees from nagging wives? Getting away from the pressures of city life? What?

And if you happen upon some of these obsessive souls as you putter up or down the river in your small boat, doing your best to navigate around the lines which they have thoughtfully cast as far out into the stream as they can, the glare you suffer is enough to scorch your eyeballs. Come too close to the line, and the language is positively footballian.

This fishing business is not confined to canals, lakes and rivers, of course. There is another breed (just as much kit, just as obsessed) which takes itself off to the beach or the rocky coast in all kinds of weather, throws a couple of lines into the surf, and stands there. Sits there. Stands there. In many, many years of living not far from the sea, and walking our dog on the beach so she can poop where it most annoys everyone, I have never, ever seen one of these poor lonely souls catch anything. Not once. And sometimes they go down to the sea in shirts, to do battle with winds that could blow the balls off a bull. I just don't get it. What I *have* got, though, is almost decapitated by an invisible line as my dog dragged me down the beach at a full gallop in a gale. Dog galloping. Me, a sort of rushed stumble.

Like everyone else though, I have tried my hand at fishing. No good. No good at all. I am capable of turning a neatly wound reel into a mare's nest of knots and loops which absolutely no-one can undo. I can achieve this mess in seconds. I tried fly-fishing for trout, once. I got the line going in that brilliantly back and forth wave, paid it all out like a pro and let go. The hook went straight into the earlobe of a friend several yards away. And I learned three new things. That ears bleed like buggery. That he knew many, many rude words I did not know he knew. And that trout can laugh.

FLUPS

Two, rapidly eating their way to becoming five

Family acronym; Fat Lumpy Unattractive Persons
I don't want to go on about this, but really, it is enough to frighten the children. Those who are not mini-flups themselves of course. Go where you like in almost all of the Western world, and the pavements will be sagging under the weight of hugely and horribly overweight people, most of whom would seem to be taking a weird delight in wearing clothing that, far from disguising their bulbous bodies, actually accentuates them. Hence the "unattractive" part of "flup".

I have seen (not very often, but often enough to know that there are at least some of the gravitationally challenged who try not to cause offence) large women who wear very attractive flowing garments which produce a pleasant tent-like effect – and good on them, I say. It is only, ever, women by the way. There is no equivalent to the caftan or similar in the male wardrobe, unless the males in question are Demis Roussos wannabe's and/or gay enough to wear female apparel with appropriate élan.

But those aside, the rest of the fluppen obesitariat will insist on wearing shorts, sleeveless upper-wear, and even, God in Heaven, those absurd and stupid little cut-off tops which have been designed by some fashion-monkey (see "F for fashion") in order to expose the female midriff. The aforementioned fashion-monkeys live in a world where everyone in sight is svelte, hollow-cheeked and professionally anorexic, and where the concept of exposing the mid-section is justified by impossibly flat stomachs and taught, tanned skin. Fine. But in the real world, most ordinary people have ordinary shapes, and the number of flat, taut midriffs constitutes never more than about two percent of the population. Does that stop flups from wearing this fashion? Nope. Wobbling putty-coloured and often hairy bulges are flaunted as if they were things of beauty. I give up. There ought to be a law.

You think I exaggerate? Then try this: watch any TV newscast, any day, and at least one story will feature a concerned mother, an outraged female hospital worker, the sister of a jailed paedophile, somebody – and she will be gargantuan, dressed in utterly inappropriate clothes for her size. A flup. Go to your local superstore, and count the number of really, stonkingly, floor-creakingly fat women wearing horribly tight clothing. You will see lots of them within ten yards of where you stand.

FOAM, EXPANDING
A million times its own volume; make that two million

You know the stuff I mean. Stands there in innocuous-looking canisters, for all the world like a cousin to tubes of silicon or something else relatively innocuous. You screw a nozzle onto the business-end, apply a bit of pressure, and book yourself into the sanatorium immediately, to recover. There is no way you can control this stuff, which erupts in all directions at the speed of light, and while still wet makes shit sticking to a blanket seem like a mildly aberrant adhesive problem. There is nothing like it. It expands to God knows how many times its be-canistered volume – and as it is impossible to estimate how much has erupted from the nozzle, it is *ipso facto* impossible to estimate what the final result will be. Have you squirted enough into the space you are trying to fill? Too much? Yes, too much, always too much. It goes on boiling and frothing and blurping and roiling and there is absolutely nothing you can do to stop it until *it* wants to stop. At which point it is on the carpet. *In* the carpet. Stuck to the wall where you did not ask it to stick itself. And stuck to you. Oh, boy, is it ever stuck to you.

A while back when my children were little, we bought a small boat for pootling about with an outboard motor which could have doubled as an egg-whisk. The boat had two flotation chambers, one at the sharp and one at the blunt end, to use the correct nautical description. Chambers full of air, they said. Guaranteed to keep the boat afloat even if it turned upside down. Hmmm, I thought. Not really convincing. If they are full of air, they could just as easily become full of water, through even the smallest hole caused by navigating onto a sharp rock. So, *I* know. I will drill a couple of holes in the flotation chambers and fill them up with expanding foam, which really *will* make the boat sink-proof.

Easy. Drill hole at point A, nozzle for the insertion of, and, as per instructions, another one at point B as escape-hole for displaced air. Proceed. Of course, everything that took place after that was invisible, so I had no way of knowing how much of the chamber had been filled, or when to stop squirting. After a long squirt, I started to hear interesting creaking sounds from the boat's fibreglass body, so I stopped immediately, and put my ear to the escape-hole as mentioned heretofore, to see if I could hear …

A jet of ultra-sticky wet un-expanded foam erupted from the air-hole like a geyser, and kept on erupting. That boat ejaculated foam like a whale. It covered me from head to navel, and started to expand immediately. I screamed, and ran for my life. Into the house, where my wife and children screamed and ran for theirs, to escape from the most terrifying apparition which lurched towards them, its bright-orange skin still expanding.

After I had set nicely, I was rescued by the simple expedient of having all my clothes chipped from my body, and my hair shaved down to the scalp. I have never touched this expanding nightmare substance ever since, and I think it ought to be declared a weapon of mess destruction.

And I'll tell you something else. Once you have started to use it, you cannot stop and hope to store the un-used left-overs for another day. The nozzle and everything within range thereof sets into concrete, whatever the instructions say about the technique required to stop that happening. So the manufacturers make their profit the same way that mustard-makers make theirs. It's what is left on the plate (or in the canister) and then thrown away which makes the money. Clever stuff, huh?

FOOD, G-M, OBJECTIONS TO
Three, but … let's see if we can change it into a four

Some nerd in a laboratory discovers that he can mess about with genes by poking a pipette into a cell and either blowing or sucking (I can't remember) and the world's busybodies get their wee-wee in a froth. The marches start, the demonstrations, the picketing, the burning of underpants. Because it is now possible to produce a strain of wheat which is resistant to disease and, what's more, can grow in a desert. Same for maize, or rice or similar basics which are the staple foods of millions of people who are in the hands of fickle fate and the wicked weather. Every year, somewhere in the world, a crop fails and people start to die. These people would kill for a strain of their staple which is more dependable than the one with which they and their ancestors have been battling for millennia.

But this is described as a slippery slope by the twenty-first century Luddites who look at GM crops and make a Superman leap of hysterics to a world where, in their fevered heads, everyone will be able to modify everything including human babies and we will be defying either natural science or God or both.

But wait a minute. Have you ever been to Crufts Supermutt Extravaganza? Or watched cattle, sheep, pigs, anything at an agri-show? They have been bred to smithereens over generations, to breed *this* trait out and *that* one in, to have bigger or smaller or longer or shorter or fatter or thinner whatevers. And have they done this by themselves? Only to the extent that they are allowed to go at it in the normal reproductive way, having had their partners carefully selected for them. Oh, except for cattle, and, I think, some sheep, of course. Here, the poor bulls/rams are fooled into endless sexless ejaculation and exhaustion every day, and cows/ewes thousands of miles away are impregnated by a giant version of another pipette. Which the operator *must* remember to *blow*.

We have been genetically modifying plants, animals, anything we can get away with, for centuries. Eons. But now, because exactly the same thing can be done in a lab, it is different and scary and makes it inevitable that we will eat GM bread and start to grow cross-gender genitalia where we definitely don't want them. Rubbish, of course. But it gives the battier journalists something to write about.

There will always be scare stories. Rats fed GM grain develop kidney problems. Mice fed GM rice develop something un-mice-like.

Endless. What the mad scientists don't tell you is that the rats and mice were fed so much of the stuff that the same amount would have caused problems in an elephant. I recall one incident which turned me into a lifetime sceptic about this kind of thing. Years ago, I worked with a soft-drinks company. In an effort to make things go better, they produced a diet drink which tasted like the leftovers from a bad chemistry experiment, but started marketing it anyway. The opposition, so the story went, got some scientists to test the stuff and announced that the product's artificial sweetener had produced all kinds of intestinal nasties in, you guessed it, rats. (Poor rats. The things they have to ingest in the name of science). So everyone at Go-better Ltd flew about in a panic, and the drink was taken off the market very fast. It then turned out that the amount of sweetener the suffering rats had been fed was the equivalent of a human continuously drinking seven thousand three hundred and fifty-two cans of the drink a month, or something. Job done, though. It's called competition, and anything goes.

In the end, it comes down to choice. If we in the West decide we do not want to take a chance on GM-anything, then let's not go there. If people in the un-developing world feel that feeding their families reliably is worth the risk of whatever GM crops might carry, then let them. Anything wrong with that?

FOOTBALL, ANYTHING TO DO WITH
Five hundred. On penalties, missed, oh dear

When I was a lot younger, I was prepared to give football a chance. After all, millions are fanatical about this game to the point of making themselves ill if "their" side loses, so how can millions of people be wrong? Easily, as it happens, but that's another matter. But I came to loathe the modern game and nothing has changed my mind.

The game *itself* is blameless. It's is not fundamentally different *as a game* from rugby, polo, lacrosse, hockey or buzhkazi; one team tries to propel an object through a goal or past a line defended by the other

team, and vice versa, and whoever does it most often, wins. Simple. Oh, yes, buzhkazi, and I'm not making this up. A hundred crazed Afghans (or is it Mongolians?) on even more crazed horses attempt to throw the beheaded body of a goat through something more or less like goalposts, while war breaks out among the rest of the players. Lovely. They have a marvellous time. Not including the goat.

It's today's football *people* I cannot abide. Both on-the-field-players and off-the-field fans, supporters, and managers. And players off the field too, for that matter. I've often wondered whether it's the sheer frustration of a game which doesn't allow anyone other than the goalkeeper to use their hands. It's maddening. Like having to juggle plates into the dining room instead of just setting them out in neat rows from a tray. And having to head-butt a quite heavy plastic bladder which has been kicked at you from fifty yards away has to have the same effect as being punched repeatedly by Mohammed Ali. Mike Tyson. John Prescott. Your brain just has to be dislocated. And having to tackle an opponent using nothing but feet and legs is terribly frustrating, especially for the bovver-boys who make it to the top of the game today and who are itching to get in there with fists and elbows, but can't. No wonder that William Webb Ellis at Rugby School invented rugby by saying "sod this for a game – I'm picking up the ball". He did it out of frustration. What took him so long?

If there's a sportsman in the news, having been caught fighting or fornicating in the wrong place, you can be damned sure it's a footballer. If there's outrage at the language being used by a disgruntled player who is spitting and shouting at the referee, a footballer will be doing it. If there's a witless teenage jerk who's paid a king's ransom per week and flaunts it in the most vulgar and flamboyant way possible, it will be a footballer. If there's mass open-air sex among members of a team who've just scored a goal, that team will be playing football. If a team member is knocking himself out, giving an Oscar-winning performance, rolling about in feigned but convincing agony in order to persuade the referee that he has been most foully fouled, it'll be a member of a football team. Talking of referees, I have always thought that in the modern game the only people who would want to become football ref's have to be masochists. Sure, they say they love the game. That doesn't stop them from enjoying being abused every week.

And the hooligan supporters. They make the case for bringing back conscription better than anything ever did. In no other sport, not one, is there a problem with spectator-supporters having to be corralled and separated from one another in order to avoid inter-fan mayhem. In no other sport is there a problem with players of off-white skin-colour being taunted and insulted on a regular basis, or having coins, bottles, false teeth, fruit, eggs and highly inventive abuse chucked at them by snout-faced, shaven headed arse-wipes. At no other sporting stadia is it necessary to build fences and sometimes socking great moats to keep fans and players apart. Only football needs that.

So, there's nothing wrong with football that a complete change in the nature of its players and supporters wouldn't cure. Fat chance. There's an exception, and that's not absolute either – commentators. For the most part, those who commentate on football matches on TV and radio appear to be decent and harmless enough – and who could be more so than everyone's favourite Nice Guy, Gary Lineker? Jolly Nice Bloke. But then there's Ron Atkinson, of course. So there are exceptions to the exceptions.

The worst thing about all this? The fact that footballers become role-models for the youth of the country. How could they *not* be? They play a *game* for shed-loads of money, achieve fame, become celebrities, pull birds or blokes of every shape, size and colour, behave like brain-damaged Nazis *and get away with it*. Who wouldn't want a piece of that?

FOOTNOTES
Three references, but see below

I have had e-mailed words with him. Does not help. He insists on using them, despite the fact that every damned footnote, bar none, could have been slipped comfortably into the body of the text where [17, 26, 47, 196] etc., can be found, and reading would be a smooth, simple and entirely pleasant experience. Oh, sorry. Him? Michael Bywater. One of my heroes. Funny and very, very clever man, possessed of an ability to see, verily, right to the invisible vest and underpants of the unclothed emperors who govern us. Wonderful book – "Lost Worlds". Go and buy it.

But he will use damned and blasted footnotes all over the place. So instead of a flowing read, where one sentence slips comfortably into the next and a smile creeps comfortably over my face, I am left having to read in a jerky stop-start, eyes having to dart hither and yon, fingers pressed into service on the page to try to keep note of where I was before I had to drop my attention down to the page-bottom in order to see what further pearl he wished to cast before me. Maddening.

Michael B is not alone of course. Several authors of non-academic works have footnoted themselves into incomprehensibility. I wish they, or their editors, would put a stop to this. Footnotes are for wrist-crackingly heavy academic tomes, where the author has to demonstrate his endless research and the height of his brow by referring to other academic works, themselves full of footnotes. Not for sensible authors writing otherwise lovely stuff.

GAS, COOKING AND HEATING
Mark five, but be afraid, be very afraid

Imagine that you are a blobby green person in a spaceship from Fuzztt in the Billtt Galaxy, circling the Earth, getting to know us a bit before touching down in Arizona. It's always Arizona. They are watching as we drill enormously deep holes in our planet, and we whoop with joy when the holes give up huge quantities of a frantically explosive gas. Then we pipe that gas thousands of miles all over the place, where we distribute it into our homes, offices, factories, hospitals, and schools. Then *we set fire to it – deliberately,* to cook our food, warm our buildings, and create electricity – when there are much, much safer alternatives available. And, it now turns out, much cheaper alternatives, too. To add to the nonsense, we in Britain are now dependant on Russia for supplies of our gas. Remember Russia? Used to be our merely Commie enemy, now the world centre for crime, and run either by very worrying steel-eyed ex KGB types, or by the Mafyia, or both. *Very* dependable.

Not only is gas furiously anxious to turn itself into a fire, it is horrendously poisonous, and odourless to boot, so if you inhale it, you don't even know you have done so – and hello, next stop crematorium, where at least they put the gas to a roughly appropriate use because the whole point is to do terminal damage by fire to the box and contents. Our space-visitors will have looked at this gas–lunacy, concluded that we are dangerously, irredeemably mad, selected double warp speed and got the hell out of here.

No, I mean, really. I have watched while my wife, newly married and touchingly naïve about things that might go bang in the day (now, now, don't be rude), blew herself clean across the kitchen because the

gas oven refused to light, so she thought she would just poke the match into the oven a little bit and take a closer look to see if something called the pilot light was working, and you know the rest. Took ages for her eyebrows to grow back. The oven door came to rest on her chest. I took it outside, took an axe to the thing, and I have never, ever used gas in any home I have ever lived in, since. It scares the very wind out of me. Why wouldn't it?

GOOGLE
Searching. Maybe 2,456,675, or possibly 3,776,298

Would not want to live without it, not really. Finally unclenched my teeth and got serious about how the damned thing works. And it works very well, mostly. So do the other search engines, but frankly I worry that Google is rapidly becoming the equivalent of Microsoft-Everywhere, or possibly, and this thought has just occurred to me, is *already* secretly owned by William Gates Esq. It is in the nature of all businesses to aspire to monopoly or as near as possible thereto, so a World Gates Computer and Search-engine Monopoly would not surprise me.

But back to Google. Do I care that it took 0.00005 nanoseconds to find 2,456,789 references to my request for lawnmowers? Does Google know that, like almost everyone else on this planet, I never look beyond Page One of the listed sites it has found for me? OK, Page Two if I am in an expansive mood. But that's it. It just seems boastful for this service to pile millions of items of completely unwanted information on my plate, and tell me how awfully cleverly and fast it did so. I hope, I really do, that somewhere in a cave in Norway or New Zealand perhaps, some pointy-headed computer freak is busy inventing the next big thing in search engines. Simple, accurate, modest. Sign me up, techie.

GREED
Four, and I'll have another, thanks

(See above under "F" for fat-cats.) If only it stopped there. But it doesn't. Greed is all around, in the form of burger-gobbling balloons on legs; binge-drinking bimbettes of all sexes bent double outside pubs, ralphing up their rings into the gutter; chinless bankers driving stupidly expensive arse-scraping sports cars or road-hogging four-by's; private collectors of great works of art who buy them, ship them to their moated and bloated palaces and hide them forever in cellars; motor-way service area operators who charge anything they like for everything you need, because they can; third-world tyrants and dictators who funnel millions in charity and aid cash into their own accounts while their citizens starve.

It's a long list. But I'm going to stop there. I have touched on some of them in this book. I'm feeling nauseous. You can fill in the rest yourself.

GRUNTING, TENNIS, MOSTLY
Forty and no love lost

Uh-**haaargh**! Yuh-**eeeerch, ga-agrgh**!! Those are the sounds of tennis as it is played in the modern era. No longer the pleasant thwang of rubber on gut and the blunk of the bounce. Too many modern professional tennis players have discovered that a massive great grunt, which is not a grunt at all, but more of a shriek, apparently helps make better contact between racquet and ball. Why? How? I have no idea. But I am convinced that if they thought it would help matters even more to produce a large fart at the same time, and a belch, they would be trumpeting away at equal volume. Possibly farting, belching and shrieking simultaneously. Oh dear. Do I understand the need for any of this?

No, actually, I used to understand, but only sort of. It is terribly obvious that in any activity which calls for feats of exertion, a sudden expulsion of air from the lungs at the moment of greatest effort does something either to add to the force being exerted, or to make us feel better about the effort we are putting in. Try lifting the side of a piano without emitting some sort of unghhh-noise, and you are not trying.

But listen to what goes on at Wimbledon and at other major tennis tournaments, and the thing has clearly got out of hand. In all started, I seem to recall, with Monica Seles, who pioneered the grunt and took it into a decibel range which seemed impossible from such a relatively small frame.

But then it moved on, until most of the top women players now have an ear-splitting repertoire of yelps, yells, squeaks, roars, shrieks and trills which are more usually heard through the thin walls of cheap hotels when a honeymoon couple are going at it next door.

Listen to Miss Sharapova, which you can do in Glasgow or Gateshead without benefit of television or radio when she is on court in South-West London, and you wonder how on Earth her opponent can stand it, when the force of sound comes over the net at least as hard and furiously as does the Sharapova forehand. Her opponent stands it of course, by bellowing right back like a moose on heat. As for the sisters Williams, their future will be assured by the time they give up top-level tennis. They can go on the road as a double act where their mighty screeches could be used to shatter railway-ties, bring down buildings, dislodge massive stones in quarries, pulverise skip-loads of glass.

During a recent match at Wimbledon, Mistress Shoutemova, having to run like buggery to retrieve a shot way out wide, and then leap on the return to win the point (great play) completely forgot to shriek, and played those two shots brilliantly nonetheless. So, what's going on here has nothing to do with adding power to the stroke. It's a deliberate policy designed to destroy the concentration of the opponent who has to attempt a shot while shutting out the shout. And when Miss Shriekemova was asked about her shrieking and had it suggested ever so gingerly that she might tone things down, she went straight into Putin mode, blue eyes as cold as ice, mouth like a gun embrasure, face as stiff as a bayonet and said "I will not change *anything*." She is six foot tall, Russian, scary. Holding a big tennis racquet. OK, she can shriek if she wants to, but this year not even her hog-calling could get her to the final. Good.

I called her boyfriend to ask if the sound level at moments of passionate climax were comparable. I still don't know. He didn't hear the question. He's stone deaf now.

The men are not free of blame either. Several of them are joining in the buffalo-honking, and it is no prettier than the ugly noises being made by the women. The overall result is a cattle-yard at feeding time, a hog-calling contest, a deafening shout-fest which is reducing the world's once most decorous and well-mannered event to decibel-hell.

I have taken to watching tennis on TV with the sound on "mute". I just can't take it any more.

GUM, CHEWING
Five-plus, ptui X seven

It isn't just that chewed-out gum is spat onto pavements by thoughtless snouted jerks in baseball caps. It's the chewing of the gum that gets my goat. Gum-chewers have no idea how deeply unattractive it is to the passing public to see their jaws on a permanent phantom-eating mission and how utterly repulsive it is when these chewers do it with open mouths, as so many do. And don't get me started on bubble-gum. That's the nadir, the bottom of a deep pit in a masticatory hell.

But back with the non-inflatable variety; I watched, as did millions, every ball bowled in the 2005 Ashes cricket series against the Aussies, who lost. Just thought I'd like to mention that again. The Aussies deserved to lose. Their captain, Ricky Ponting, chewed gum throughout, in close up. He rolled it about his lips and teeth in a highly charged manner. He did phantom-spits with it. He prodded it towards me on his tongue. It was impossibly disgusting, but the Channel 4 camera-people seemed to revel in sticking a lens down his throat the better for us to see it all happening. Yeeeeuch. And the same damned thing went on with the coach of the French national rugby team M. Bernard Laporte during the 2006 Six Nations Contest. Every time the producers cut to him having an orgasm at a French score, one was also treated, if that is the word, to his jaws grinding and heaving as he did it to a wad of gum. Somehow, seeing Frenchmen chewing gum is particularly disturbing. I can't help the feeling that they, of all people, ought to know better.

When it comes to public mastication, I come over quite nauseous when I see people eating in the street, whether they intend swallowing or not. I make an exception for ice-cream cones on a hot day. And

there's an exception to the exception; some cone-lickers go at it like fellatio, and somehow the sight of a large pink cow-like tongue working its prehensile way around the knob of ice-cream makes me uneasy. But I'll put up with it. However, nothing else is allowed.

And then comes the gum-excreta. Local Councils are having to spend millions every year cleaning up the gum-shit left by the chewers, now even more slack jawed than before, having defecated through the mouth. The Polluter-Pays rule is going to be applied, I hope, so that the cost of the cleanups is borne by the manufacturers within the price –

but that will not stop my shoes and yours being subjected to stuff which is on a par with dogshit. Nor will price alone stop the chewers from spitting their foul globs all over the place, any more than putting up the price of cigarettes has deterred smokers from blowing their reeking gases into my face.

GYMNASIUMS
Five, six, seven, eight, and ... five, six, seven, eight

OK, gymnasia. Pedant. See "Exercise" above, but I have more to say about these God-awful places. First, there's the gear. Do you think you can turn up to a gym in a sagging pair of track-suit bottoms and a stained sweat-shirt? Not if you want to avoid a lot of sniggering, eye-brow-raising and surreptitious pointing, you don't. Trainers? The things you wear for gardening or the occasional breath-robbing jog? No, no. It has to be the very latest Adiboks or Reedidas Super-Flite Magi-Daps, and white, please – nothing else. Towel? That old thing your significant other chucked at you last time you asked for something with which to mop the brow? No, again. A branded special, either idiotically emblazoned with the name of a famous sports-goods maker, or with your own discreet but clearly legible initials. Now you are set. You are a pretentious prat, but you are set.

Having paid your gaggingly huge annual sub, you are anxious to get on with it. You know you have to be sensible about this; you don't want to be carried out of the place wheezing and grunting with a drip attached or, possibly, very, very silent, so you give yourself a target number of minutes or miles or repetitions, possibly under the supervision of a "personal trainer" who does this because he can't find a proper job. You reach your target, stop, glance to one side and see another person of about the same age, still pedalling, pulling or pumping for Britain, and you started *after* they did. Your pride instantly consigns your brains to your buttocks, and you will not stop until they do. Or just after. Your muscles quiver and wobble. Your lungs are working like buggery, your heart is double-timing, your face is puce and you are sweating like George Forman. You know that you will be in agony tomorrow, if you survive that long. And you have only done the first of ten torture sessions on machines designed by the Marquis de Sade.

Eventually, feeling seriously ill, you totter to the change-room and divest yourself of your gym-armour. Then you will be asked if you are all right, by some showering bronzed freak with rippling muscles, far too much pubic hair and, as I may have suggested elsewhere, a disturbingly unnecessary interest in your genitalia. And that goes for all sexes.

I have heard it said that gymnasia have a higher turnover in membership than supermarkets have in pimply checkout assistants. No wonder.

HEIGHTS
Four deep pile inches and two attacks of hysterics

I know that I share this problem with millions, but that does not make me feel any better. I am utterly terrified of heights, and it takes a colossal effort for me even to take a lift. Three feet off the floor and I break into a sweat.

Business used to force me to New York City quite a lot, and as everyone's office there is on the 245th floor, I know that I sat through several meetings with my eyes averted from the windows and my anus forming a suction-cup on the chair. I was once persuaded to go to the top of the Eiffel Tower. I have no recollection of the view whatever. I was glued to the central wall, facing inwards. I also went to the top of the Empire State Building once – *obviously* only once, but at the time I was prepared to do anything to impress a nubile blond American princess and get her into bed. When I reached the top, and I did this without oxygen which is pretty impressive, what did I see? A very large man, lying prone in front of the elevator from which he had just emerged, his finger-nails embedded in the carpet, his hands curled into talons as he whimpered and blatted in terror. Someone had to fetch a very sharp knife and cut him free, after he had been sedated with enough stuff to render him virtually unconscious. I came within an ace of joining him, and I was prepared to beg for an injection. The nubile American etc? Forget it. She left without me and I never saw her again. "Limey wimp," I think I heard her say.

One person is able to stand on the rim of the Grand Canyon and strike a Cortez-like pose without a care, as the ground disappears two miles straight down, five inches from his toes. Other schnooks like me get that horrid greasy feeling in the lower gut, knees and ankles just watching a documentary on TV featuring lunatics who saunter along the exposed beams of skyscrapers under construction. Just writing about this, I promise you, makes me feel uncomfortable.

Someone once told me that in certain brain-types there is a primeval instinct which tells the owner that he does not belong anywhere other than firmly on the Earth with nothing below that but earth. So, should he find himself at any height above that, his natural urge is to get the hell back down by the shortest possible route. Which accounts for the seemingly almost irresistible urge to jump instead of going back down the stairs. Terminal, via terminal velocity, but definitely the straightest route. Others, equally mysteriously, have no problem with heights. Indeed, they get their odd jollies by climbing up sheer rock faces while attached to the mountain by string threaded through a not terribly big nail.

And yet, here's a thing: I fly small aeroplanes and I love it. I will happily show off by putting myself into a spin or a loop and flying out of it at anything from 800 to 18,000 feet. No problem. The floor of the 'plane becomes my "ground level"? Yes, OK, but how do I manage *not* to think of what is *not* below the floor of the plane, when, by the same logic, I know that if I am on the 134th floor of a building, there are 133 solid ground levels below me, and I *still* freak out? Next.

HILLS, WALKING UP
Two, gasp, possibly three

I can walk miles. No, really I can. Miles and miles. Provided that the terrain is as near flat as makes no difference, I am off into the distance. And I am reasonably fit, without being toned and tanned. I am not even seriously overweight. Alright, about ten pounds. Twenty, maximum. But there is something in my metabolism or cardio-vascular machinery which causes me serious discomfort if I have to walk up hills in the course of my rambles. I have very small lungs? Very narrow tubes? Bad aerobic conversion from oxygen to energy or something complicatedly

89

chemical? I don't know. But if any of that were a problem, why can I walk for a long, long way, and at a good pace, without any ill-effects, provided the terrain is more-or-less flat? Because walking on the flat requires minimal cardio-vascular exertion? I suppose.

Problem is, the Earth is not flat. Revelation! You mean Magellan or was it Copernicus got there first? Damn. Anyway, it is *certainly* not flat in the county where I live. Wherever I go, the terrain either suddenly takes a dive down to what others see as a charming wooded valley, or decides to become a mountain. In either case, it means trouble for me. What goes up/down must go down/up. I wheeze. I pant. I huff and puff and blow. I stagger. I go sufficiently red in the face for my wife to get that anxious look on her sweet face and suggest a little lie-down.

And it's no good telling me that it is all a question of fitness, and that I am nowhere near as fit as I think I am. I know all that. A little while back, we planned a walking holiday in an area where the up/down element is not avoidable, so for weeks beforehand, I strapped on a rucksack filled with a few bricks (OK, two) and did some training. No good. The *training* almost killed me, and the actual holiday brought me even closer to an early demise. Any ideas?

HONOURS
Four lords a-leaping but once a knight

I dealt with our specially, uniquely genteel British form of corruption somewhere else and I suggested that at the core of this problem lies the giving and receiving of honours – especially peerages and knighthoods. Right on cue – thanks, Mr. Blair – came the scandal exposed by blameless Dr Chai Patel, confirming once and for all that if you know what you're doing, and you know the right people, you can simply buy an honour if you want one and you know you won't get it any other way. And the right people? Someone, somewhere in the bowels of the political party of your choice. But not the treasurers of course.

I still think that we don't do a lot of overt corruption in Britain. Not the kind where public money is siphoned off into private bank accounts, Italian style, by clever accountants and lawyers, some of them possibly British. No. We do most of it another way. We allow the Prime Minister and the leaders of the so-called main parties to dish out titles to people who should never be allowed anywhere near a title of any kind, but who are so desperate to be called Sir or Lord, that they will do almost anything to get one.

Twice a year, or perhaps more often (I have lost count and I don't care) the lives of a number of people in Britain are changed forever by the acquisition of titles. These are dished out at various times, including the Queen's Birthday, which, in true Brit style, isn't her birthday at all, just her *official* birthday, because her *real* birthday … oh, never mind.

People selected by some deeply mysterious, and, it turns out, highly suspect method are given titles and must be called Sir This or Lord That or Lady The Other, if you will pardon the expression. Does this matter? Oh, indeed it does.

One day, Mr. Jones, is plain Mr. Tom Jones. The next day he is Sir Thomas Jones. One day, Mr. Even Fattercat becomes Lord Fattercat. Oh, and if the new knights or the new peers are married men, their wives automatically become Lady Jones and Lady Fattercat. And what have their wives done to become Lady This or That ? With some rare exceptions – nothing. Nothing at all – except marry the men in question, lie back and think of England (or Wales or Scotland etc.,) and then, as the wisdom has it, stand behind them, amazed at the achievement of the men they know to be poltroons.

And what's even more mysterious – if Sir Thomas or Lord Fattercat divorces his wife, *she* can *continue* to call herself Lady Jones or Lady Fattercat – and if the knight or peer remarries, the *new* wife is *also* known as Lady Jones or Lady Fattercat. Wonderful, isn't it? But if a *female* member of the great-and-good is given a title, does that entitle her spouse to be called Sir Something or Lord Anything? Absolutely not. And while I'm on this subject: now that gay marriage is upon us, as it were, will the spouse of an ennobled partner be entitled to a title as well, provided that he/she declares that they are the, ahem, female equivalent in the marriage? Not yet? Just a matter of time, then. But why does a female spouse have an automatic entitlement to a title? For the same reason that so many other things are seriously wrong with the way Britain is governed and managed. Tradition, old boy. Can't go mucking about with tradition. The wheels of state will fall off. Hello. They have fallen off already, or haven't you noticed?

Titles have the strangest effect upon the people who swim around the be-titled. Yesterday, plain Mr. Jones couldn't get a table at that fashionable restaurant for love nor money. Today, a table is *always* available – please come this way, Sir Thomas. Please come this way, My Lord. And when that new Government committee is being formed to look into mad politician disease or drug-abuse by sheep, or why corn flakes go soggy in milk, the chairman always turns out to be, you guessed it, Sir Thomas or Lord Fattercat. They know nothing about the subject, but it's assumed that they carry with them, in the same bag as their title, a sort of automatic authority and the knowledge to go with it. And it's assumed that they deserve unquestioning respect. Tossocks of course, but how very British. And how very stupid. Small wonder that so much of what quangos do is cock-up.

So, who *is* on the receiving end of titles these days? It's all very mysterious, as I say, and whatever anyone in any of the political parties tells you, it's going to stay that way. Retired, or even current captains of industry get titles for services to their own bank balances. Civil servants get knighthoods automatically as soon as they reach a certain rank. The same with judges, no matter how stupid or out of touch with life. Actors receive knighthoods or peerages. (David Jason, bless him, already had a title before he was recently dubbed by Her Maj. "David Jason". That was and is his title. You can't improve on that. Dear old David could get any table at any restaurant just by saying he was David Jason. He does not need a knighthood). Managers of football teams are knighted. Retired party politicians, no matter how bad or incompetent they've been, are knighted or made peers on a conveyor belt basis. Some senior Bishops automatically become Lords. Raddled, retired or should-be-retired rock-stars are knighted, for heaven's sake.

And one final category, which no-one liked to talk about, but it's well out into the open now. If you give a political party enough money for its campaign funds, you get your knighthood as well, if you ask for it. Just like that. You might even get a peerage. Depends on what you paid, and what you asked for.

The reasons given for conferring these titles are for "services to …". It's all dressed up as services to Charity, Industry, Education, Medicine, and so on and on, or whatever business sector in which you have made your pile. It's usually nonsense – for the most part, they are given these titles for services to themselves and their own bank balances as I've said. Just occasionally, a title goes to someone who is genuinely deserving, but that is oh, so rare. And even then, was it right for Steve Redgrave, Ellen MacArthur and Kelly Holmes to be knighted and damed? Wasn't it good enough that they won their medals and achieved their goals without having to give them titles as well? Gold-medal winners are not turned into Counts in France or Germany or anywhere else. Just like David Jason, their names and their achievements *are* their titles. That ought to be good enough.

Does any of this matter ? Well, it matters enough for the Government to have appointed a committee to enquire into how it all works, because there have been rumblings, rumblings. And who heads up this new committee? Why, Sir Borpher Brittan of course. Will anything change? Of course not. I rest my case.

No, I don't. The whole thing ought to be discontinued, immediately. I have no problem with awarding people some sort of recognition for truly outstanding charity work or heroism – something similar to the MBE, but for heaven's sake let's bury that particular piece of outdated stupidity and call it the Order of Britain. Or replace it completely with something that is already there and under-used, viz., the Order of Merit. Also forget grades, such as Member, Order, Commander. Make them all equally valuable and equally valued. If someone is good enough to get a gong, why grade the gong-getter? The Order of Merit says exactly what it does on the gong.

But there should be no honours simply for having done the job you were paid to do. And let's get rid of titles altogether in the Britain of the twenty-first century. And I don't just mean stop dishing them out – abolish them altogether. And absolutely *NO* titles for politicians, past, present or future. Ever. And finally – get rid of the Honours Committee or whatever the secret thing is called, and give the job of awarding recognition honours to a publicly-appointed committee, open to scrutiny, with debates in public. *Now* I rest my case.

HORSES

Two. No, make that four, one at each corner

Careful. Very careful. My nearest and dearest is a horsy-person. Talks a strange language involving metal and leather bits which look and sound

like things out of a medieval torturer's kit-bag. Puts a horse-blanket on the nag; takes it off; puts it on again. Takes it off. Spends all kinds of money on small turd-like pellets, horse-shoes, electric fences, batteries.

Rides the thing once in a blue moon. But loves it.

Me, I only have to go within six feet of any horse, and its ears go flat, it flashes the whites of its eyes, and the huge muscles which control its ability to kick the corpuscles out of me start to twitch in anticipation. I stay the hell away. Horses scare me to quivers.

I suppose that it has something to do with past experience, when I spent a lot of time as a teenager on a farm with relatives who had sheep by the squillion – and several horses, which we were all forced to ride. I was bucked off a miserable nag's back about twenty miles from home and had to walk back in the baking sun. The damned thing took fright at a twig. It took me the rest of the day and well into the night to get home. My water and rations were in the saddle-bags, which went home with the horse. Bucked off? I should say so. Another time, I was taken for a ride by a pissed-off gelding (well, he would be, wouldn't he) at lots of miles per hour round the farmyard until the damned thing ran out of oats or steam. A change of underwear was needed. I don't know how I stayed on board. I know *why*, though. If I had come off, I would have hit the ground head-first, doing ninety.

I went to a point-to-point, could not see the point, and retired to sit on a bank at a safe distance. Or so I thought. One of the competitors parted company with her massive, snorting beast, which galloped *way* off the track and roared down the bank straight at me, farting angrily, nostrils flaring and squirting steam, teeth akimbo. I had to dive into a nettle-filled ditch. Any one of four hooves, each the size of a dinner-plate, would have driven me into the ground like a tent-peg. I was a long way from the action. The cursed thing sought me out. I *know* it did.

I have a rule: never get on the back of anything that has a brain, however small. And with horses, we are talking *really* small. At least those small brains have not yet figured out how to put a large piece of heavy leather on my back, festoon me with straps, force a metal thing between my teeth and then make me carry them around. But I know that if they could, they would. Horses are huge, powerful, unpredictable, and capable of being very, very nasty. I don't care what Monty Roberts says.

"HOW DO YOU FEEL?"
With five fingers, and no brains

Here they are. Media reporter-interviewers. Note-books, microphones, cameras thrust up the noses of some poor soul who has just lost a loved one in a fire, or a road accident. And then comes the question to this sobbing individual. "How do you feel …?" The interviewer knows *perfectly well* that the interviewee is desperate, distraught, destroyed. But the reporter/interviewer/arsehole asks them, "How do you feel?". Same thing if the subject has just won the pools, the lottery, the FA cup, a gold medal. "How do you feel?"

I have been in the happy position from time to time where I was asked to recruit and train news reporters for TV and radio. I warn them. Say **** and **** on the air if you absolutely have to. Fall over a cliff while interviewing a wildlife nut-case chasing the lesser twatted grabdick. Vomit copiously to camera while talking about the latest offal-disposal problem at the local abattoir. Your job is safe. Say "how do you feel?" just once, and you are fired. And I will know *exactly* how you feel.

HYENAS (IN RESTAURANTS)
Your shout, and rising with plonk

No, this is not some sort of Hurst-Emin foray into surreal installation-art. This is about groups of people who arrive in restaurants half-sozzled, proceed as fast as possible to fill up the other half, and start braying, yelping and hooting at the top of their disgusting voices, like hyenas at a kill. The women are worst, because their laughter is pitched higher than the men, and they laugh at absolutely anything. At everything. If the waiter arrives to take their order, all he has to do is stand there, and the female contingent falls off its chairs in drunken hysterics. Then one of the party recounts the latest unfunny episode about Mr. Nobwick in Accounts, and they go off into paroxysms of forced mirth, banging the table and one another's shoulders.

Usually, the parties in question are collections of People From The Office. But not inevitably. I have endured a couple of hours of this torture while twenty or so teachers – *teachers!* – from a prep-school shrieked and gabbled, not a yard away from me. Letting off steam, I suppose, after a term of dealing with intelligence-free children and aggro from shaven-headed, earring-wearing parents, so fair enough. But also enough to cause me to adopt a new rule when booking a table. I ask if they are expecting any large groups or tables of six or more. If so, no thanks, another time.

Killjoy? Me? Nah. It's just that noise-pollution is a particular hate of mine, and I don't care if it is made by jack-hammers, helicopters, idiots playing "music" in cars, mobile phones in trains – or packs of hyenas in restaurants. Or indeed music in same. Wait until I get *there*.

HUNTING WITH DOGS
Four tallies and a mounted ho

I wish that the hunting fraternity and sorority would just tell the truth. They don't go out with packs of dogs trained to tear a live fox to pieces because this is a service to the countryside which is infested with foxes killing one's chickens and lambs. There are much better, more efficient and more humane ways to keep the fox population under control, if this really is a necessity. They do it because they love the whole scene, just as people who play golf love doing that. If part of playing golf involved using one's mashie ritually to smash in the heads of rabbits which keep digging up the greens, we would be on the golfers like tons of bricks. And if they were to compound the lie by saying that they play the game as a service to the control of rabbits and the ball-hitting part was just an extra, we would string them up by their niblicks.

The fact is that hunting with dogs is entertainment dressed up as a sport. Which is fine, but the hunters have to come clean and admit it. Then, maybe, they would get the respect they so crave. But they can't do this, can they? Who, in the twenty-first century, would ever give them licence to behave as their forefathers did with bear-baiting or cock- and dog-fighting if they actually came clean and said that hunting foxes and stags with dogs is actually about a damned good day's entertainment or sport on a horse? Talk about non-PC. Whoo-hoo.

The theatre of the hunt is a wonderful thing to behold and, no doubt, to be part of. It all looks like a lot of fun if you like sitting on the back of a huge dumb beast that can move at forty mph, go airborne for several minutes at a time, and throw you the hell off its back whenever it wants to, if that's your pleasure. And let's face it, some of the gels who do this stuff look utterly stunning. Most of the men just look like pompous pink-coated prats, but that's another matter. I also happen to believe that there *are* countryside jobs and traditions which deserve to be preserved, and I hate the idea of packs of hounds being put down because *their* jobs have disappeared. So, let's keep the ban on hunting with dogs, encourage the hunts to keep on using drags and find other ways of having a good gallop over the hills and dales without having to watch cruel and unusual punishment being meted out to foxes, stags and hares – and then leave the hunts alone. Including, especially, the dogs.

But will we ever be able to persuade the hunters to tell the truth? No. That's why His Blairness and his city-slickers have passed That Law. Maybe some future Government will repeal it, but the hunt-people had better come up with a better story than the one they currently want us to buy.

I

"I MEAN"

Four y'knows and two likes

No-one is immune. I mean, where did it come from? I mean, how did this choking bit of extraneous verbal foliage arrive fully formed into the English language and take up residence in the brains and mouths of everyone? I mean, why has it become impossible for anyone to utter a sentence without this irritating pseudo-introduction – and I mean, *I mean* anyone? Including that wonderfully self-important but entertainingly aggressive interviewer, quiz-master and guardian of our language, John Humphrys. Also Lynn Truss.

I do my utmost to avoid it. But I know that I fail more often than I succeed, because it is simply against the nature of human oral-aural communication to have to listen to oneself all the time in case an "I mean" slips out. You try it. You'll find that you are talking strummocks in no time, with half-formed thoughts spilling out onto the carpet while your mind tries to filter what your mouth has already decided it is going to say.

There are all kinds of odd verbal punctuations of this kind. "Well", "y'know", "ahm", "erm", and in the mouths of teenage persons and actresses, "like". Not to mention "actually" which is my personal second-most hated after "like". Until recently, and thank heaven for mercies it is no longer necessary because I have been able to sever my connection with this offending and offensive jerk, I had to do business with a man who actually said "actually" between every third and fourth word. It made conversations around meeting-tables almost impossible for me, because I sat there waiting and wincing for the next onslaught of "ackshly's" to hit me, rendering without meaning almost everything he said. The fact that he talked arrant

nonsense most of the time anyway, did not help, and his poisonous personality made the mix uniquely unbearable. I digress, but I did enjoy getting that off my chest.

The ubiquity of "I mean" almost makes me look forward to listening to those call-centres in Bangalore, where they struggle sub-continentally with English – but do not speak it fluently enough yet to allow the use of extraneous conjunctions to become a habit. But give them time.

I taxed a friend with this "I-mean-ness" recently and he gave me a slant on it which I have to make space for. "It's about making the spoken language seem softer and less edgy," he explained. "If you speak a thought without some sort of introductory slider or softener, you can sound like a robot, or one of those machines used by Professor Hawking – the communication is there and clear, but sounds the way it is – inhuman". I can see this, sort of. Speech needs embellishment the way a salad needs dressing. So perhaps I should not be too hard on the, um, look, er, y'know, like, people who, I mean, can't help it, actually. Absolutely (which, these days, tumbles out of mouths instead of just plain old fashioned, "yes".)

Robert MacGregor

ISRAEL, ARABS AND
One body, two heads
_____

This is awful, but I am suffering from Middle-East-Fatigue and I know I shouldn't. It's just that I feel that sick-making revolving-door syndrome and I want the become a Super-Giant with power to knock heads together and tell the both the Arabs and the Israelis, very, very loudly to stop behaving like brats.

They are all descended from the same semitic ancestors. They have very similar cultural norms. Some of them even look alike. They have more in common than they have differences. They are among the most intelligent and resourceful people on Earth. So, why?

But then, I suppose, anthropologists and historians said something similar about the Germans and the English who knocked the crap out of one another for a century. At least we seem to have stopped now. But the Arabs and the Israelis? Any end in sight? Can't see one.

So, I will just have live with being tired of the daily Middle-East dose of mindless mayhem, and switch channels to watch cartoons again.

INCIVILITY, DRIVERS GUILTY OF
Two fingers, one on each hand
_____

I live in an area where A to B frequently involves single-track country lanes. If you comes across a vehicle going the way you have just come, one of you has to reverse to the nearest passing place. And talking of reversing, this is a skill which is rapidly being lost, especially by those who have made enough money by the age of eighty to afford a new and comically expensive German or Swedish roadster. It's the neck, you see. Can't turn an eighty-year old neck more than a few degrees this way or that, so trying to look backwards over the elderly shoulder will put the driver straight into physiotherapy for a month. So, when you come across one of these, no point in waiting – just do the reversing yourself, however far you have to go. Saves a lot of time.

Usually, this ends up with the aforementioned eighty-year-old creeping past you at 0.6 mph, but mostly you do receive some form of thanks, ranging from a smile and hand-wave to a repressed English raising of just one finger from the steering wheel. But far too often after you have let the other driver through, he will sail past without so much as a glance, as if he owned that stretch of road and *you* had been trespassing. I swear, this makes me so angry that I would, if I could, jump out of my car, run bionically after the manner-less jerks, overtake and force them off the road, where I would deliver an epithet-loaded lecture on courtesy and good manners. Only once, so far, have I had the immense pleasure of being able to do this, and no bionic legs were needed. The axe-faced driver squeezed her immense 4X4 past my car while it and I crouched in a slight widening of the lane, and she steamed on without so much as a glance. She only managed another ten yards when she had to stop for a truck. I *did* get out. I *did* saunter over to her driver's window, which, with an expression of supreme distaste, she wound down. I let her have it, involving, I seem to remember, quite a few inadvertent flecks of spittle.

I don't think anyone had spoken to her in such terms since she left St Lesbia's School for Rich Snooty Gals. *Boy*, did I enjoy that.

INSURANCE
Clause 703 applies, but see exception under clause 905

Talk about grudge purchases. Paying the TV licence-tax, or a road-fund tax disc, or petrol, or BT line rental, or dentists. But the worst for me are insurance premiums of any kind. It has something to do with the endless forms which only insurance companies know how to generate, ranging from proposal to claim and everything in between. It also has something to do with the corporate policy which assumes that every claim is a fraudulent one, so all claims must be treated with suspicion and if at all possible, refused. It *also* has something to do with the fact that with all the other grudge purchases, you get something back right from the off, whereas you get "peace of mind" and nothing else until you have make a claim – and *that* requires that you have either (a) been injured, (b) been robbed, (c) had your property damaged, (d) fallen ill, or (e) died.

If some insured calamity strikes, your next premium, because you had the nerve to make a claim, will be a lot higher, unless you have been prepared to buy a protected no-claim policy, and that is not always available. And if you foolishly indulged in unprotected insurance-claim, they might not be prepared to renew your insurance at all, because you are now a bad risk. A story: we had a power cut recently. Powerless freezer unfroze everything, of course, to the tune of about £75 replacement value in veg, meat, fish, stuff. Claim met, no problem sir. Premium on renewal? Increased by a fair bit. Ner ner na ner ner.

And even if you made no claims at all, the chances are that your premium will go up next year anyway, because some other sods made hefty claims and, well, they just *do*, don't they? Will your premium increase by the same amount as inflation? No, no. The insurance industry has its *own* measures of inflation, and when they say inflation, they mean skin-bursting, tyre-pressure, blow-out-causing inflation. No matter what has been happening in the rest of the world or the rest of the economy, things that insurers have to pay for in order to recompense you for what you have lost, cost a lot more than anything else. Strange, that.

JAMS, TRAFFIC, TRACTORS CAUSING
Five miles will take you ten times longer than …

I live in the country, sort of, as you have, by now, gathered. Nothing could ever persuade me to go back to town or city life, and civilisation will only decline further than it has already done if the drift both of, and to, the cities continues. But there is one aspect of the rural idyll which raises my blood pressure and in common with thousands of people who have become spoiled by the relative freedom of countryside travel, I am borderline-apoplectic when my gentle and steady progress is brought either to a halt or to a crawl in a traffic jam which ought not to be happening at all. Many of my fellow country-siders fulminate at the presence of large caravans and mobile blocks of flats masquerading as "motor-homes" which crawl everywhere as they have a perfect right to do – but in this congested, over-populated, badly managed island of ours, anything (including caravans and motor-homes) which causes the road-arteries to clog results in motorised thrombosis. So I am not exactly enthusiastically supportive of anything, no matter how righteous its cause, which causes jams.

But I stop a long way short even of tolerance when it comes to tractors and damned great JCB-type vehicles which have a maximum speed of about twenty-three mph (and that's dangerous enough) which amble along roads where overtaking is simply out of the question. They are driven either very slowly by elderly, grizzled, pipe-smoking, hat-wearing, infuriatingly smiling escapees from The Archers – or at a heart-stoppingly fast weave by young, bearded, cigarette-dangling, baseball-capped, surly wanna-be boy racers. Behind them, sometimes for miles, there is a country-made jam of cars, mine included. Watch closely if you can, and you will see me biting chunks out of the steering wheel. Rarely, very rarely, the tractor-driver will pull over into a lay-by and let some of us past, and he does it reluctantly because he knows that once he does this, the dozens and dozens of vehicles which have piled up behind him, are going to keep on going. He might be stuck there for a long time. When a tractorised Samaritan does let us past, after we have followed him for miles at 5 mph, he always receives a "thank you" wave (at least he does from me) in the vain hope that he just *might* remember my car next time he glances into his cow-shit encrusted rear-view mirror, and *might* just let me past, again. What I really want to do is throw an incendiary device into his cab as I accelerate past, but he won't know that. I smile, I smile.

The question is – what the hell are these rolling road-blocks doing on relatively main arterial roads at all? They can, like tanks, be driven over anything, and that includes fields of any kind. But that would mean the long-way round to the other part of the farm, so onto the road for several miles, why not? And always in the middle of the day, usually at the busiest times.

In Britain, our roads are just not tractor-friendly. Nor am I.

JELLYFISH
Ten foot tentacles approaching two testicles

Into aphid territory here. What the hell are they for? As far as I can tell, nothing eats them because how much utterly tasteless or possibly utterly revolting jelly can one eat even if one is a starving turtle or a demented dolphin? Jellyfish pulsate about the oceans in an aimless fashion, and occasionally fetch up in swarms (shoals? herds? flocks? jams?) too close to beaches for their, or our, comfort. They sting buggery out of us, and then flop helplessly onto the shore to die. They cause mayhem ranging from mild annoyance as in hell this jelly thing has stung me on the ankle and it burns a bit, to instant death if you happen to tangle with an Australian box jellyfish. This Aussie charmer has tentacles in great fronds several feet long and if you get caught by one of them, the amount of venom which is then injected into you is enough to cripple a ship.

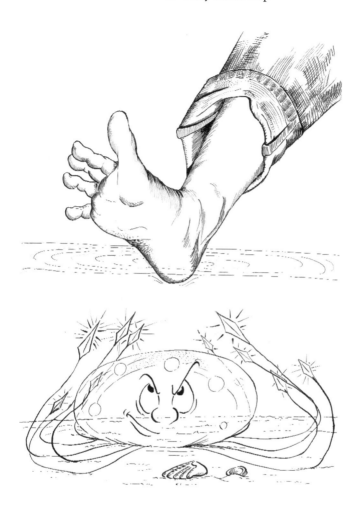

Now what the hell is *that* about? Why does anything, never mind a blob of useless jelly, need to be equipped with such a terrible weapon? When its rudimentary nervous system (it has no brain that we would recognise as such) does not even "know" that it has just knocked over a whale, or you, what's the damned point? I have watched David Attenborough waxing just-audibly lyrical through his face-mask while glooping about watching from a safe distance as a flotilla (fleet? squadron?) of millions of these things lollopped squelchily by, prettily reflecting and refracting light this way and that, to make what I have to confess was quite a sight. Why were so many of them in one place? He didn't know. Where were they going? He didn't know, and nor did they. All I wanted to know was whether or not they were headed for the beach near me. He didn't say. I stayed out of the water for weeks. Jaws? Forget it. Jelly. With a very bad attitude.

JINGLES
Seven twangs and two thuds

I have had things to say about radio and TV commercials, and I could have included jingles in that category, but they are so deeply irritating that I have created a separate category for the little dears, all to themselves.

In the past, in the long-ago past and far away, there used to be commercial jingles we could remember, sing along with, and actually enjoy. Today, the advertising ear-muggers who are responsible for them are creating stuff of such mind-sapping inanity and forgettableness that the Government ought to Pass A Law banning them altogether until such time as the advertisers and musicians have been re-trained in a Siberian Jingle Camp and are allowed back into society having rediscovered tune-making, rhythm, rhyme and scansion.

Jingles are not confined to commercials. Radio stations are keeping the writers of these jingles in vodka, nose-candy and spliffs, so that the station can be identified to the dumb-shit listener by means of a string of discordant notes and disconnected words. Why? Because radio stations assume that simply *telling* the listener in simple words what station they are tuned to, does not do the trick. You have to hit the poor mush-brained slobs in the ear with a jingle wrapped loosely around the station identification, or they won't get it.

And do we think that the non-commercial BBC is above all this? No. With the possible exceptions of Radio 4 and Radio Three, BBC radio and TV are at it all the time. Beeee Beeeee Ceeeeeeeeeeeeeeeee ... R-a-a-a-a-a-dio Tooooo! Urgh.

I have simple musical tastes and requirements, really. I want musical phrases to resolve, so that they feel complete, rather than ending in. I want words, if they are set to music, to rhyme if they are intended that way, and to scan so that they fall easily on my brain. Clearly, it has become impossible for any of this to be done by the writers of today's jingles. Can't someone find them proper jobs?

JUDGES (and magistrates)
Several tresses short of a wig or two

As you will come to see a little later, I am not enamoured of the legal profession. Why am I being so bloody polite? I despise and detest everything to do with the parasitic bastards who have made themselves responsible for the administration of the law and as a result, I have kept my nose as clean as possible so that I do not have to come into contact with lawyers and courts. And, especially, judges.

Which is not to say that I have always succeeded. And which is not to say that close friends of mine, and family members, have always been able to keep the legal profession at bay. In the past two years, I have been in court and watched, my mouth hanging open in disbelief as ...

A magistrate found friends of mine guilty of keeping a dangerous dog when the only "evidence" of danger came from a local Policeman, known to be as bent as a corkscrew and a dog-hater par excellence. The magistrate's findings flew in the face of a stack of clear evidence to the contrary, some of it given in court, some by written statement. The prosecution lawyer was a concentration of gimlet-eyed nastiness, while my friends had to make do with a chinless, voiceless, brainless gump. The judge was an arse.

A district judge found in favour of a known local crook who accused one of my relatives of having deliberately rammed his (the crook's) already severely damaged boat in harbour, when all the evidence pointed in the opposite direction. The judge's whole demeanour was sour, dyspeptic and querulous. He was A JUDGE and he was not going to allow anyone to forget it.

The father of a six-year-old daughter, outrageously falsely accused by the estranged and psychotic mother of sexually assaulting his daughter, was told by a smiling simpleton on the bench that he should be patient while those who managed the court calendar found a convenient date for a hearing – likely to be two months into the future.

Meanwhile, the mother is making life hell for her own daughter. Could the father persuade the judge that there was an urgency attaching to this case? No. The judge just smiled and smiled and refused to budge. The father was almost put away for contempt of court when he asked the judge what the hell he was playing at.

A judge, having taken leave of his senses, decides that nine Afghan 'plane hijackers can stay in Britain without fear of prosecution, and can live off the welfare state too. He said that was what the law says. No, it doesn't.

How many more such idiocies are being perpetrated by judges every day?

We are supposed to accept the infallibility of those who claw their way to the top of the legal profession. Becoming a judge automatically imbues the person so elevated with wisdom and an extra helping of knowledge, intelligence, and humanity, does it not? Not in my experience.

KISSING, TELEVISION, CINEMA, CLOSE-UPS
Four liver lips and two slurps

It's bad enough if one happens to be seated alongside an amorous couple on a train or a 'plane, where they are trying to use their tongues as scalpels to perform tonsillectomies on each other. But it gets a lot worse when directors of TV dramas and movies insist on showing the stars trying to eat their way into each other's throats, in close-ups tight enough to show saliva swilling about their teeth. In the cinema this is happening on a huge screen, so the effect is magnified many-fold, and the facial parts of the actors take on the hue and consistency of whale blubber. All this to the accompaniment of whooshing and sucking sounds akin to the sort of thing you might hear if you had a stethoscope and could listen to your bowels in full peristalsis. Which I do not recommend.

I appreciate that love scenes have to have the stamp of authenticity when portrayed on film, or we would simply not believe that Hector was desperate to get into the nether garments of Hortense. So we end up with the revoltingly explicit osculatory close-ups which some directors insist on. By contrast you watch something like the wet-shirt scene involving Colin Firth (poor sod, he will forever be remembered as D'Arcy diving into that duckshit- and weed-infested pond). Boiling, passionate sex without any touching. Or equally, some of the scenes in Out of Africa involving Redford and Streep, where steam could be seen rising from their waist-bands before they got within ten feet of each other. And you realise that aching passion and the nearness of one's be-lusted *can* be portrayed without all that open-mouthed wetness and lip-swallowing.

If I happen to record a drama I want to see at a later date, I have fun

putting the videotape into fast-forward on playback when the actors are having at each other's oesophagi. It is hilarious. I really do recommend it. This, you can try at home.

KITES

One or two, can't get it up any higher

Kites? What do I mean, kites are crap? Those enchanting gossamer creations that flutter, swoop and dive? Things people *play* with? Yes, kites. You will remember how I think fishing is crap because it involves miles of very thin line which only has to see me coming and it starts to copulate and twist itself into a ball beyond untangling. Same with kites.

I go to the beach with my family. The wind is doing its best to divest me of what little hair I have left. Six-year olds roll out the strings and in a flash they have something that looks like a B52 swooping and

shrieking all over the place. Then it's my turn, whether I like it or not. How kind. In an even shorter flash, the kite has turned on its head, and kamikaze-ed its way straight down into the picnic which a family at least a hundred yards away were about to tuck into. The lines have strangled their family dog en route.

The kite, which previously firmly declined to fly, is now jumping up and down in a bowl of Waldorf Salad. Having Gone To Earth, *now*, it is trying to fly, the damned thing. How do I know it is a Waldorf Salad? The kite is scattering walnuts and celery every which way, instead of just lying there and sucking up the dressing. I am being advanced upon by a very large bald-headed man with a paunch and loads of attitude. I grovel, and wind in a tangled mess of line. I offer to buy him a plate of chips to make up for the salad. He glares.

No. I do not do kites, I do not do fishing, I do not even do long bootlaces. Spaghetti, I carefully cut into short pieces. I have always kept the hell away from girls with long flowing hair.

I watched, one day, while my eldest son (six foot two, strapping, etc) decided to help a kite-surfer with a problem. Being a kite-surfer is enough of a problem, I feel, but this one had actually lost his grip on his kite, which was just a bit smaller than an Airbus, and the stupid thing was towing a load of handles and straps and other apparatus across the beach. The surfer was in the surf. My son leaped to the rescue, got a hand on the line and was immediately hoisted ten feet into the air, his flailing legs making an interesting BLUNK as they connected with the head of a bystander, standing by. The surfer was now out of the surf, running and screaming for everyone to leave his ★★★★★★ ★★★★★★ ★★★★★★★ kite alone. I am expecting a postcard from my son any day now. He has just landed in Goose Bay, Canada.

KORMA

Three heaped spoons and a pinch of what, exactly?

That's *korma*, not karma, OK? I don't do karma.

In common with millions of people whose palates have been colonised in revenge for the Raj by Indian food, I love curries. I do not love curries as produced by most of the street-corner curry-houses, who get through tonnes of monosodium glutamate every week, but I adore curries made lovingly by people who know what they are doing, starting with fresh spices carefully ground and ... better stop, as I am salivating onto my keyboard.

For me, a curry does not have to feel as though someone has thrown napalm down my throat, and it is sad to watch lager-filled cross-eyed morons stumble into Indian restaurants and demand a prawn vindaloo, chop-chop, with extra chillies, OK, Rajah, narmean? I was lucky enough to have a proper Indian market close to where I once lived, and I was given a once-in-a-life-time course in the choice and recognition of a good curry, where flavour mattered far more than the extent to which it could explode your teeth. Which is not to say that these wonderful dishes were bland – far from it. They were plenty spicy enough.

And then I came back to the UK, where I found the cultural invasion which had spawned an Indian restaurant in even the most remote parts of the country, poppadom-by-chapatti in every high street. I often wondered what an Indian, Pakistani or Bangladeshi family made of the culture and weather in, say, the Isle of Man, but that's another story.

And I chanced upon korma. I learned that korma is a description which anyone in India, Bangladesh or Pakistan would recognise, because it was developed there as a contribution to the curry range, at the mild-but-tasty end. In Britain, a korma has degenerated into a gloopy mess in order to cater for those who want a curry but want it to be devoid of any of curry's characteristic spiciness and to taste of nothing but coconut.

I don't get British-made korma at all. It is so ... beige. You may as well be eating a thickened, slightly savoury, lumpy custard.

There is of course another side to this curry business. I once shared a flat with a bloke whose parents had lived in Rangoon, and ex-Indian Army Colonel Thing's taste-buds had been beaten into submission by eating very hot curries, and nothing but, for decades. He announced an impending visit, so in preparation his son alerted the local Indian curry-house to the imminent arrival of the taste-challenged Colonel, who could sense the heat of a curry in his mouth, but as to flavour? Forget it. The cook excelled himself. He produced a beef curry which had no name – way, *way* beyond vindaloo – and it arrived in a heap of visibly pulsating black chunks. I took a tentative forkful.

My eyes bulged, my throat went into spasm, my tongue curled up and resigned. I don't think I have ever fully recovered. But Colonel Thing took a large forkful. "Waiter! Bring the chilli sauce, chop, chop!" I think I fainted at that point. It sure as hell made the case for *something* nearer the korma end of the range.

LAWYERS
Seven hundred thousand, and a refreshing coupla grand

Equip yourself with a glass of something strong and a sandwich. I have a lot to say. With many of the things to which I have given vent in this book, my displeasure ranges from mild to mighty. But with this lot, my rage is apoplectic, incandescent, towering and eternal. I hate these pernicious parasitic swine with all my heart and soul.

Because I had absolutely no idea what I wanted to do with my life after school, I went along with the limp suggestion of the brainless nerk who did duty as our careers adviser, and read law. For five years. That almost did me in. Then I spent a few miserable weeks as a solicitors bum-boy, most of it comatose, having keeled over trying to make sense of Farnesbarnes vs Barnes Farms. Or what the judge, clearly paid by the word, was trying to get out of his system. The rest of my time was spent fetching and carrying, and endless hours of unspeakable tedium in the courts listening to the lawyers boring one another, the judge and me to sobs. That *did* do me in. I got the hell out of the legal profession as fast as my mummified mind could make me go, and got a life.

There is nothing anyone can say that is either remotely insulting or defamatory about lawyers, because it is all true and in the public interest, which is a perfect defence, and they know it. It's like dealing with street gangs. You call them every rotten name you can think of, and they say, "Filthy, ear-ring-wearing, shaven headed, snout-nosed arse-wipes? That the best you can do?" There is no insult you can throw at them and expect it to have an effect. The more vile the insult you try to concoct, the more pleased they are with it. They are completely immune - just like lawyers, who come top (or is it bottom?) of every crap-poll in the land, and love it.

118

A typical London solicitor will charge £375 per hour in fees. Per *hour*. Plus VAT. A London barrister can charge £2,000 per day. And given that important cases at High Court level have to be heard in London, the clients pay London rates. What entitles these gouging, jumped up parasites to charge this kind of money I have no idea. Well, I do, and it's that old dog indulging his genital fixation again. Senior medical consultants, who are not shy about charging like the Light Brigade themselves, would blush and cringe if they dared to demand lawyer-level fees, and some of these medicos are out there saving lives, rather than just saving or making money for their clients, which is what most lawyering is about these days.

Lawyers have, over the centuries, developed a very neat trick which forces every one of us into their reeking caves if we have any kind of problem which can only be sorted out by recourse to law. They write

119

the laws themselves, and they write it in a language which only very remotely resembles English (or French, or Italian or Hindi etc - they are all at it, worldwide) so that they alone can understand and interpret it. Lawyers love to remind with glee anyone who decides to represent himself that he has a fool for a client, and the practice of the law is such that they are usually right. I recall one very experienced solicitor who told me (but not until he had retired) that in the bad old days before there was the Rule of Law, people settled disputes by hitting each other over the head with a club until one or the other fell down. "Not substantially different today," he said, "but instead of clubs the disputing parties use lawyers wielding cash, and the methods and outcomes are roughly the same."

One of the most utterly hateful things about these parasites is the game they play. Lawyers will take on any case where they smell money. Today, a barrister will argue a case on behalf of an insurance company being sued by a customer who has been shamelessly diddled out of a payout. Tomorrow, the same barrister will take on an almost identical case, but this time arguing for the customer against the same insurer. Any sense of what's right, wrong or fair? None. Go to any of the whine-bars or fashionable and horrendously expensive restaurants in the City of London, and listen.

"Ay say, erld by, jolly werl darn in thet case. Sheohed the buggah warts wart, eh? I heah he's hed ter sell his hice ter pay corsts. Wifey nort tebly happeigh, lookin' fra dvors. Kids hev ter gota rahly orfl Guvmint school, nigh. Har, har. Werl done, werl done indeed". I exaggerate? Go there and listen.

I learned very quickly while I was studying law that I should never confuse the administration of the law with the dispensation of justice. Those matters are only very distantly related and only occasionally coincide. It still comes down to who has the biggest club in the form of the deepest pockets; who can afford to take a case ever upwards on appeal after appeal, while the costs go through the roof. But, whoa, again, what about Legal Aid? Surely those who are skint can get help that way? Yes, but only up to a point - and they involve means-tests. Means tests? Demeaning tests. Except, if you are a footballer, earning

£40,000 a week, but French-speaking, whereupon under Rule 256 Subsection 29 Clause 36 (b) (iii) of the Exceptions to Common Sense Act of 1973, you can have Legal Aid, *pas de probleme*, Monsieur. The Law is not an ass, as the old aphorism has it. That represents cruelty to asses, which are gentle and helpful things. The Law is certainly nothing to which any animal can be compared. Less ass than assassin. Really, truly, terminally hateful.

Does my diatribe mean that all lawyers are greedy scumbags who operate in a principle-free zone? No, of course not. There must be several, who are full of decency and honour, long on service and helpfulness, free of greedy thoughts and generally good eggs. If you are a lawyer and you are reading this, you are one of the good guys, of course. Pity is that so many of your colleagues actually seem anxious to polish the opposite image and take pride in being precisely what most people think they are.

The good guys are, most usually, civil rights lawyers, and they try to do what they can from the pittance of the public purse for people chucked into chookie, taking such fees as they can from Legal Aid. They appear to have consciences and feelings for their fellow beings. But they are exceptions. The rest are crocodilian opportunity-eaters, and the bigger the carcass the better.

I wondered, when I started writing this, how I could encapsulate my thoughts in one perfect example. It did not take long. Look at the list of Members of Parliament (both houses) and analyse that list according to previous or current profession. Like to guess how many either still are, or used to be, lawyers? No, don't - you will depress yourself almost as much I did. And what were all three leaders of the so-called main political parties before they turned their attention to self-aggrandising politics? Barristers. QED.

(And do you know what is the largest group of ex-somethings in Parliament, just beating lawyers to the winning post? Teachers. A bent bit of unfair logic says, "Those who can, do; those who can't, teach." Now we must add to that, "Those who can't even teach, become politicians." That says something dreadful about the teaching profession, don't you think?)

Robert MacGregor

LETTERS, CHAIN
Seven streaks of bad luck and two letter bombs

The Internet and e-mailing have made this menace worse, because it has made it easier and cheaper. And the most irritating thing about them, however they are sent, is that they tend to come from people who *know* you. So you, and most civilised people, have to curb a natural inclination to reply using every possible curse, informing the sender that they should drop dead. One does not wish to offend one's friends, or even one's acquaintances. Now I appreciate that there is a difference between a proper chain *letter* and its e-mailed second-cousin, because at least the senders of the now old-fashioned letter variety had the decency to lick and stick, not to mention actually write. Sometimes using a pen. With tongue stuck out of side of mouth. Now, the whole thing is made childishly easy with a click-click here and a click-click there, here a click, there a click etc., etc.

Part of the problem is the sheer cheek of others who think you could *possibly* be interested in forming a link in one of these chains, and the other part is that most people harbour at least *some* residual superstition and are scared witless that failure to keep the chain moving actually *will* result in some personal calamity. They don't have to *imagine* any of this. The chain letter invariably says so, right there in the final paragraph.

"*The last person who failed to send this letter to ten friends or family fell under a bus, and his family discovered that in his lifeless fingers he held a scrap of paper on which he had scribbled a set of numbers for the national lotto, and he was on his way to play it. These numbers came up as the week's jackpot*". Or some such twaddle.

Me, I take my chances, having reached breaking point some years ago. I reply to the sender in terms which leave no room for ambiguity or any other kind of misunderstanding, and that, I am afraid, now includes friends and acquaintances. I tell them to print out the letter, roll it into a tight cylinder, and with the help of a mirror if necessary and some cheap margarine, to shove it. I decided that I do not need friends who send me these things if they have been dumb enough to try to cover me in chain-mail. I am perfectly capable of accepting that if any calamity befalls me, it was going to happen anyway. Kismet I can handle. Chain-doom I cannot.

LETTUCE
Four leaves, or six strands, with with-sauce

Of all the pointless …

Start again. Who decided that this tasteless and unmanageable slug-fodder would make a good addition to the human diet? The same wastrel who invented goats' milk cheese, no doubt. For the sake of humouring my loved-one, who consumes lettuce by the wagon-load, I have tried every variety under the sun. Curly, flat, pale, vivid, floppy, crisp, purple – they all taste exactly the same to me. Of nothing. To make any of the stuff palatable, it has to be soaked in maximal amounts of dressing, and for those who eat lettuce because it contains zero calories, the exercise is futile once the calories in the dressing have been calculated.

I agree that it can look decorative. But decoration is taken to comic extremes in certain restaurants where everything from salmon to sorbet is wrapped in, or served on, a load of greenery which does double duty as décor and filler, to make the dish look more generous than it actually is. If you go to a place which serves smoked salmon and it arrives on a bed of lettuce, have a care. The amount of salmon you have bought is enough for a couple of small toothfuls (toothsful?) while the plate overflows in all directions with green tarpaulins. Order a dish as simple as fish and chips in certain pubs, and along for the ride comes a heap of lettuce in which crouch two embarrassed tomato-quarters. And if lettuce is off, the chef substitutes several strands of something like green knitting, which comes from some other tasteless plant.

But the world lettuce-eating champions are the Yanks. When it comes to a meal-starter, the restaurant will dump before them half of a football-sized iceberg lettuce, onto which has been poured (poured? ladled, mechanically loaded) two gallons of a salad dressing with an entertainingly bizarre name such as Caligula, Snake Island, or Blue Grease. No-one, irrespective of the level of their hunger, can *possibly* eat that much lettuce and then be ready for a prime rib *with au jus*. (*With* au jus. That is the way it appeared on a menu I once saw, those particular yankeedoodles being in a state of bliss-less ignorance as to the meaning of the French "*au*".) But Americans are always lettuce-ready, and they eat the whole damned thing. Where they put it is beyond me. When visiting American friends, I chop and chomp my way through a ton of the stuff *pour la politesse*, but barely manage a quarter of what I am given. That is my lettuce quota for twelve months. Years.

"LIKE"

Like, five, yeah, or seven, yeah?

Where did this come from? American hip-hop or rap? Slough? I cannot find out. But almost everyone is like-ing away like mad. As with "I mean", it has become an infuriating almost-conjunctive inserted at very odd places in speech, meaning utterly bugger-all, and making the like-er sound like some sort of agitated insect. Watch them being interviewed on TV as eye-witlesses to a train crash …

"And I was like, standin' there by the like crossing, like, and the, like, train was, like, comin' down the, like, line, too, like, fast for the, like, driver of the, like, car to, like, move away, like". I want to strangle the stupid sod, or persuade the interviewer to do so, but that would be cruel, because the twerp has no idea that he is doing it. It has become automatic. And it has become a verb among teenagers in particular and not in the sense of "being pleased-by". No longer do these brain-challenged youths use the word "said" any more. " So I was like yeah, and he was like yeah, and I was like so, and he was like no, and I was like no way". Hateful. Utterly, totally, indescribably hateful, like.

"LUXURY"
Penthouse. Five, please, and two tubs of marg

The undisputed champion of all of the over-worked words in the meagre vocabularies of marketing muppets. Luxury toilet roll. Luxury holidays. Luxury mints. Luxury seating in cinemas. Luxury fleeces. Luxury apartments. Luxury Crunchy-Coo Breakfast shale. And luxury margarine. *Margarine,* for heaven's sake!

The origin of the word is the Latin for "light" (lux) and it pains me to see the meaning of a word so horribly corrupted and put to such base use. It has simply become one of those trigger words, like "new" and "improved" which sucker the snail-brained into parting with ever more cash. It is a word which is quickly losing its meaning thanks to the under-educated imagination-free zones which are the brains of so many marketing people. A pox on them.

M

MAKE-OVERS
In line with dropping TV ratings, definitely not a ten

Talk about silk purses and sows' ears. Most of what I have to say is second hand, via members of my family who watch some of these awful programmes the same way a hypnotised rat watches a snake. They tell me that they can't believe that anything can really be so bad, so they watch from time to time just to make sure. I tried once. Some limp-wristed drooper with the world's most irritating voice was making a reasonably comfortable house into an unreasonably pretentious mess. I muttered a lot. My wife told me to go away and shut up. Happy to oblige. The audience, and that of all other similar crack-papering mwah-mwah's is now at least one less than it was or might have been. Mercifully, my wife is gradually losing the will to live through any more of these "programmes" too.

Talentless and unattractive schlumps are turned into painted caricatures for forty-eight hours, and then revert spectacularly as the paint falls off, the hair-do collapses and the clothes pop at the seams. Gardens are destroyed by covering most of the surface with bricks, throwing monstrous loads of decking over the rest, and putting the three remaining plants into pots. Oh, and the gardens must have a water-feature, to go *drubba drubba bloop bloop phnink.*

People queue up to be made over. Or to have it done to their homes and their gardens. But then taste-challenged people of a certain kind will do absolutely *anything* to get themselves on the telly. They actually seek, avidly, opportunities to be humiliated in public – the more public and the more humiliating the better. For these sad-sacks, making an utter arsehole of yourself on TV is a million times better than not being on TV at all. And if you happen to be a D-list celebritette, you prove my point by taking part in "I'm a celebrity, get my ego in there". Who was surprised to see Germaine Greer behaving like both the front- and bum-end of a pantomime cow? She's Australian. She has a Blair-sized ego. She's over here. Next, she'll be made over. Into what? Bad Thought of the Year. And, while on the subject of Greer, did you watch Balderdash and Piffle on BBC2? Who was given (or possibly just took) the opportunity to explain, in a lot of detail, the meaning and origins of the "c" word? Who else? Next.

MAKE-UP, TEENAGERS, USING
Four blotchy patches and three hundred pots of goo

We have friends who have a sixteen-year-old daughter, and to borrow the marvellous phrase coined by Raymond Chandler, she is enough to cause a bishop to kick a hole in a stained glass window. Gorgeous enough to cause my sons' eyes and other things to pop out. Absolutely bound to end up as a film star or something. Not a model (pronounced in such circles as "moddewl") though. She has a proper body with curves and bumps in the right places, and she is far, *far* too intelligent to do anything like modewling. But. Each morning, she spends hours and a great deal of money putting on enough make-up to increase her overall weight by several pounds, and at night, she smears some more horrible grey goop on her face. Then she takes it all off again. No discernible result or facial-skin difference of any kind. Does she suffer from bad skin and typical teenage facial eructations and explosions? No, she does not. She is perfect. But she is following the flock. Baaaa.

Walk down any high-street and you see girls, some of them *impossibly* young, wearing enough slap to cause envy in a Japanese Noh-play actor. Is it fashion, again, or is it that children, their brains fried by watching hours of Estuary-enders, Neighbrooks and the rest of the angst-filled soap-operas which bloat the TV medium, decide that they have to look like the actors? Who, by definition, are made up to the eye-balls? Who knows?

I just hope that someone, somewhere, will eventually tell these moppets that their youth will fall off suddenly one day like a discarded snake-skin and they will be middle-aged. At which point they will need every lotion and crevasse-filling facial cement they can lay their liver-spotted hands on. It's no good, I know. They won't listen. I can carp and weep with regret all I like. They will keep on slapping make-up onto their little faces – just as they will keep on having their little bodies tattooed with stuff which, as they grow into adulthood, will be there to haunt and embarrass them every single day. Wasting my time, sadly. Will they listen to their increasingly desperate parents? Parents? *Parents?* What the hell have *they* got to do with teenagers?

MANUALS, INSTRUCTION
Blood pressure rising; two hundred over apoplexy

I am not alone in this. Everyone is doing more and more DIY, and much of that involves assembling something. Or we buy some piece of equipment and we have to know how to make it work. And I am not even going to take a single step towards IKEA or any of the other flat-pack merchants, because everyone knows about that, and how these torturers stay in business defeats me.

One can be caught out anywhere. The other week, our vacuum cleaner finally went *pffttt, weeeowww, ughhhh* and died. Bought a new one. Household name. Well, it would be. Motor like something perfect for a Jumbo Jet, and a no-bag job, which is helpful. (See "Cleaners, vacuum")

After fisrt use, said the manual, *chek for al filtrs and cleen with knoking or wash.* (I quote). Made in China of course. Should be grateful for any instructions at all in something vaguely resembling English. So, when it clogged itself into no-suckee, I laid the beast on its back, opened the book of words, and had to be revived with strong drink an hour later. In my world a vacuum cleaner has just one job. *SUCK UP DIRT.* That's it. I do not ask it to make my lunch, tell me the time, warn me of objects in my path, monitor my state of health or, and here's the nub, *protect me from anything*. This monster has seven, count them, *seven* different filters through which dust has to pass before it gets to the bit where it is collected. Or where the air has to go after it has collected the dust. Whatever. The manual tells me what they are and how to get the damned thing working again.

To cleen Filter A, Hypoallergic de-fibrillating atmospheric recycler (I think that was what it says). *Remov out cover B by gentry prise open catchs D and F, not use screwer-driver.* (Scream for wife to bring sticking plaster as attempting this instruction has broken three nails and produced a cut several inches long on thumb, while the cover remained closed. Open cover with screwer-driver). *Gripp tab Z, pul filter out, use only fimgers.* (No go, Mr. Ho. Use pliers, with one foot firmly braced against cupboard). *Do gentel knoking axtion to remov dust.* OK. Will the filter go back whence it came? Will it buggelly.

And there are seven like this. If any one of them is even slightly full, a warning light blinks in a threatening manner and then the motor cuts out altogether. (Again, see "Cleaners, vacuum").

No problem. I now have a little bag in which permanently reside all but one of these Chinese nightmares, and the thing, having been fooled by my extracting its filters like bad teeth, works fine. There is one I can't remove. Don't ask.

It's the same with everything. Miles of tripe composed by a technician in Shanghai, possessed of just enough English to be given the job of producing these maddening manuals, but not nearly enough to make them make sense. I have nothing against the Chinese manufacturers. Well, actually, I do, but that's another matter. They are making stuff, almost all of it, designed in Europe or the USA or Japan.

But I do hope that somewhere in Wanking or Bang Kow there is a Mr. Long Dong doing his nut while he tries to make sense of Mandarin instructions written by Doreen Clove in Telford (two years Chinese by distance learning, failed) as he tries to get his Blitish-made car to work. Levenge is sweet. Ying tong.

MESSAGES, ANSWERING-MACHINES, ON
Four, and I say again, four, after the ...

I can be driven daft by the knowledge that someone made a telephone call to my number, but left me in the dark as to who they were and what they wanted. No message. But then again, there are people who *do* leave messages and they *must* wonder why I don't return their calls. The reason I don't return their calls is because *they* are so familiar with their *own* telephone numbers that they assume everyone else is equally familiar, so they gabble it and expect me to (a) hear it and (b) write it down accurately. They draw breath, rear back and deliver their phone numbers, just the once, at a speed which ought to be the subject of scientific investigation. And do they have the courtesy to repeat it, just in case? Of course not. Even when I ask them to? Seldom.

So the OGM (out-going message) from me is, these days, a whining beg, pleeeeeeze to leave a message and pleeeeeeeeeeze to repeat the phone number. Most callers do just that on both counts, but there is a rump who do neither, and I want to shoot them, slowly. Their message usually terminates in a barked "*ba*" which is their cute-idiot way of saying "goodbye".

It's a sort of unthinking arrogance, an assumption that I can listen as fast as they can speak. And if I ever mention it to them once I *do* make contact, boy, do they get huffy. And while I am at this; why do people who leave outgoing messages on their message services or machines still tell you to leave a message *after* the tone? Who, after half a century of answer-machines, is still trying to leave a message *before* the tone? Oh, well, I suppose there must be a few. Crosses to bear, crosses to bear.

MIDRIFFS, BARE
Middle to very low

You have already had the benefit of my thoughts on fashion. Now a word or two about this particular crap example. As I explained, it is all

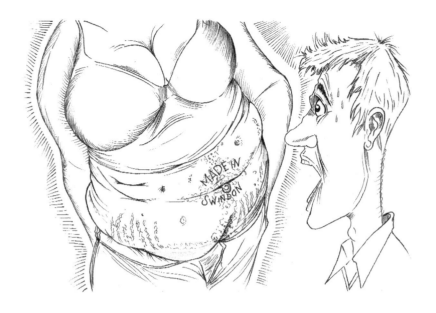

very well for modewls who are stick-thin and six-foot-three to wear stuff which is utterly comic, with the "designers" sniggering and capering in the background, having highly successfully taken the piss out of *ze pooblique,* again.

But when *ze pooblique* fails to see the joke, takes it all in po-faced seriousness and proceeds to wear it, things have gone too far. This bare midriff thing is almost the last straw. Almost, but of course next year a coven of French woofters will decide that exposing the arse-cleft all the way down to the fundament is the next big thing, and away ze female pooblique will go, wobbling, flaunting and exposing. Meanwhile, the sights to which the rest of us are subjected are enough to cause severe illness.

This fashion for indecent exposure is taken up by people with bath-foam for brains and the bodies of hogs. Especially girls (and some older women who really, *really* ought to know better) with bulging guts, often covered in hair and almost always the colour of dough.

One day, I was at my desk when one of the secretaries hove into earshot and pulled up alongside, with an urgent message from Mr. Big. I turned to listen, and found myself with her midriff at eye-level, no more than a foot or two away. The midriff in question was bare and cellulite-rippled, thick black hairs sprouting between zits and blemishes of various size and hue. I recoiled in horror, pushed my chair backwards on its castors too fast, and my head collided with a shelf several feet away. Hard. Bleeding. I said ★★★★★★ and ★★★★★★ and ★★★★★★ you ★★★★★★

You see? Not only horrible, but positively dangerous.

MIMES, NEEDLESS
Two fingers, both hands and an elbow

The most natural thing in the world is for us to use our hands when we talk. Except for Dr David Starkey, the TV history teacher and all-round bad-mood champion. He never smiles, and his hands are clearly clapped around a live ferret or something else in his lap, because, when seated, he never moves his hands, not for a second. Whatever he has in his lap might escape? I don't know. And when he is talking-and-walking, which he does a lot, his hands hang lifelessly at the end of his highly-tailored arms like bunches of bananas. Inhuman, really. It's as though someone told him "don't use your hands". I wish someone would un-tell him. It is true that the hand-waving thing can be over-done so that some TV presenters and others look like talking wind turbines, but the talking tailor's dummy effect perfected by Dr Starkey is positively *unnerving*.

The rest of us are natural hand-wavers, and we do it to emphasise, to add sense and colour, to clarify and so on. But when we are faced with that silly and irritating thing with the thumb and pinkie, hovering the hand near the ear, to indicate "telephone", I want to slap the mimer. I even saw Jeremy Clarkson do it recently. Slap him too. Now *that* I really would enjoy. Time he got slapped. He is always doing it to someone else. Fat bully.

And then there are people who form curled "v"s with the fingers normally used to give the two-fingered salute, only they use both hands, hang them in the air palms outwards, and the fingers are flexed up and down to air-hook "around" a word they would otherwise put in quotation marks. (God, it's hard to explain this in words. Like trying to describe a spiral staircase to anyone who has never seen one, without using your hands.). But you know what I mean – this set of poltroons makes this mime instead of saying "quote, unquote". Infuriating.

What about those who use the thumbs-up sign all the time? Or using a certain unmistakeable gesture learned from the drivers of white vans, to indicate to other drivers what they think about (your) constant unaccompanied sexual activity? Well, those are useful, and I don't mind them, not really. I must get myself a white van.

MORGAN, PIERS
Off the scale, beyond measurement, squillions

That wonderful Radio 4 programme "I'm sorry I haven't a clue" hosted by Humphrey Lyttleton (107) regularly asks its team of clever-dicks to come up with new definitions of words they have found in the Ox Eng Dic. One of them suggested "Countryside". Definition? Killing Piers Morgan. Can't improve on that.

"Was it something I said?"

MOTORWAY SERVICE AREAS, PRICES AT

Four-stars, and no conscience

The old dog again. Motorway service area operators can charge anything they like, because they know that you are completely captive, and short of walking back to your car through empty crisp packets and used condoms, then driving to the nearest town, you have no choice.

A litre of unleaded which will cost you, say 90p in the nearby town, costs 99p at the Go-Stop Motorway Rip-off Experience with all the free air you can breathe. A cup of coffee? £1.75, compared to £1.10 or so elsewhere, and I am not talking a Moltolattacino Chocospresso (will that be a Regular? Super-regular? Ultra-extra? Massivogrande? With or without cream, sugar, milk, foam, ice, salt, nutmeg, or a sprig of genuine artificial Mexican cactus?). I am talking just a mug of coffee, should you be lucky enough to find one. Would you like a Danish pastry to go with that? You'll find a bank just around the corner, and someone there will be happy to arrange an on-the-spot loan so you can have one of our pastries.

What is going on here? Are the Motorway service-area owners claiming that all their stock has to be trucked in from far away, that the transport costs are horribly high, so they have to charge more to make up for that? They are on a MOTORWAY for God's sake, where trucks of frightening size thunder up and down all day and night, and where delivery is a hundred times easier than battling traffic in British towns and cities. Does it cost more for staff? No. Maybe staff have to be paid danger money as compensation for being abused by customers incensed at the prices they have to pay, caused by the wages which have to be paid to staff, which causes ... etc.

And it is not as if the quality of the fare at these places is worth paying extra for. It is almost universally bland-bleah and yuck-muck. There is talk of these ghastly rip-off-areas being upgraded. Whoopee! Bigger and better opportunities for the owners to charge even more. I have to stop at these rip-stop areas to pee (free, for the moment, but I just know they are working on a way to charge for that). But food and drink? Home-made sandwiches for me – and I now have a very efficient vacuum flask for keep-awake coffee. So Motorway Stop-ins have become Park 'n Pee 4 Free, 4 me.

MUSIC IN RESTAURANTS
... AND IN SHOPS OF A CERTAIN KIND
... AND SOME FRIENDS' DINNER PARTIES
Doh, la, soh, stone mee, off the scale

It's an Anglo-Saxon thing. Imported I have no doubt from the USA. What has persuaded the managers of restaurants that the service is not complete without forcing the customers to hear some half-arsed pop artist accompanied by clanging dustbins and howling guitars?

Thing is, I go to restaurants to eat, and, cautiously, to drink. I want some interesting, possibly unusual but certainly not pretentious, food. I want some pleasant company, and the congenial atmosphere which goes with people having a pleasant time. I enjoy the clink and dink of cutlery and crockery and the hum of conversation. What I do *not* enjoy is music I do not like, nor did I request, being thrust down my ear. I do *not* appreciate having to shout above the screeching of Madonna or worse in order to place my order or convey my pearls of wisdom to my dining companions. Or having to stretch my neck across the table to hear what they have to say, getting my necktie in the soup en route.

Why do restaurateurs in Britain think that music *they* like, and which (I have heard one tell me) keeps their teenage waiting staff from turning into pillars of, well, rock, is also music *I* will like? And having taken the decision to impose *their* musical tastes on *me*, why do they compound the crime by turning up the volume to somewhere near rock-festival levels? Is it that the British are so reserved and timid that, if they happen to be among the first to arrive in a restaurant, they feel uncomfortable about sitting there either in silence or in embarrassment because their muted and in any event boring domestic mutterings can be heard by other people?

OK, let's allow that this may be the case, so while the restaurant is slowly filling up, by all means let the management play some gentle music so that the socially challenged British have an aural crutch to lean on, but as soon as the level of conversation reaches a certain level and the British can hide behind normal and pleasant dining noises, *TURN IT OFF AND LEAVE IT TURNED OFF*. But have you ever asked restaurant managers please to turn down the music, or preferably, turn it off? I have. You would think I had asked them if I could do unspeakable things to their mothers.

Then there is the hurry-up-and-eat music trick. This is used by places which serve pizza, burgers, and other "fast" foods, where the marketing people and the accountants have created an unholy alliance which centres on turning over as many covers in a given time as possible, so that profits can be maximised along with indigestion. Here's your food, now get on with it. Gobble it down as fast as your little chops can go, and then get the hell out of here, because we want to lay that table for the next party of dyspeptics. To speed up the eat-and-go, they play some of the world's worst up-tempo music, which has the effect of making you eat as fast as possible and finish as quickly as possible. That's what "fast" food means. Not just that it is prepared and served too fast (it is) but also because you are encouraged to eat as fast as possible. Buuuuuurrrrrrrrrp.

Go to France or Italy, or Spain and tell me you find the same thing. Fact is, you won't, in a proper French, Italian or Spanish restaurant. You might, of course, in a French, Italian or Spanish McBurger. That's not European at all − it's American. Continental Europeans understand what restaurants are about, and they encourage the natural sounds of people talking and eating together and taking their time over it. And if they happen to be the first to arrive, they chat happily without embarrassment or inhibition.

And then, the shops. Loudspeakers like truck-sides are positioned right at the doors and throughout the stores. This is to attract the attention of passing bimbos of both sexes, who are so inarticulate anyway that they can't ask the (usually non-existent) shop-assistants for anything, so the shop managers reckon that they may as well play even worse music at even greater volume, both inside and outside their emporia. I did an experiment recently. I walked into such a shop, and from a distance of about four feet, said, loudly, to the shop-manager, while taking in his merchandise with a sweeping gesture, "Good morning, you prime imbecile. Why are you trying to sell this garbage to anyone?" He said "Wowozat". For one ghastly time-flash I thought he had mistaken me for a compatriot from somewhere in Asia–Minor. Experiment complete. I shrugged, and moved on.

And finally. We have some acquaintances in London (of course) who invite us to dinner from time to time. They are among the most educated, cultured and articulate people you could wish to meet. Conversation with them is a delight. But, until we could stand it no more and protested, conversation was almost drowned out by "background" music which originated in far away places, performed on the *rambam, bangalang* or *fahoo-ha* with accompaniment by the famous Delhi Belhi on *blabalab*. (I did not have a lot of time to check the CD cover properly, but that's what I think it said). In its way, and in an appropriate context, fascinating. As an accompaniment to conversation, incomprehensible and annoying.

N

NAMES, CAR
Two syllables, three with turbo

If ever you wanted a sure sign that our civilisation is going the same way as all civilisations before it and that dumbing-down has become both an art and a science, look no further. Somewhere in offices, dimly lit to reflect the low cerebral activity of the occupants and to protect their squinty little eyes from the glare of daylight and intelligence, there are "creatives" who think up names for new cars.

The starting point for these poltroons is, I suppose, the "global economy" which really exists only in the minds of lunatic economists, so the "creatives" nurse the belief that cars have to be named in ways which anyone, anywhere, can pronounce. Car manufacturers and their "creatives" are enough to make small children weep with embarrassment. There are some exceptions at the top end of the market where residual intelligence still resides, such as BMW, Mercedes, etc., and where silly names are few and far between. But then the Germans really *have* to be exceptions to the rule on names because they start with throat-clearing, hawking and scratching noises anyway, so they avoid names altogether and stick with numbers and letters. Mostly. I still don't know what a "Kompressor" is, other than a mis-spelling of a machine for inflating stuff. You can see this word on the backsides of certain models of Mercedes. Remind me to find out.

But – beyond that exception. Aygo, Bupo, Lupo, Cada, Nada, Lada, Nana, Filo, Uno, Polo, Mako, Jimny, Jumpy, Bravo, Twingo, Zingo, Tuto, Disco, Lumo, Pupa, Focus, Cazzo, Corsa, Vectra, Dildo. Almost anything with two syllables, and vowels in roughly the right places, as long it does not actually mean anything. Yes, OK, I made up some of those, but not all of them. Can you spot the real ones? Bet you can't. (But I promise you − Twingo *is* the real thing. Small and French. *Twingo*, I ask you). And that's just the two-syllable garbage they stick on the bums of the cars they make. There are plenty of three-syllable examples as well, but never more than three, naturally. Lipido, Bipido, Kakapu, Ibiza, Monaco, Manaco, Manoca, Maniac, Tipico, Picanto, Fatuo, Buffalo, Bippity, Bappity. One of the Asian manufacturers make something called an Emina. Looks like what it sounds like if you happen to be even slightly dyslexic. Another maker has a lumbering thing called a Sharan. Would I been seen by anyone, anywhere, driving something called, barring one letter, Sharon? It's all mobile Esperanto for idiots.

I have decided to give the people who have to give names to cars, a little help. Let's have the Toyota Todja, Turdo, Testos and Tossa. The Vauxhall Vajeena, the Ford Gonnad and Farkov, the Nissan Numpti, the Peugeot Peenys, the Citroen Blomi. You think that's just silly? Yes, it's a bit ruder, but why is it any sillier than Yaris, Avensis, Kangoo, Leon, Bora, or Berlingo, all of which are actual, real names?

This sort of thing does not go on in the USA. There, they still tend to give their cars hairy, muscular, sweaty names. Blazer, Fireball, Thunder, Lightning, Mustang. Mustangs became quite fashionable with a certain kind of Parisian at one time, but they pronounced it "Moose-tong" of course, which gives us a clue as to why lots of other manufacturers elsewhere have gone for the nursery names above-mentioned. Even the French can't really mangle those. And talking of the French (briefly − it's all I can stand) at least Peugeot have got it right by giving all their models numbers rather than nursery names. But not Citroen. (More to say about this under "X").

Infantile car names are relatively recent as a phenomenon. There was a time when the Japanese in particular outdid themselves and everyone else with the hysterical dottiness of the names they gave to their models, but they were charmingly strange. It is best encapsulated by the immortal and sainted Alan Coren, when he invented the Datsubishi Loganberry. Or did he? I could swear I followed one in mint condition the other day.

NAMES, SLAV, THE BBC, PRONUNCIATION BY
Two wrong syllables, and three bad accents

Now I know you probably don't care much about this but I am going to attempt it anyway.

It is about tennis, mostly. Because suddenly, countries such as Russia, Slovakia, Czecho, Poland, Serbia, Croatia and others are producing stonkingly good players, and because the BBC gives us hours and hours of the blonk-donk-love-game every summer.

What a shambles the BBC commentators make of pronouncing the names of those players, and almost always the females. They consistently place the emphasis on the wrong syllable, and it sounds so *wrong* to anyone who has a feel for any language and respect for all of them. Example: Sharapova. The BBC says Sha-rap-**OV**-a. It says Petr-**OV**-a. Cer-van-**OV**-a. Han-tuch-**OV**-a. Pan-**OV**-a. Pas-tik-**OV**-a.

But in all the slav languages, the accent is placed on the syllable immediately before the -OVA part of the name. Thus:

Sha-**RAP**-ova. **PET**-rova. Cer-**VAN**-ova. Han-**TUCH**-ova. **PAN**-ova. Pas-**TIK**-Ova. Easky peasky. And then, *mirabile scriptu et dictu*, they find themselves perfectly able to say Kuz-**NET**-sova. Which is perfectly correct. But that is the sole exception.

It seems that the linguistically-challenged commentators are knocked flat when they see anything ending in "-ova". It comes out as "O-ver" with the accent on the "O", when the whole syllable is actually supposed to be suppressed and almost swallowed, coming out almost as ".... Uh-vuh" if correctly pronounced. Not difficult at all.

I know what you are thinking. In Britain, we say Paris, not Paree. Rome, not Roma. Moscow, not Moskva. (In America, they say Moss-cow, as if it were a green subspecies of milk-giver). So we English-speakers can pronounce other-language names any way we damned well like. But the point is that those place names have become anglicised through usage over years, and this does NOT apply to the names of tennis players. Harrrrumph.

Have you ever been next in line at an immigration desk anywhere in the non-English-speaking world, to watch the annoyance when some Brit ahead of you, with a name like Featherstonehaugh or Cholmondeley is being processed? Or even Jones for that matter? The invariable mangling of the name sends the beetroot-Brit into the cardiac danger-zone. How dare these foreign johnnies not know the correct way to pronounce *our* names? Eh? *Eh?*

You still don't care? OK.

NANNY
Three, but five if you don't eat your greens

Nanny used to be a Good Thing. Mine was. That is to say, mine *were*. My mother was faaaaar too busy going to parties and flirting with everyone in a pair of trousers to be involved in the ghastly business of feeding me, especially as I obeyed the Law Of All Babies, viz., fling all food-goop at the wall. Still less did she wish to walk me about in a pram, out of which I wanted to throw myself. No, all that was for a succession of lumpy women ranging from the hardly- to the definitely-un-trained. I know there were lots of them, but not one face comes to mind. They would come and go according to my mother's mood, state of sobriety or digestion. And their degree of terror of my mother ranged from suppressed quivering to abject shrieking and leaving on the first bus out.

But now, only the very rich and idle have nannies as they used to be, and "nanny" is now the word we use to describe a slithering phalanx of gimlet-eyed Health and Safety Inspectors, Insurance Executives, Lawyers and similar jobsworths, whose word is Law and whose Law is Absolute. It is obvious that we cannot be trusted to look after ourselves, let alone look after others, so nanny is there to make damned sure we don't even *think* about stepping over that line between safety and risk. It seems that nanny is too dumb to understand that everyone, other than those who are certifiable, prefers being safe and healthy to living in danger and disease. See S for Safety, Health and.

The utter nadir of nannyism gone berserk? You cannot buy more than sixteen paracetamol capsules or tablets at the same time. The Government says so. Paracetamol, provided you swallow lots at a sitting, will kill your liver and then you, in that order. It is a very effective way, or so I am told, to a relatively pain-free suicide. But you can't buy more than sixteen in any one place at any one time. So, with topping yourself in mind, you buy sixteen at Tesburys, get into you car, drive to Phriendly Pharmacy half a mile away, and buy sixteen more. Then on to SuperDooper and sixteen more. And so on. All within the hour. You are set. Good bye world, and up yours, nanny. Did the imbecile who came up with the sixteen-max rule not realise that if you are absolutely intent on suicide, this utterly stupid regulation shows itself up for its comical lack of point? Clearly not. So (and it will not be long in coming) all painkillers containing paracetamol will be banned and those who want to kill themselves will have to buy a Japanese skewer, dagger, sharp pointy thing and learn how to commit *seppuku*.

Somewhere in a fetid pit in Whitehall squats a reeking rat who works for the Department For Pissing Off The Proletariat. Do you think that imbecilic regulations arrive out of the air during a meeting of the Nanny Ministry? They don't. They are presented to the Minister by one of his senior minions via the dribbling creep in his pit. It is what he does for a living, and we the taxpayers pay him a salary for doing that. I think of it as minderbation.

NEWS, BAD
Five nice explosions and several arrests

Dear Old Martin Lewis once got himself into hot water by complaining that TV news editors were obsessed by bad news, and that good news never gets a look-in. He ought to have known better, having been a TV newscaster for years. He was right, but he was wrong. Fact is that we, the sag-brained public, take a special delight in wallowing in disaster, mayhem, murder, suicide and bad politics. We get what we deserve.

Martin's diatribe made not the slightest impression on anyone. But it really has gone too far when it becomes possible to record the TV news on, say, Monday, and play it back on Thursday without having to be aware that any time has passed at all.

Baghdad ... bomb ... insurgents ... helicopter ... bomb ... George Bush ... Eurofollocks ... bus overturns ... flood in ... earthquake ... bomb ... fire ravages ... price increases ... industrial action ... Baghdad bomb ... superbug kills ... Darfur ... judge wrong ... cold front ... bomb ... killer 'flu ... refugees ... poison in ... jail riot ... suicide bomb ... cancer causing ... paedophile ring ... bomb in Baghdad ... police brutality ... World Cup Exit ... profit warning ... politicians, sleaze crisis ... Rumsfeld ... Home Office balls-up ... Eurovision, last again ... bomb ... bird 'flu ... more Home Office cock-ups.

Any day you like. Fully transferable from Tuesday to Friday or any other day. It's all bad. Good news is non-news.

I am not expecting, nor would I especially care for, a permanently grinning newscaster with endlessly joyful stories pouring from his excellently be-dentured phisog, but a little more leavening of the eternally sour and flat news-bread would make a pleasant change. Fat chance. News editors are not inclined to look on the bright side of life. They would feel queasy and stupid if they did. Even more than usual. But I suppose their excuse would be "giving the viewing public what they want". And how do they know what the public wants? Because we, the public, appear to have an insatiable appetite for bad things happening to other people. It's called mass schadenfreude. Serves us right.

NINETY-NINE PENCE (99p)
A pound's worth of bull and some change

Nothing costs a round pound. Or round pounds. Everything is £24.99, or £99.99, or £9.98, or 99p. Even cars, costing thousands, are advertised at £25,998. And 99p.

I am told that the practice of pricing stuff this way started in the USA (of course) in the first large department stores, where sticky-fingered sales assistants would pocket full dollar bills, whereas they had to make change if the price was, say, $4.99. And the change had to come out of the till, which had to be opened, so the sale would be registered, and the customer would see this happening, so, etc. But that was in the days when everything was done with great clanging tills of the Ronnie Barker Open-all-hours type, involving payments in cash – and those days are long gone.

But the nonsense lives on, and now it is used by retailers because we, the thicker-than-porridge consumer, believe that if something is priced at, say £24.99, it is actually £24.00 they want from us, not £25.00 and *that* is going to make all the difference between our deciding to buy it and deciding not to. Or that we think (they think) that we are spending £24 when we are actually spending £25 (see below). In any case, I am prepared to bet that the vast majority of all purchases are made with credit or debit cards these days. Who gets change when buying with a credit card – and who expects it? We actually put up with this tillocks, because, like appallingly bad service in shops and restaurants, we have become used to it, and we never, *ever* complain because although we are British we are actually English under the skin. Also because virtually everything we are prepared to accept encourages retailers in the dead certainty that we are all dumb and deserve to be treated like the cluck-suckers we are.

I have not the slightest doubt that the advertising agencies who advise their clients on marketing (which includes pricing of course) have researched all this to within a cent of its life, and can prove that an item marked £24.99 is 37.974 percent more likely to be purchased than if it were priced at £25.00. It appears that retailers rely on our feeling that we have got a bargain at £24.99, but that we have been ripped off at £25.00. Are we really as dumb as all that? Probably.

It's the fuel retailers I understand least and despise most. Given that the vast majority of us buy our fuel at the same filling station year in and year out, and use credit/debit cards when we do so, there is absolutely no point whatsoever in pricing a litre of petrol at 95.8p or 99.6p in order to give the impression that *this* filling station's prices might be just a bit lower than *that* one down the road.

What other reason could they possibly have for this nonsense? I have more to say about this (See P for Petrol, Pricing). And when they change fuel prices, do they ever drop or raise them by these pathetic fractions of a penny? No. They go up (frequently) and down (rarely) by whole pennies at a time. Of course.

NUDITY
Usually two, and some other bits

I am not a prude about the nude. There are plenty of human bodies which are a delight to behold and to hold, usually in that order if you get lucky. But nudity on the part of people whose lack of muscle-tone is matched only by their lack of decent cover is too much, really it is. Less is emphatically less. Usually, this fetish for baring all is confined to groups who are a few stitches short of a jockstrap, and who cavort in the name of naturism, as if it were some sort of religion. To some, I suppose, it is. But it seems that while some otherwise apparently normal people

are drawn to wander about in the altogether, sadly this normality usually stops at the neck, and, going south, disaster is piled on awfulness, yea unto gagging point.

Male or female, and in late middle-age, it is those with the largest tits who flaunt them, and the tits have become sagging bags of shrivel, punctuated by nipples which leer mottled-brownly from navel-level. Once rounded apple-bottoms which jutted pertly are now pleated pachydermous pouches, the lower reaches of which threaten to be caught up in the backs of the knees. Bellies, swollen by decades of *pate de foie* or bacon baps depending on social class, cascade in unsightly folds almost, but not quite covering pudenda which have seen better days and done better things. Pendulous scrota form unsightly backdrops to bloodlessly depressed and hangdog penises, the whole framed by unsightly grey pubic hair. Wobbling labia flap like gills out of water. How do I know all this? I have had to walk through a nudist beach on my way to the non-nudist area, and, well, one can't help looking, can one? If you are walking along a beach and you see a shell, an umbrella, a towel and a dick, what are you going to notice most noticeably?

And when naturists gather, their first instinct is to go for the sun-protection bottle, and smear every last square inch of someone else with much exaggerated spreading of limbs and accidentally deliberate brushing of knuckles on knobs or knorks. How do I know all this? Am I the voyeur you are starting to suspect I might be? No, no. See above. On beaches all over the Med, nudist beaches are slap bang (sorry, I am getting fixated) alongside those where bathing apparel is *de rigeur*, and it is impossible not to see what is going on.

It is all harmless and sexless? Yes? Really? But what's this flabby short-arse doing just over there by the flag which says "Nudist beach boundary". He has his bathing shorts around his ankles and he appears to have some sort of small baguette in his hand, positioned oddly just below his sagging gut, pointing outwards. No, he can't be. But, yes, he is. With enthusiasm and a wide smile. I rest.

OF-ANYTHING

Six excuses and ten un-civil servants

Office Of. Ofsted (more on this, in a moment) Ofcom, Ofwat, Ofgen, OFT. Ofthis. Ofthat. Far too many and far too Often. We are Off-our-heads allowing this bacterium-like growth. Supposed to be the watchdogs who bite transgressors in our name, allowing this, disallowing that. Us, we the public. Not in my name, and not in my experience. Have you ever tried, as an individual, to get any of these Offices to *do* something about a problem you face with a regulated industry operator? I have, and I am a lot less than impressed. Off-pissed, in fact. So off-pissed that I have a whole section on these and other quangos (see Q for them).

Most recently, I complained to the Office of Fair Trading about a well-known computer and printer manufacturer and distributor, whose policy in terms of ink-cartridges was straight up and down anti-competitive gouging. Blatant. The response? "Unfortunately, blah, blah, we don't have the power to blah, blah blah, please see page 975 of the attached guidelines especially blah blah. Summary? "Can't help, won't help. You are on your own, sunshine. Don't like that? Throw away the printer and get a new one from a supplier you prefer". Next?"

Ofwat. Ofwhat exactly? Water to our premises regularly looks like Brown Windsor soup, and is not half as flavoursome. Complain to the monopoly supplier. "We dunno, squire. Must be a problem at your end of the pipe. Get a plumber". Plumber: "No problem *here* guv'nor. That'll be £250 plus VAT thangyoo." Phone Ofwat again. "Sorry, but this is a matter you have to sort out with your supplier. Not within our powers". Water bills keep going up? Whenever the supplier feels like it, and Ofwat always, always approves.

They operate, all of them, on the Bostonian closed-coterie system, where it is held that the Lodges speak only to the Cabots and the Cabots speak only to God. The suppliers speak only to their Of, and the Of speaks only to the Government department which is there to protect it. Good arrangement or what?

And that brings me neatly to …

OFSTED
Failing, unsatisfactory, minus five, F-grade

And of all the Of-Phenomena, of all the Government agencies, this one is the most vindictive, capricious and downright nasty. And do I think so because I have been reading too many newspaper stories about it? No. I have been right at the centre of an Ofsted shit-shower, and once it had passed, so to speak, I made contact with other schools at both primary and secondary level in my county to see how typically – or un-typically – our local prep school in question had been treated.

You could have heard the roar of hatred and rage in the Alps. Not one of the head-teachers I spoke to had anything good to say about this tyranny, but that gave me scant comfort. On the strength of our experience at our local primary school, I wanted to drive very sharp pencils through the temples of the gulag-worthy inspectors who fouled the precincts, and the back-room administrators who, despite being proved one hundred percent wrong about the outrageously unfair and wrong-headed decision they took, refused to back down, apologise or correct anything. The school in question was graded as "under-achieving" despite having a waiting list of parents gagging to get their children enrolled; despite having SATS results which were nothing less than sparkling; despite a fully supportive PTA and LEA; despite a head teacher who was loved and respected by everyone; despite the fact that this school was a happy, thriving place; despite the fact that those children going on to the local high school from this particular prep were and still are universally acknowledged as being among the brightest and best-prepared.

Robert MacGregor

Of the two inspectors who carried out the Ofsted assessment, the male of the species was clearly out of his depth while the female was a hatchet-faced sour-puss of a scarecrow who barged about the place terrorising the staff and the children alike, interrupting conversations, putting everyone on edge and generally disrupting the school for two full days. How she got out of there alive I will never know. One of the teachers, reduced to a nervous wreck by the presence of this harridan with her miserable, interfering demeanour, did not acquit herself as well as she would normally do in one – *one* – of her lessons. Her nerves were rattling. On that basis, the school received its "under-achieving" assessment. Ridiculous, gratuitously damaging, unbalanced, spiteful, immoral, and wrong, wrong, wrong.

The Head-teacher, a clever, tolerant, amusing, dedicated and experienced person of the kind the teaching profession simply cannot afford to lose, very nearly resigned as Head, and even more nearly left the teaching profession altogether. She suffered the nearest thing to a nervous breakdown I have ever seen, and a combination of all of these events and factors left the staff demoralised, frightened and devoid of confidence in themselves for months. Worse, having been down-graded, the school had a further Ofsted inspection scheduled for two years down the track, instead of the normal four. How they all managed to pull themselves together after this disaster was nothing short of a miracle. They have recovered now, but the scars are deep and livid. So am I. Livid, that is. If this Stalinist agency had deliberately decided to destroy a school, it could not have done a better job. It failed, and it is a tribute to the mettle of the school and its people that it pulled itself out of the Ofsted-made mire and went from strength to strength. By the way – the school sailed through the second inspection having adopted, under the Head's specific instruction, a policy of Ofsted? What Ofsted? Which involved utterly ignoring the inspectors from start to finish, preparing nothing special in advance, and answering questions politely but tersely.

Ofsted horror-stories emerged from far too many of the other schools where I spoke to the head-teachers. Ofsted is regarded with loathing, fear and disgust. When an Ofsted inspection is scheduled, it is dreaded. And what's more, these inspections are flagged up months

150

ahead of time, so the schools, paradoxically, behave as though a Royal Visit were in the offing. Everyone tries to be on best behaviour, including the children. Everything is scrubbed and polished. Absurd. If these inspections were conducted at random and without warning, there would be no months of dread building to a crescendo, and what the inspectors would see would be the school as it operates every day. But that would be messy and untidy in the minds of the jobsworths who manage this frankly frightful agency.

It seems to me that Ofsted is programmed to treat every school as if it expects all of them to be like inner-city sink-schools with all kinds of problems. I have no doubt that inner-city problem-schools need all the attention they can get, from any source, popular or not, and that Ofsted is, just possibly, a necessary evil in sorting them out. But schools well away from the cities, especially small country schools which are doing a great job? I say – keep these vindictive busybodies the hell away, and leave it to a combination of parents, LEA's and teachers to sort out their problems. If they have any. The time has come for most schools to treat Ofsted the way it deserves to be treated, and start to boycott the visits en masse. Shut them out on the grounds that they disrupt the teaching of children. Which is what the schools are *for*.

If enough schools did this, the Government would have to re-think the whole Ofsted cess-pit. *That* would get the attention of whoever happens to be the Minister in charge of the Department of Ballsing Things Up In Education (See also "Educationalists"). And possibly bring about the one reform which education really needs – an instruction to Ofsted to wind its bloody neck in.

OKRA
Two dear little ladies' fingers and a barf

I eat almost anything. Some stuff I do avoid because it is too gross for words and I refuse to go there. Still-alive fish in Japan, as I have explained; disgusting Australian grubs; sheep's eyes; stuff like that. And I don't do snails, either. Even if they are disguised as *"escargots"*. Things that make the gorge rise, create that greasy backwards feeling behind the tongue and cannot be swallowed at any price.

At the top of my small list? Okra – originally a plant indigenous to West Africa, it has now become a staple in Indian food, and has a Hindi or Urdu name I take some pleasure in having forgotten. It is also known as ladies' fingers, or gumbo and lurks in vegetable curries waiting for me to arrive. It clearly hopes I will eat it without being aware. Wrong. I can spot even a smidgeon of okra no matter how hard it tries to disguise itself.

It looks like the fingers of no ladies I have ever known. It is grey-green, small-boys' uncircumcised dicks in shape (I have three sons, so I know) and whichever way it is cooked, it remains revoltingly slimy, and … and … Excuse me. I have to … I'll be back as soon as … I have to ….

OK. I'm back. Better now. Gah. Whew. Close run thing. Just *writing* about it, you see.

OLD, GETTING
Four bits dropped, oops, make that five

I am not there yet, not by a long row of candles. Merely an observer. For now. But I have watched while relatives and friends *did* grow old, and I dread it. My dear departed father used to say through gritted teeth as he fought off the latest bout of pain or irritation, "There is *no* compensation for growing old. *None.* By the time you are into your early sixties (no great age any more) you are as wise as you are ever going to be. Power? Yes, it is sadly possible for old men and women to exercise a great deal of power and *that* is the only possible compensation for decrepitude".

Anything else by way of compensation? No, seriously, *anything*? What makes up for joints which join but will not swivel? For muscles which have no tone or strength – or have simply disappeared? For skin which belongs, clearly, to someone much bigger than you, but which has decided to take up residence on *your* frame and then turn itself into sagging camouflage? For teeth which are fine in gums which have packed up, or vice versa? For eyes which see progressively less, ears which hear ditto, taste buds which have caved in and dropped off? And, if you are a male oldie, what compensates for a once-proud little soldier who would stand to attention at the merest suggestion of a thigh, thing or thong and which now hangs its little head in shame and stares eternally at the ground?

You can't run. You can't even swing a golf club with any real malice. You definitely cannot even *think* about walking onto a tennis court. Sport is something you watch. Period. Small wonder that most old people are so damned bad-tempered. You have some idea that I am not always the most patient and gentle of people. Wait until I am eighty-plus, and believe me, I am genetically programmed to be. Stand clear.

ON-HOLD
Seven hundred rings and four Mozart bits

We have done call centres. This is not about call centres, but if the cap fits … It's about *any* company which one has to call, and which does not have enough personnel to handle the average number of daily calls. Credit card companies. Banks (of course). BT (of course). Mobile phone operators (particularly). The people who sold me an extended guarantee on my computer, and once I get through to someone, that someone cannot spell my name or the name of my house, my town, my county. They are in Bangalore or Chennai. (See under B.)

While we wait, and wait and wait, our ears get hot with the pressure of the ear-piece, and while some music we positively *detest* is played to us, our rears grow numb with the sitting and waiting. A message, informing us that our call is *really and truly* important, is played over and over again. *If it is so goddam important, then employ enough people to avoid having to give me this repeated non-message until I could scream.* Have screamed.

Not to mention audio-menus. I can hardly bring myself to keep my temper by the time I have jumped these menu-hurdles. Press this and that and the other, *and*, you poor stupid berk, don't do it until *all* the options have been given to you.

You can't remember what Option One was by the time you get to Option Six? Start again. None of the options suits your particular question, so you sit there wondering what to do, while the metallised voice prompts you over and over again. That assumes you have reached a series of options which seem vaguely in the area of your problem. By then, you have selected Options 2, 4, 3, 4, 5, 2 and 4. This is supposed to make sure you are directed to the person best qualified to handle your particular problem. Phonnocks. It is there simply to keep you on hold while the *same* person who deals with *everything* is handling calls way ahead of you in the queue.

It's about saving money, as usual. And that is about making even more gaggingly disgusting amounts of profit, as usual. For the shareholders, as usual. And who are the shareholders ? Many of them are people who are also known as customers or consumers and ... oh, forget it.

OPERAS, SOAP
Average weekly angst rating; five, but six on Sunday

I selected this item as a target some little time back, because I thought it would be a good one. But then I realised that as I never watched soap operas, never listened to them, therefore how could I comment on them? So I tried to correct that by spending several miserable hours watching, in order to catch up a bit, and it turned out that I was right to start with. They are abysmal. And it seems that the lives of so many people who watch them are so dreary, so empty, so *bleaaah*, that immersing themselves in these make-believe lives is an improvement on reality. How infinitely sad.

Here's a test. Turn on your TV, mute the sound, select a channel showing a soap opera, and close your eyes. At random, whenever the urge takes you, open your eyes. I'll bet you large amounts of, that the screen will be filled with the creased and angst-ridden face either of a teenager or a middle-aged mamma, brow furrowed in consternation as part of an overall facial expression brought on by moral constipation, and she will be saying, probably in an Australian accent, "*But Shane (or Wayne, or Dwane) ya tole me onie yesdi ya wozin luv wimmie". Neaow ya wanna temme ya doan lummie na mor. Ut's thet Sharon, innit? I'm goanna killa".*

Then she will flounce out of shot, leaving Shanewaynedwane standing there densely, like a pillar of fog. The girls (all ages) go to flounce-school to get this exactly right. Now change channels. Same thing. Different actors, possibly. But same story, same setting. And there are millions of people who watch this. No, no, not just *watch* it. Drive over whole crocodiles of schoolchildren in order to get home in time to see today's episode start. Run right over their dear old mothers in the hallway in case they miss a second. And not just TV either. I mentioned The Archers right back under "A", did I not? Same thing. Soap Operas? You do know where the name originates, of course, so I won't insult you by telling you. But the name is all wrong now. No soap manufacturer in his right corporate mind would sponsor this stuff. Soap operas? Soup operas. Slush operas. Schmuck operas.

Years ago, as a result of a terrible misunderstanding with a radio producer, I was cast as the hero of a radio soap opera. I need to explain that, while I am an astonishingly talented person, a veritable renaissance man, I cannot act worth a damn. Not even on radio, where I could *read* the lines I would otherwise never, ever, be able to *learn*, and where no-one but fellow members of the cast could see my crimson blushes and suicidal embarrassment. But I got the part because the sponsor's radio producer was apparently half-deaf and blind, but appeared to fancy me. Well, not *me*. She said she fancied my voice. Well, she *actually* said my voice suited the part. Can we move on now?

It was dire. For two years, while audience ratings inexplicably shot through the roof, I hammed my way through situations of such fatuousness as to beggar belief. The writer was terribly kind. He knew I could not deliver a line with anything close to conviction, that I had no idea how to act any kind of emotion whatsoever, and that my timing was from the Gerald Ford walking and gum-chewing school. So he wrote carefully sculpted lines for me, which conveyed a kind of lackadaisical boredom and deep ennui with the rubbish going on around me. I was in character at last. Frozen insouciance I could handle in my sleep. It was terminal crap. But the audience loved it.

If the producer had hanged himself at the end of the series and blamed me in his suicide note, I could not have escaped justice. It would have been true.

OXBRIDGE, ACCEPTANCES, "SYSTEMS" FOR
At least five A levels and nerd-rating of ten

"System?" Not a lot. Have you had the miserable experience of watching the beloved and quite high-flying son or daughter of a friend (or possibly your own progeny) go through the agonies of the damned as they try to get acceptance from either Oxford or Cambridge, either one being a university they really, *really* want to attend and are plenty good enough to? Four A levels at A Grade, first team everything, etc., for example? And then watch as having failed (sorry, having had their *success deferred* in the modern PC-bullshit-speak) they have to settle for second best while an acquaintance with a similar sixth-form record and absolutely no bodily co-ordination whatsoever gets accepted, unconditionally, before his results were even known, and made an offer subject to getting three C-level passes?

How could this be? Same university? Same year, same levels of scholastic attainment? Ah, yes, but … The College System. One does not apply to Oxford *University* or Cambridge *University* – one applies through a College within the University, and *that's* where the wheels come off. The college through which Boy A applied had a positive tsunami of applications for *his* chosen course, while the college selected by Boy B had almost none for *his*. The latter lad sailed into Oxbridge to read for a course which everyone including himself knew he would never, ever, put to use, while Boy A gave up in disgust and went elsewhere. Boy A wanted to study his subject at the best possible faculty in the country. Boy B just wanted the Oxbridge life-style. He said so.

I'm not complaining about the inescapable fact that competition for places comes into it; that's a given when there are more applications than places available, but a system which allows students into the two most prestigious universities in Britain on the basis of a lottery is downright perverse. The College system is a *lottery?* What could I possibly mean? Just this: I don't suppose that more than a single-figure percentile of applicants to Oxbridge target a given college on the basis of knowledge of that college, if you see what I mean. How can anyone know in advance that in applying to be accepted to study at a university faculty, you have to know how full, or how empty a particular college is going to be? And, leaving aside applications for different types of degree, and making the playing field level, that if you apply to Saint Whatsit's to do Law you will have a ten-to-one chance at best – while applying to do Law via Saint Whosis' almost guarantees you an acceptance if you have the right qualifications? Deciding where to apply is a pin-and-list matter. Unless of course one is talking about entrants from Eton or Harrow or similar, where there is a form of post-pubertic Masonic mystery at work, involving the earld-by network, late night phone calls and dropping in on old Buffy who tutored one thirty years ago at John's or Balliol and having a quiet word, provided that young Tristram has good A-level marks. Otherwise, lottery. Choose the wrong college, find that too many of your year-group have done the same thing, and you are out. Or, rather, not in.

There is something called the "pool" system. Failed applicants to a college who are nonetheless thought to be good enough for the university by the college Tutor for Admissions can have their names placed in the pool, so that some other college can pick them up if they have room. On the basis of what? Masonic connections again, perhaps, or just another lottery? Who knows, but the reality is that every place for any of the more serious academic subjects (Law, English, History, Medicine, Sciences etc.,) were filled ages ago, so those who succeed through the pool-system consist of those who have applied to do Tractor Maintenance, or something suitably obscure. And in they go, accepted by a college they have never seen, whose name they can neither spell or pronounce and which they can't find.

Any hope of a change to this absurdly nonsensical non-system? None, unless The Government gets involved, I suppose. God forbid. But maybe, one day, the Vice-Chancellors of the Universities will get their heads out of the clouds which cosily enfold their ivory towers, come down to earth and talk through a system which is fair, open and logical. Such as dropping the silly via-the-college nonsense, processing all applications through Central Admissions, and allocating the successful candidates to this or that college, on the basis of a proper system which spreads talent and ability throughout the colleges.

Unless and until that happens (holding my breath I am not) and if you happen to have a bright son or daughter who is Oxbridge material, don't expect their path to be anything less than strewn with haphazard rocks. Wish them luck – they'll need it, just as they would if they were playing the lottery.

PACKAGING
Four layers, two broken nails, one lost temper

We are rapidly sinking under our own garbage. Land-fill sites are land-full. Recycling is barely making a dent in the rubbish pile. Fly-tipping is on the increase. Small hills of old fridges, TV sets and so on are turning into mountains. What 30th century archaeologists will make of the dead civilisation they find, and the midden which crushed it, heaven only knows.

And somewhere near the centre of this pile of crap is the detritus left by us as a direct result of the uncaring and irresponsible activity of The Packagers. Have you ever taken stock, say, at the end of week's shopping and consuming to see how much unnecessary packaging you have bought? How much air has been packed into tubs of this, packets of that, jars of the other? How much space is taken up by acres of unnecessary foil, cardboard, paper, plastic? An example: I had to take a course of pills recently and the packaging defied belief. Each pill has its own little press-out compartment in a foil-type sheet, and is separated from the next pill by at least a square inch of totally flat foil, doing absolutely nothing. Each sheet holds seven pills. One a day with the days of the week marked so, being irredeemably dumb, I cannot mistakenly ingest more, or less, than one a day. For a month, four such sheets. Over a few weeks, enough to make a good start on a shelter for a family in Africa. And each week's worth, i.e., each of four sheets, is transported in its own cardboard box measuring four inches by three. Criminal negligence, deliberate and unspeakable waste. As a family we have a stunning array of vitamin pills in little pots, each pot exactly the same size, distinguished from one another only by variously-coloured labels and a lot of reading if you are in the mood. In *this* pot, sixty little pill-lets of Vitamin D, which crouch in the very bottom, embarrassed by three

159

inches of air between themselves and the lid. Same for three other similar pots of vitamins. Then a tub of small aspirins. About half an inch of pills in the pot. Two inches of air.

Almost everything comes in boxes and packets which are arse-tearingly difficult to tear open. A box within a bag within a sleeve within another bag within a box. Wrapped in an Enigma™ . Containing a plastic bag which, one is warned, should not be allowed into the hands of small children, as it could cause them to suffocate. (Or cause them to suffocate some other nearby child. The warning is not clear on this). I wish I could take the plastic bag and force onto it the head of the poltroon who put the packaging together. Then tie it up at the neck with any one of the several yards of tape which came with the item.

Vacuum packing. Bubble wrapping. Small items such as spare car headlamp bulbs in a vacuum-bubble pack with very hard cardboard backing, the whole being about four times the volume of the two small bulbs. Impossible to open without several sharp tools. What the hell are the manufacturers thinking of, on the assumption that thinking plays any part in what they do? The chances are that some designers have been let loose on this, which would explain everything. (See D for Designers).

And all of this ends up in a massive pile of stuff, most of which cannot be recycled, or, what is worse, that people cannot be bothered to recycle. I would say that taking the total of all items brought into a typical household over a week, well over half of the volume is packaging of one kind or another. We are packing ourselves into a serious problem, and the time has come for The Packagers to start thinking about it. Or for us to start thinking for them, and refusing to buy their packaged air.

PARTIES, COCKTAIL (ACTUALLY, PARTIES, ANY)
Two vile wines and a ton of small-talk

How do you feel about parties? Me, I'm about average-gregarious, I suppose. Fairly sociable, quite enjoy meeting new people. I have catholic tastes in booze and food. No canapé fazes me, no matter how weird. No Chateau Pissoir gets poured into the aspidistra when I can pour it into myself.

I'll hang in there, talking, munching, slurping with the best – until, without warning, a shutter clangs down in the far reaches of my brain, and it's time to go. I suddenly wonder why the hell I am there, and what's this gathering of the gormless about? Can I do without it? Will my absence ruin my career? Will anyone even *notice* if I slip away?

I'm supposed to be "networking", aren't I? I'm supposed to be making and nurturing contacts who'll be helpful to me. I'm supposed to circulate, strike up conversations, exchange views, all that. It never even crosses my mind that I might be of help to someone *else*. Why would I, of all people, be networkable, I start to wonder? After a short-lived attempt at circulating, striking up, exchanging, suddenly I can't be bothered any more. I remember that I much prefer the company of family and close friends in small groups around a dinner table, *sitting down,* where the food and drink will be what I *really* enjoy as against providing some form of lubrication for social intercourse. And most of all, I just don't want to be here any more.

The abovementioned intercourse factor offers me a neat link to the other thing about parties. They are preliminaries to the other kind of intercourse for the sexually frustrated, voracious or simply curious. Mating eye-dances across crowded rooms. Hands brushing thighs and pert protuberances. Phone numbers (mobile, naturally) exchanged. Trysts made for later in the day or the evening or the week. I'm past all that. I have an absolutely wonderful collection of lines in brush-offs, put-downs and offers declined. What are they? You don't think I am going to tell *you*, do you? You might be the next vamp to accost me across the rim of your glass of that amusing little Guatemalan Shirazernet, while I try to swallow that Cajun curried snail on a stick. I'll have to get rid of you.

Robert MacGregor

PLANNERS, LOCAL GOVERNMENT
Four refusals, no reasons, but re-submit in three years.

In my area, we have lost God-knows how many new job opportunities because our local planners simply refuse permission, as a matter of course, for anyone who wants to put up or convert a building for a new business. But hang on, if the applicant is refused permission, he can appeal to the Secretary of State For Interfering With Local Decisions, can't he? Fine theory, but given the hair-tearing delays and the cost, most businesses faced with the No-Way-Man in Planning simply go away and look for another site, in another county.

And while this is going on, the same Planning Committee shoves through, on the nod, the plans submitted by a local semi-big-wig for a house which will cause Prince Charles to come all over boils. But the local biggie's brother/cousin/uncle/godfather is the Chairperson of the Planning Committee, so that's that. Next, please? I exaggerate? Not in my District I don't.

But _you_ want to put a modest conservatory onto the side of your house? No. You want to put in a window in the ... No. You want to ... _No_.

There are supposed to be Great Big Proper Area Plans for Everywhere, designed to ensure that the progress we make is sensitive to preserving the environment, while allowing enough room for progress. Each document is about a foot thick, and written in Bureauglish. It is ignored, over-ridden, forgotten by Local Planners. There is supposed to be some major review of the entire planning process country-wide, to make it more sensible, cheaper, and more logical. It will do none of those things. It will also leave an appeals process in place. As soon as I see the words "major review", anyway, I grab my boots and head for the hills.

In common with increasing numbers of people, I would like to see a hole open up in London and swallow Whitehall and all its words in one great gulp followed by a satisfied burp. I would like to see _local_ matters handled by _local_ people without a John Prescott crouching behind, ready to over-bear, over-ride and over-turn.

But local administration consistently lets itself and us down very badly by displaying incompetence and nepotism, because it attracts, at the level of elected councillors, far too many people who are seriously under-educated, functionally illiterate and deeply bent. Been to a local council meeting recently? Go. You will see and hear what I mean. Solution? Start by creating a climate at local government level where intelligent, independent, honest, caring and courageous people are attracted to the idea of serving as councillors, and we might end up with local planning decisions which make sense. But until then ...?

POLITICIANS, AFRICAN
Several million, any currency will do

What follows is correct, politically, but may well be politically incorrect as in "non-PC".

I detest and despise racism, because it is the preserve of those who are severely intellectually under-equipped and/or psychologically warped. I am not interested in the colour of skins – just the colour of souls, and when it comes to the psyches of so many who attain power at any level in Africa, there is no shade of black deep enough to do justice to the depth of their venality. Many. Not all. There are some wonderful exceptions. A few. It is not confined to Africa, of *course* not. South America and Asia far-and-near have more than their fair share of despots, tyrants and worse. But Africa is the world standard by which awfulness-in-power is judged. And awfulness-in-opposition, too, for that matter. Human rights? Bah!

To make matters worse as we all know, brain-damaged big bankers all over the Western world have been throwing galactically vast sums of money at African Governments for decades, but then that's bankers, big bankers, for you. And far, far too much of that cash has been shifted, one bounce, into personal accounts managed with po-faced insouciance by secrecy-obsessed Swiss who ask no questions. Neat, really. From one set of banks to another, via the cumbersome but oh-so necessary medium of an African despot. Here's a truism; with a few shining exceptions, people become politicians in Africa in order to get rich, and someone had better tell "Sir" Bob Geldof about this the next time he creates an Aid-Band-Wagon and encourages everyone to throw some more cash at Africa.

Has Africa benefited from all this money? Hardly at all. Soft-centre governments in Britain and other countries with more gross national product than sense continue to describe most of Africa as "developing", and throw "overseas aid" onto the pile of loans already pocketed by the politicians. Developing into what? When? For the good of whom, exactly?

It is all a horrible shame. While Africa's people die by the million of AIDS, malaria, hunger and thirst and perish in disgustingly purposeless tribal and political wars, most of their "leaders" shrug smug shoulders, and laugh all the way to, well, to the bank, actually. And the worst part of it? Some of the very people who now take their countries to ever-deeper levels of hell on Earth have been educated in Britain, the USA, France, and elsewhere in the West, and have done very well both studying and working there. But as soon as they get back home, the evil spirit of that uniquely African form of corruption takes over many of their souls, and they rush their suffering subjects into poverty as fast as they can.

"Let's make poverty history" – that's the latest well-meaning campaign. Who could object to the sentiment? But back in Africa, the bloodless bloody tyrants smell the enticing aroma of yet more money coming their way, and smile that singularly African smile of happy anticipation.

But there's another side to all this. Listen *carefully* to the words of Archbishop Desmond Tutu, one of Africa's saints. He reminds us that while we get all hot under the collar, clerical or otherwise, about Africa and its inability to behave itself, The West has, in the past one hundred years spawned Two World Wars, the second one of which included The Holocaust, and the first one of which was utterly, comprehensively stupidly pointless. Plus Korea, and Vietnam. The West has on its bloodied escutcheon (and this includes near-western countries as well) Yugoslavia, Stalinist Sovietism, Northern Ireland, Basque Separatists, etc., etc.

So, provided we give them time, Africans will move towards the wonderfully civilised standards of behaviour which we enjoy in the First World. So that's alright, then.

POLITICIANS, NORTHERN IRISH
Nine hundred and ninety on the Paisley-Adams

The ordinary people of NI are, for the most part, a delight. When they are demonstrating their wonderful Celtic love of *craic*, and being funny, they are the best. But when their leaders are being dour and prune-faced, they are the worst. This has bugger-all to do with Catholic vs Prod, with Nats vs Repubs. There are best and worst on both (or is it all?) sides of the NI community. But just look at the politicians and their hangers-on. And in that I include the amateur politicos in bodies such as The IRA, The Immediate IRA, The No We Are The Serious IRA, The Look We Really Mean It IRA. And in the Ulster Freedom Murderers, a.k.a., The Northern Irish But Wish We Were British Freedom Fighters.

Has there ever been a more snarling, scowling, bad-tempered, ungracious, depressed and vicious collection of people? In few places in the world do you find such relentlessly *unsmiling* unpleasantness.

Ian Paisley could curdle milk at a hundred yards even before he opens his mouth and lets loose with his particular version of the Belfast adenoidal snarl. Gerry Adams peers like an aggravated chipmunk from behind his owl-specs and face-foliage and you just know he has permanent indigestion. Behind both of them stand phalanxes of hatchet-faced acolytes, xenophobic stomach-acid etching displeasure into their faces.

I just wish they would all be more *Irish,* that's all.

POLITICS, BRITISH, POLITICIANS, AND

Three small majorities and a thousand massive egos

Weep in frustration, in anger, in disgust. Weep for democracy slowly being strangled. We, the people, to borrow the slightly purple American phrase, have allowed the creation of a politico-governmental monster of Jurassic proportions, and have given it talons and teeth the better to rip into us. With a massive digestive and excretion system which can chew up everything in its path, then crap on us lavishly and from a great height. And the breath which emerges when it speaks! Peeeee-yoo. Government as T-Rex. Despair, for that is all we can do. Or is it?

Democracy is not a world panacea, whatever the Americans say. It is possibly the best system we have been able to invent so far (more-or-less civilised nations for the use of, as Winston Churchill explained a great deal more elegantly) and the problem is *not* the concept, nor is it the various incarnations which democracy takes upon itself, which lie at the root of the problem. It is the way people bend and twist the democracy under which they live. Those people whose inflated opinions of themselves and the delusion that they can somehow "serve" others, sends them into the unrealities of the political arena, leaving the rest of us to watch them swarm up the greasy power-pole at its centre. And the higher they get, the more our view of them is confined to their arses.

Politicians in democracies use a wonderful trick to gull and lull us. "If you don't like what we do or don't do, you can vote us out". So if we are utterly disgusted by something the politicians have done, we have to wait until *they* call an election, at which point we can chuck out the present lot and replace them with clones wearing a different-coloured rosette – and that could, and usually does, take *up to five years*. Brilliant, isn't it? There was a time when an argument could be made in favour of giving a new Government a reasonable spell at the wheel, and not changing things too often, but those days are long gone. Our world moves too fast now, and every aspect of our lives changes with blistering speed without any intervention at all from our not-terribly-good lords and masters. But our l's and m's depend on a system which puts years between today's idiocy perpetrated by them and tomorrow's revenge taken by us. For them, excellent. For us, deeply frustrating and destructive. This system gives them time to cover over today's pile of rubbish with layer upon layer of newer and better rubbish, so that, come an Election, we no longer have sight or memory of anything that happened so long ago, and as soon as the Election looms, the politicians suddenly start trying to behave themselves. Maybe too late by then, but this you can be sure of; if we do vote out those in power, it will not be because we remember what they did four years ago, but because we are watching them, now, bugger up our lives, and we have grown weary of them.

And then we have Unity. Possibly the greatest political curse of our age. If we don't think together, we sink together, we are urged to believe. Unity is strength. In particular, political parties cannot function if they are not united, or at least put on a united front whatever back- and chest-stabbing is going on behind the scenes. Or so we are made to think. The fact is that unity usually means *uniformity*, where members of a group are urged *not* to think for themselves, but to follow the Thoughts Of The Great Leader, whoever that may be. Don't step out of line, because that gives the impression of woolly disparity and lack of purpose, and we can't have that, can we, if we are going to win that election?

What? Somebody muttering in the back row about needing to have freedom of thought and discussion *before* we become a Government? Bloody fool. Politics is about winning elections and getting into power, idiot, and the only thing the great brainwashed British public understands is Being United. (Being United lives in the same part of the brain as Manchester United, Dundee United, West Ham United, Lower Faffington United). If we, the politicians, start arguing and disagreeing now, we haven't a prayer, they say to one another. But stay united, and win the election, so when we sink our fat backsides into those lovely leather ministerial chairs, *then* we can fight like ferrets in a sack and we almost certainly will – but by then we will be able to do what we bloody well like for years and years.

In passing, this unity business is not confined to politics, not by a long hard shout. Armies come the most colossal croppers by trying to do things with their troops too close together, while, on the contrary, the history of warfare is stuffed full of the names of heroes who not only acted on their own initiative but allowed others under their command to do the same. Yes, the Romans created formations under massed shields, called themselves tortoises and rammed their way through everything and everyone in their path, but that was about *cohesion*, not unity. And yes, I do understand about the need for togetherness and a common purpose in trades unions (among other types of human groups) but when the chips are really down, it is the bloody-minded individual with a sense of his own power and destiny who makes things happen. These days, there's just too much unity around, and it is bad for us.

The whole thing is hateful. Government is not advancing us as a nation any more, nor is it responsible for such personal life-improvements as we make. If our lives are better in any way than those of our parents or grandparents, it is not as a result of things that have been done by governments. It happens *despite* what government gets up to. There simply isn't room any more for truly big ideas such as The

Welfare State or the NHS, introduced when the social slate was desperately blank, so government today tinkers and faffs at the edges. And tinkering and faffing is dressed up as "radical reform" and we are so dumb that we buy it. How sad is that?

And something worse: When an election is called, just listen to yourself piss and moan about how boring it all is, what a *fag* it is to have to schlep to the polling station – once in four or five years! And then having *not* voted because you could not be arsed, you spend the next four or so years pissing and moaning some more about the stuff being done in your name by a Government you did not elect. To get around the second lot of moans, I would make voting compulsory (it works for Australians – *Australians,* for God's sake).

And in any case, voting is a lot less of chore and a lot more quickly done and dusted than supermarket shopping with all that trailing about, heaving a trolley and standing in a checkout queue. But we happily do *that* on average *once a week*, never mind once every few years. Apparently we place more value on a packet of Chewey-Chunks than we do on a vote.

But it is not just about the fag of having to vote, and the attached boredom – it will not be too long before polling stations are things of history and we will all vote by Internet, Telephone or Interactive TV anyway. The problem is that the whole process is flawed at its core by the feeling that *however we cast our vote it will make not the slightest damned difference.* So why bother?

Are we are getting what we deserve? Probably. Should we re-think the whole damned charade so that we start to believe that we deserve better? Yes, and soon.

PRICES, HOTEL
Three hundred, four-fifty with sea-view

This, I really, *really* do not understand. It surely must fall into the dog's privates category. These days, because I am self-employed and run on a budget tighter than a ... than a ... can't remember, and because I have to travel a bit, I stay in Bed and Breakfast places which seldom charge more than around £30 per person per night including breakfast. That's £60 for two people if I am really in a mood to splash out and my wife is travelling with me. And B&B's are wonderful. Some of them are Five-Star-Plus.

Staying somewhere overnight usually involves getting there fairly late in the afternoon. Even later if there has been the wrong kind of traffic on the M-something. Over*night*, see? Clue there. So, a meal at the B&B, often available, usually very good and excellent value, or a trip to a nearby pub. £15 total. Then to bed. And away again the following morning at 10.00 a.m. at the latest (and often a lot earlier) after an excellent breakfast, all included. Total spend; +- £45, if I am travelling alone.

Exactly the same time-pattern applies at a hotel, so I never use the bar, swimming pool, gymnasium, squash or tennis court because I don't have time – and sometimes these "facilities" require extra payment anyway. Hotel prices start at £45 *single*, which often (and certainly in London) gets you a room in the attic with a shower like a phone booth. The evening meal in the restaurant is never less than £30 plus overpriced wine. Plus tip for mediocre service. Breakfast is extra, of course, and never less than £10 an egg. And that's the bottom end of the scale, with a total expenditure of about £100. Per person. In some places, usually involving the word "Inn", it is very easy to pay £150 a night for a room with everything else extra. Per person. That's £150 and sharply upwards. Did you say that you want to *breathe* in your room? £25 extra, thank yoooo.

I have asked hotel managers about it. How do they justify prices like this? The answers are always the same. Building-cleaning-maintenance-staff-water-electricity-rates-taxes-raw materials etc. Oh, and profit. Fine. Got that. But how do B and B places manage with more or less the same array of costs, except for staff?

I don't know. What I do know is that hotels will never see me again if I can possibly avoid it. I don't do sleeping at £20 per hour.

PRICING, PETROL
No lead and no points

I utterly hate buying petrol. With each litre I pump into my car, I see the grin of Mr. Dracula Brown in the little windows of the dispenser, and fume at the tax I am paying for the privilege of being able to move about in an area where there are no trains and the arrival of a bus is greeted with a celebratory party.

Environmental campaigners and the Government keep telling us that the more we are forced to pay for fuel, the fewer cars and trucks there will be on the road, while, despite decades of steadily climbing petrol and diesel prices, inflated by criminally high rates of excise duty, *exactly the opposite* has proven to be true. The Enviros who support the high-tax policy, simply do not know what they are on about and/or they have they have their heads so far up their green backsides that they can't see the truth for the trees. The Government is motivated purely by the amount of tax they can extract from the motorists and hauliers – and nothing else. You and I can safely forget protestations about Government policy concerning the environment. They talk the talk, but that's all they do.

With that off my chest and into my carburettor, let me ask you a question: do you see any real relationship between the price of petrol at the pump and the price of crude oil?

I have watched the oil-price go up and down like the proverbial tart's netherware, but down at Exxaco and Bshellp, the pump prices go either up or nowhere *whatever* the oil price happens to be on a given day. When the oil price goes down, either the pump price stays the same or mysteriously goes up a tick or two. Oh, that's because the stuff in the petrol station bowser was priced according to the oil price several weeks ago, was it? Really? Pull the other one. It's got a special additive.

And then there's the "price-watch" hoodwink dreamed up by some marketing gink who works for the company which I forbear to name but which is associated with an endangered species of large cat. According to this campaign, we were asked to believe that the cat people are watching everyone else in their immediate area, cat-like, to see who is changing prices, and then adjusting theirs to match – the implication being to match downwards. This really clogs my fuel line. Just who is watching whom? Everyone is watching everyone else, in which case – *who makes the first move?* Why do they expect us to believe this rubbish?

And why, if any of this is true, are there noticeable variations in price as between competing petrol stations, all the time? The fact is that local pump prices are set by a computer operated by a zombie in London, and all this "we're watching" stuff is exactly what it appears to be: full-fat four-star twaddle.

Here's another question: how is it possible for the Exxaco station in Blimpwater to be selling petrol at 5p a litre cheaper than the one in Lower Upper, when the Blimpwater station is just up the road from the refinery, while Lower Upper is in the middle of nowhere? Eh? Eh? Transport costs? Don't think so. There goes that old dog again, flopping onto its side.

PRICES, WINE
Seven hundred percent mark-up and rising

I don't do restaurants much these days. It's such a lottery in terms of what you get for your money. But when I do decide that I have loaded the dishwasher as many times this month as I can stand, I head for restaurants which operate on a bring-your-own-booze basis. I refuse to submit to the bare-faced robbery practised by the "fully licensed" ones.

I have no problem with anyone who wants to make a reasonable profit. But when I know that a bottle of not-very-special Chardonnay has cost the restaurant owner £3.00 or less, and I am expected to pay £12.75 on the rare occasion I do go to licensed place, I cry foul and order water. I love drinking wine with my meal, and I am totally in agreement with the Italians who say that a meal without wine is like a day without sunshine. But *not* at any price.

I have spoken to many restaurant wine-robbers about this. They moan that they have to buy a very expensive wine licence (interest on the bank overdraft) buy the wine (more interest) transport it, if it is not delivered (petrol, wear and tear on the car/van) or pay delivery charges, then store it (cost per square foot of space) chill it if it is white (cost of running the refrigerator) walk it to the table (shoe leather) pull the cork and pour it (waiter's time and effort) and store the empty bottle (more space-cost). Then wash the glasses and put them away. Oh, and the cost of buying the glasses in the first place. And buying corkscrews. Almost forgot. And medical expenses for the waiters/waitresses who suffer from Repetitive Strain Injury from all that twisting and pulling.

All of this terrible burden means that they are scarcely making any profit at all. Or so they would have me believe. One restaurant owner told me with a straight face that he had *had* to put up his wine-prices, because the drink-drive laws now resulted in his customers drinking less, so he sells less. So he puts up the prices so that … I leave you to work that one out.

Because I once foolishly owned a small share in a restaurant, I know that there is a rule of thumb on restaurant costs and charges. One third for the raw material, one third for the cost of preparation and serving, and one third profit. The average charge for a main course runs at around £12.00 these days (a lot higher in London, but then in London, people will pay anything for everything and I am not even *thinking*, here, about the snob-eateries run by TV chefs and the like) and it is not unreasonable for the restaurant to apply that rule-of-thirds and justify the charge. They have, after all, actually *done* something with the raw materials, transforming them from lumps of meat and veg into (sometimes) delectable dishes, so they deserve a decent reward for the effort.

But they do absolutely *nothing to the wine* other than pull the cork, and pour it (if you are lucky) so they have no right to apply a rule of tipple-tripling at all. If they applied a rule of doubling, putting a one hundred percent mark-up on the cost (in itself a liberty) I would grit my teeth and pay up. That bottle of Chardonnay would cost me about £6.00. Still too expensive, still unreasonable. Still leaves me feeling dyspeptic.

Behind it all is the *real* reason why restaurants charge so much: many of them just cannot make enough profit on the food, because they manage things inefficiently. But they are *restaurants*, not wine-bars or pubs, and the wine is supposed to complement the food, not stand as the main profit centre. So what is really happening here? My belief is that the wine-rippers are charging these outrageous prices for a simple reason. In many cases, restaurants would go to the wall without the profit they make on wine, so they charge whatever they can, because they can. And *why* can they ? Because you, you poor put-upon British person, are too embarrassed and timid to complain. Arise, I say, and whine.

'QUAKES, EARTH
Clear off the Richter

Have you ever been in or near one? No? But you have seen stuff on TV, and read about it, yes? Recently? Good. But I have *been* there, too close for comfort. I watched as the ground did things which showed that terra is not always as firma as it is cracked up to be, because it cracks, spectacularly. I watched while some very old and beautiful buildings juddered, swayed and then bit the dust, right down to ground zero. Buildings, then rubble. In about thirty seconds. Me, blubbing and piddling in terror, convinced I was going to disappear into a hole in the ground, realising that I would never again express the metaphorical wish to have the ground swallow me up no matter how serious my social gaffe.

My atheism kicked in big-time. Just as I wonder about snakes, about which a LOT more later, and nettles, and funnel-web spiders and other stuff which appears to exist for the sole purpose of pissing us off or hurting us, I wonder about an all-powerful all-seeing, all-doing Creator who so completely mis-designed the Earth that it has socking great rips and holes in its crust. Why would earthquakes be part of some great divine plan? When they cause the kind of death and destruction we saw in South-east Asia, not to mention dozens of other places where they have happened and will happen again?

I wait for the ground to settle down and then I rise up in loathing and disgust. Our planet has been around for four or five billion years. That's more time than it is possible for anyone to imagine, especially when even the longest-lived of us just about manages 100. Surely four billion years is long enough for it to sort itself out, settle down and stop chucking itself around like a spoiled celestial brat?

For a while, and I would much prefer to forget it, I lived in Los Angeles. It is the worst place on the surface of the earth, and the people who live there are all more than slightly loopy, every last one of them. But can you blame them? They live on the wrong side of the San Andreas Fault, which is actually God's, and one day there will be a noise like, like, I just can't imagine, and the entire shooting match is going to fall into the Pacific Ocean. If you live with that hanging over you, or crouching under you, and you know that it is not a matter of whether but when – no wonder you are as crazed as a loon.

But I don't wish it on them. No creatures have evolved, despite the age of the Earth, to cope with the ground heaving and splitting beneath their feet. Paws. Hooves. Aside from being caught in the path of an erupting volcano's pyroclastic flow, or an avalanche, there can be nothing more horrifying than being on top of the Earth when it moves. So I have never understood that phrase when applied to sex. Who would want that?

QUALIFICATIONS, TOO MANY
More degrees than a compass, few of any use

What do you feel when you are introduced to some gink who has a Ph.D, MA, BA., MBA, LL.B etc.? How do you know that the gink has all these degrees? Because the gink will take the first possible opportunity to hand you his business card, upon which are engraved all of them. Or you will have received a letter from him or his Highly Personal Assistant, with all degrees flying.

If the gink happens to be in business and not an escapee from academia, ask any of his colleagues how they rate his education in direct proportion to whether or not he gets the job done. You will find that half of them will reach for forelocks and start tugging, because they are simply over-awed by all that lettering, while the other half say very rude things I could not possibly repeat here. Especially if the gink has an MBA. Master of Business Administration. Master of Bullshit

Advancement. Which, for certain, he will have acquired after his MA or BA or similar.

Now don't get me wrong. I am fully in favour of giving intelligent young people the opportunity to go to a Uni and acquire whatever it is they acquire there. For the most part, and for most undergraduates, that tends to focus on copulation and alcohol in equal measure, but they will, unless they are totally socially unacceptable, have a hell of a good time – a better time than ever before in their lives, and certainly better than anything they are likely to experience afterwards. And they will come out the other end with a degree of some kind, probably. Which is supposed to stand them in good stead for the rest of their lives. Which is, possibly, why The Blessed Blair wants to see fifty percent at least of all young people going to Uni. I think. Maybe he just wants them to have a good time. I don't know.

And what about student debt? When will they, and we, stop worrying about this? Anyone with half a brain-cell will know that any students who can't pay off their debts after a few years, will be able to go to the Department of Soft and Furry Landings, look forlorn, fill in a form, and have their debt written off. If we can write off the debts owed by whole countries who never had the slightest intention of repaying them then we can and we will, mark my words, do the same for our poor under-employed students. This only applies to the un- or under-employed, of course, because those who manage to get into Big Law Firms, or Big Accountancy Firms or just Big Firms will have their debts paid for them by tomorrow morning. Or will be earning mini-moggie fat-cat salaries so that they can pay the debts themselves, p.d.q.

Where was I? M's of B.A. Yes. I keep meeting people who have employed these over-educated degree-hunters and they keep saying, "They give great theory, but when it comes down to the deal, they seize up solid." All of them? No, not all of them. But, put most of them up against people with built-in drive, instinct, perseverance and bugger all by way of thermometers attached, and guess who wins, every time? But do I really view them as complete crap, as this book implies? Nah, not really crap. They are just very slappable, is all.

There is one saving grace in this country. In happy contrast to Germany, where multiple-degree'd personages must be addressed as Herr Doktor Doktor Professor Doktor to celebrate his multiplicity of degree, we don't go overboard. But we do still refer to people with Ph.D's as "Doctor". Even if the Ph.D is in Meejah Studies. I'm old fashioned. A doctor is a bloke (yes, any sex) with a stethoscope, bad breath and worse hand-writing. And as for those jumped-up hobbledehoys who have honorary doctorates in Ph and insist on being addressed as Doctor, gahooey.

QUANGOS
More = a lot less, but mounting

THE RAMPANT QUANGO

Thought to have evolved from a cross between a hyena-like creature and a vulture, the quango reproduces by sex-less cell-division provided that sufficient quantities of Prime Ministerial patronage are present in the air.

Proliferation is now a problem, though, and steps are being considered to organise a cull.

The quango has developed a long, sharp nose so that it can stick it into every other animal's business, a permanently irritated disposition with expression to match and sticky fingers to which everyone else's money adheres with depressing ease.

There are almost six hundred quangos in Britain. They cover the country like a rash. And would you like to know how many have come into existence since the Blessed Anthony Blair took office in 1997? No, you wouldn't. It would make you very, very cross, so I will spare you that. But it's lots. *Very* lots.

Have you ever looked at a list of them, or even a list of *some* of them? It is enough to cause you to gag in disbelief. Try some of those I have listed below and decide what you think they do. By the way, I have made up some of them. Can you spot the real deal against those I dreamed up? But play the game, OK? Don't look at the answers opposite until you have had a guess at each one on the list

> **Apples And Pears Board**
> **British Anti-Piracy Commission**
> **British Potato Council**
> **British Retread Board**
> **Cakes Licensing Commission**
> **Export Group On Vitamins And Minerals**
> **Milk Marketing Board**
> **Mobile Phone Investigation Committee**
> **Ofcome**
> **Ofcom**
> **Offer**
> **Ofnav**
> **Ofpurse**
> **Ofwat**
> **Pig Development Committee**
> **Plaster Board**
> **Statistics Commission**
> **Topsoil Management Testing Committee**
> **Veterinary Residues Committee**
> **Weather Investigation Board**
> **Weir Board**
> **Wheelchair Control Council**
> **Whelk And Cockle Board**
> **Zoos Forum**

I can't take any more crap

And here are the answers

Apples And Pears Board True, but doing what? Inspecting stairs?
British Anti-Piracy Commission False, but tomorrow, who knows …
British Potato Council True, but what the hell…?
British Retread Board False, but badly needed
Cakes Licensing Commission False – cake slicing commission, geddit? Come on.
Export Group On Vitamins and Minerals True, dunno, ask Don Foster MP, Chairman
Milk Marketing Board True, but why? Cows do it, goats do it
Mobile Phone Investigation Committee False, but there ought to be one
Ofcome False but could be the self-abuse promotion body
Ofcom True, but see above
Offer True. No idea
Ofnav False. Ofnaff?
Ofpurse False, but almost Ofpiss
Ofwat True, but almost Oftwat
Pig Development Committee True, but how? What?
Plaster Board False. Come on.
Statistics Commission True, counting what, exactly?
Topsoil Management Testing Committee False, but close. Ofdirt maybe.
Veterinary Residues Committee True, true, and don't even think about it
Weather Investigation Board False, but not for long
Weir Board So are we
Wheelchair Control Council False, but something has to be done
Whelk And Cockle Board False. What about mussels, then?
Zoos Forum True. But I'm agin 'em

And so on and on. Tragedy going as comedy.

Robert MacGregor

QUEUES
Number 3 but moving up and we really appreciate you

A very old joke, the business of Continental Europeans and other breeds without the law who just do not understand the civilised business of orderly queues. But somehow, on the queue-less Continent everyone seems to get served, and it all looks like a lot more fun. According to the Royal League of Stuffing the British Way Down Your Throat, that is definitely Not For Us.

I am supposed to blame The War for British queue-ism, where it became the national sport and a daily dose of standing in a line never did anyone any harm. I seem to remember having to attend compulsory classes on queuing, at University. But I think it goes more deeply into the British psyche than that. It would not surprise me to learn that ancient Brits queued up for their woad ration in a nice straight line. *Buggerate me*, the Romans must have thought, those Iceni don't half look *stupidi* standing one behind the other like a human *viperus*. Some sort of religious ritual, *supposimus*.

But here's an odd thing. There is not a lot of difference between the shapeless scrum which forms at counters in Europe and what happens in pubs or bars in Britain. There is no queue at the British bar, on the (usually groundless) assumption that there are several people on the other side ready to serve, so no point in standing one behind the other – just join the back of the scrum, behind the rear-most feet to be rugby-correct and use a bit of judicious elbow to move both forwards and sideways at the same time. No-one seems to care. But jump a queue in Britain and it is a capital offence. You have your head bitten off.

I used to play a silly game when I was a schoolboy let loose into the nearby town with friends. We would form a queue at some convenient lamp-post or similar, standing quietly one behind the other. It did not take long for a collection of the gormless but Pavlovian to join the line, waiting for nothing to happen. After a while, we would peel off, one by one, in feigned exasperation at the time it was taking for …. nothing to happen. I never learned how long it took for the rest of the queue to disperse. Possibly, they are still there.

QUIZZES AND GAME SHOWS
Four sets of Forsythes and a signed Vorderman

By quiz, I mean the TV kind where one of the tribe of over-excited mincing presenters, or their faux-po-faced colleagues put collections of pudding-faced and muesli-brained contestants through excruciating attacks on their ignorance. And the pudding-types cannot get enough of it. There are always herds of them screaming me, me, me, sir, me, me, me, please sir, let *me*. Is it *really* the opportunity to win a lot of money or a third bathroom suite? Just harmless fun? Or is there something more sinister at work here? I don't know and don't much care, which is usually more than can be said for the people who stage-manage the quizzes and TV game-shows so that somebody always wins something, and occasionally, someone stages public hysterics at having won a lot of something or other. I can't watch much of this.

Is it much better away from TV in pubs when they put on "quiz-nites"? (Always spelled that way, of course). No. I have, on mercifully rare occasions, been hauled blatting and protesting onto a pub-quiz team, on the basis that I am such a mouthy know-all that I must be able to help the team win. Very flattering, very good free pint of pilsner, thanks ever so, and then my brain goes into hibernation. My eyes take on that far-away glaze, my tongue sticks to the roof of my mouth, and I have not the slightest idea as to what the capital of Lithuania might be. Or the name of the male lead in Casablanca. Or anything else. Until I get away from the pressure zone with its beads of sweat, clouds of smoke and bulging eyes. The moment I get outside, I know the answers. Of course.

RACING, HORSE-, TV, ON
Three two one, and off to the bar

I appreciate that at least a dozen or so people love watching horse racing and several million of them are dumb enough to bet on it. So the TV people cover horse racing every weekend. And *boy* do they *cover* them. If there is absolutely nothing else to see on a wet Saturday afternoon then lethargically I flick over to one of the channels and ...

A fifteen minute interview, each, with a trainer, owner, jockey, stable-person, horse-expert from The Horsy News, the horse, all conducted in the broadest Irish (usually). Pictures of the horses being led about a ring. Pictures of the same horses, from the arse-angle, no jockey. Pictures of the jockeys hoisting their tiny little rumps into kiddie-saddles, and more of the horses parading around in a circle. Oops, one of the jockeys fell off. Ten minutes of analysis. How did he fall, where, why, what happened to the horse, the jockey, the trainer, the owner, the odds? Pictures of jockey back on horse. Pictures of horses lolloping down the course, and back up again. And so on and on – not to mention the amount of time devoted to screens full of utterly incomprehensible charts and tables giving the betting odds now, yesterday, the day before. Lists of mind-crushing detail about the horse's parents, grandparents. Half an hour of this stuff – for one race. Then the race, which is over in about four minutes maximum.

Then interviews with ... analyses about ... comment from. I am happily asleep by then. Best soporific in the world. Beats a party political broadcast any day.

RAIL, BRITISH
Five, but change the crew at Crewe

Yes, yes, I know, it's not British Rail any more. It is a collection of pirates riding the rails owned by something called Not-work Rail, and it is a shambles. Furthermore … no, to hell with it. It has all been said. If Isambard Kingdom B, or Robert Stephenson were brought back to life they would take long, sad looks, emit pained and terminal sighs, and forthwith die again, this time of embarrassment.

RECORDERS, VIDEO
3456678865, bugger, 346776884, no, oh sod it

I am too mean to buy a digital DVD re-recordable whatsit and in any case, the great Nipponese, Taiwanese and Koreanese industries still cannot decide which system to settle on, and my technological luck says I am certain to buy the wrong one two days before it becomes utterly obsolete, just as I did when Beta was eaten up by VHS. So, I stick with a pile of video bricks and I try everything in my power to record programmes which I can watch later – *and* so I can whiz through the terrible commercials and the endless, equally awful, repeated-ad-vomitem BBC promotions for future programmes. And fast-forward through eighteen minutes of Helen Mirren (whom I otherwise adore as does every red-corpuscled properly male male) deploying her angst and bosom against some simpering twit in over-tight trousers. Because even Helen at her best is capable of palling if she is required by the writer and/or the director to go on and on. So I record a lot of stuff. Or try to.

But getting a recording pinned down? Eschewing all other methods, I have settled on something in my particular brand of video recorder, called Video-Plus, whereby I am supposed to enter the code helpfully provided by the published programme guides, hit several

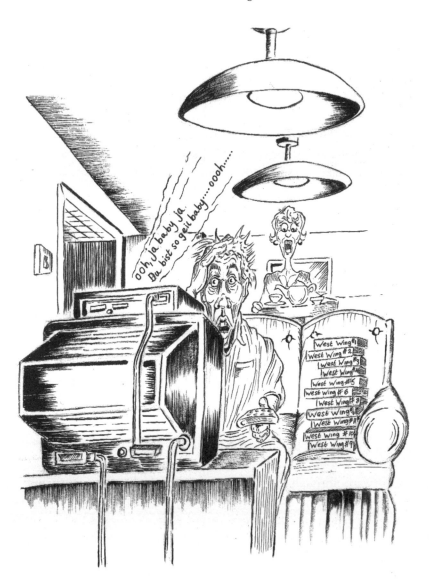

buttons, and start living in hope.

I *have* to hope, because in about fifty percent of my attempts I have set the machine to record a really interesting documentary about the mating habits of something cetaceous, and what I actually get is a soap opera about the mating habits of East-End Coronation Neighbours. I know I entered the right numbers. Well, I am *almost* sure I know, because I get my wife to check me and she is a stickler. Still does not help. The machine records what it likes. And don't tell me that I can use some fancy setting to make sure that I get what I want if the programme starts late. I have tried that. The machine can only handle this if I am setting it to record one programme and only one. Try setting it to record more, and the first programme comes to a shrieking stop exactly five minutes from the end. The villain was exposed one minute after that. The shrieks come from me.

Try the other method. Set it by the time and don't rely on published numbers which may be full of typos. No good, because this involves more thumb-tapping on the + or − button than anyone should have to put up with, and not even a txt-addctd tnagr wth mnky thmbs cn mnge tht.

So, I miss a lot. But the next day I have forgotten what I missed the previous one. Happy again. Video amnesia.

REICHS, KATHY and CORNWELL, PATRICIA And SLAUGHTER, KARIN (real name, honestly)
Not very high, just slightly off, but read on ...

I am addicted. I love the whodunit stories which these ladies construct brilliantly, even if you think you know whodunit right from page three. Page one. The characters are wonderful; just slightly larger than life, as befits a good thriller, and the research all these authors undertake into aspects of our modern world is hugely impressive. I know things I did not think I needed to know about north-American biker culture, loony quasi-religious cults, paedophilia, all sorts. I have also learned so much about human anatomy and the way it twists, burns, changes colour and decomposes, that I could pass any tough medical exam you care to throw at me, while throwing up.

In case you don't know any of these authors, they are actually the same person using three names and she writes the most blood- and gore-drenched novels in the universe. No, only kidding. I know they are different people, competitive to a fault, and possibly hate one another. Possibly not.

But I have a real problem. I love the writing, the style, the brilliance of imagination, wit and page-turning excitement. I look forward eagerly to their respective next books. I'm hooked. But I am seriously up to here with the magnified gore they appear to delight in. I just don't want to be put off my lunch for days.

The heroines of their novels are involved in criminal pathology or similar, which requires the dissection and examination of corpses ranging from freshly-done-in to bare bones, with everything in between. And I mean *everything*. In the kind of detail which makes gratuitous violence in the cinema, TV and computer games look tame and lame by comparison. If Kay Scarpetta (Cornwell's heroine) has a victim to cope with, you are thrown head-first into the putrescent liver and guts, only coming up for air when you know those organs much, much too intimately. Then you are plunged up to your elbows into the deliquescent bowels, just long enough to make you fully acquainted with the contents at close range before you are handed the rotting brain.

If Tempe Brennan (Reichs' corpse-wrangler) is faced with a body that has been shallowly buried for a few months and has had most of its limbs gnawed by scavenging rats or wolves, you are right there. And I mean *right* there, down and very, very dirty. Up close and far too personal. You get the minutiae of the life-cycle of the fly which lays its eggs in, the maggots which eat their way out of ... and the ... and the ...

Let me give you some examples from the authors whose rights (and those of their publishers) I recognise and respect. Here are some passages from their work: (Brackets are mine, of course).

KATHY REICHS

"*Someone had collected shards of bone and brain pudding ....(Yeeeeergh!). Projected blood results from someone running through,*

stamping into or slapping a pool of blood...... (Mmmmmaaaaagh!)
.... *The woman's hands had been sawed at the wrists, the rest of her limbs detached at the joints. Her belly had been slashed along the..."*

" ....*dipping her hands inside the bag of frigid, soupy organs and feeling her way through them".* " *I'm happy to report you didn't miss anything on the tongue".* "*She drops it back into the bag, where it rests on top of the other tan pieces of Gilly Paullson's rotting organs".* (Blaaaaaargh! Yaaaaaark!! Nyeeeeeerg !!! Spit, spit).

NOW, PATRICIA CORNWELL

"*Her hair is matted with dried blood and her face swollen and deformed by contusions, cuts and smashed bones (Unnnnngh). Her belly, breasts chest and neck are clustered with stab wounds".* (Yuuuurgh. Bleurrrgh. Aaaaaaaaargh!)

AND KARIN SLAUGHTER

"*The bullet had entered her skull at an upward trajectory, breaking the spheroid plowing (!) along the lateral cerebral fissure then busting out through the occipital bone "* (Mnnnerhghgh).

And so on. Believe me, I have spared you the worst. There is miles of it. Piles of it. And what do they look like, these purveyors of gore which would gag Jack the Ripper? Unless all of them have used a particularly talented make-up artist, a lot of plastic surgery and a super-clever photographer, they are all very attractive. They do not look remotely like Cruella de Ville crossed with a Russian female weigh-lifter, as you might expect. Butter would not melt, etc.

But behind those lovely looks, lurk female Caligulas, Ghengis Khans and Vlads the Impalers in very bad moods. You don't want to be reading these gals during your lunch break. What you are able to choke down will soon be back up again.

P.S. I have now discovered Tess Gerritsen, another clearly delightful and beautiful person, and another American writer in the same genre, who almost out-Reichs Reich, out-Cornwells Cornwell and out-Slaughters Slaughter. Gore galore. What's going on here? All four women, all four

American. In the blood-and-guts stakes, there isn't one Brit who comes close. Well, I suppose that we are just roo polite and nicely brought up to write stuff that makes people throw up. I must investigate.

RELATIONS, PUBLIC
Five column inches and three pork pies

Forget prostitution. *This* is the oldest profession, but the means and methods are roughly the same.

It is accepted practice for politicians to tell waddling great porkies but they do at least have the good grace to tell the lies themselves. Usually. But a trade whose practitioners lie for a living, and who tell those lies for *others*, is bottom-feedingly inexcusable.

You may remember that I mentioned back under "B" the way banks bump along the bottom of the barrel, content to stay there because their public images are so bad that nothing can be done to make them either better or worse. So they do what they like, and we can be damned. But they have to say something, occasionally, so big businesses like banks pay PR agencies vastly fat-encrusted fees for doing the work of patting the public head and lulling us all into a nice warm cocoon where we will lose the will to question what they are up to.

Stephen Fry at his awful arch best headed the cast in a TV series set in and around a PR consultancy. "Absolute Power", it was called. It was wonderful stuff, so far over the top that it almost met itself coming back. I used to think about it as some of the best satire I had ever seen on TV. Then I stopped and thought again. It was not satire at all. It was documentary. You simply cannot satirise something which is so crammed with hilarious crapology. The stuff that PR people have to do simply pickles the brain.

Some years ago, at the request of the Chairman of a company for which I was doing some copywriting, I went to work in the company's PR consultancy. Request? Chairmen do not request. They bark orders.

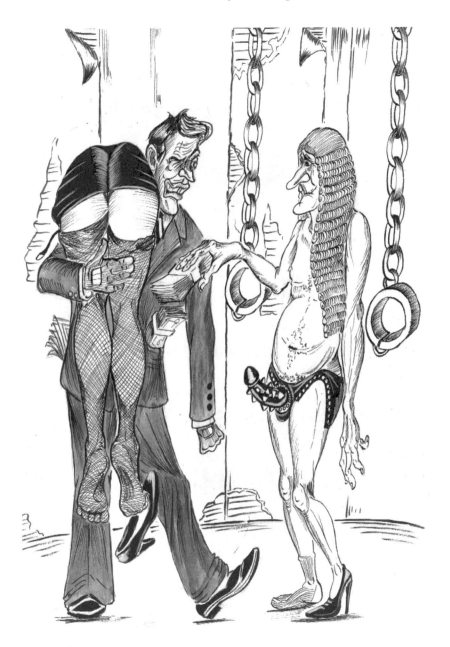

"Thenk you Mr. Farnesworth, she'll do naiceleigh."

So I went. I was working late one night (the Consultancy was less than affectionately known as Smith, Jones and Worktillmidnight) when the phone rang and, mechanically, I picked it up. Wrong move. On the other end, one of the top three honchos of a client company. Bladdered. Leathered. Skunk, Lord, Newt.

"Hellllo, lissen, I need a flavour. Favour. Tee hee. I'm at the good 'ol Dog 'n Duck an' I've met this verrry nice lady, y'see, an' y'know how tiz, we wannna have a liddle fun, but I'm a bit shorta readies atha moment, and she won' take plac ... plac... plastic, the silly, the silly... You boys've always got lotsa lolly 'angin' about. Get on yer bike 'n come over here, fas' as y'can OK?"

Dial tone.

I could not believe it. So I rang the Managing Director at home for instructions. What should I do?

"You'll find a couple of hundred in my office, old boy. That ought to be enough".

"You mean you actually want me to ...."

"Yes of *course* I bloody well do. He's an important client. *Haven't you worked that out yet?*"

Dial tone. Public Relations? *Pubic* Relations.

RELIGION, ORGANISED
One deity, or several, but only my way is True

As I may have tried to persuade you, I am not actively atheist – just very sure that I don't know. Oh, the hell with it. Let's tell the truth. Agnosticism is just the atheist coward's way of hedging bets. There are either believers in a deity/deities or there are atheists. Stop mucking about. I'm an atheist. I don't believe because I can't.

As a boy, I was forced to attend a boarding school where the headmaster was a determined God-botherer who made us trudge to church once on Wednesday and twice on Sunday. As a result, I know the words to all the most-sung hymns. I was baptised and confirmed. Not bad for someone born of a Jewish mother and a Scottish Presbyterian father, eh? Bets hedged. Thought you ought to know. Escaped *bris melah* and *bar-mitzvah* by the skin of my … skin of my.

The day I left school, that was *it* as far as religion was concerned. I had done my time. Since then I have become progressively less impressed and more depressed by what I have seen of organised religion. And that range includes the big-league players such as multiple-choice Christianity; at least two-sided Islam (where one faction says killing is bad and the other says *jihad* and *fatwa*; hydra-headed Hinduism; and Judaism which talks unity and barely practises irritated tolerance with itself. Not to mention the truly frightening cults and sects which are all over the place in every sense thereof. Intra-religious intolerance is a truly disturbing thing to watch at work. Now move to *inter*-religious similar, and you have hateful world mayhem, all practised in the name of God or gods.

Intolerance? It's the cornerstone of all organised religion, as far as I can tell. God is love? The God of people other than your own seems happy with whatever human mood happens to be on the menu at any given time. God is revenge? That's fine. *Organised* religion? The religions in whose service people gather and in whose names they construct mighty edifices and fight mighty wars seem to me utterly *dis*organised but very capable of inspiring mass hatred and murder. Neat trick, that. Other side of the coin, I hear you say? Great works of religious art, saintly saints who never harmed a fly, great good works by endless columns of nuns and monks? Yes, all that, but why *should* there be two sides to this particular human coin, when a religion ought to be *religious,* concerning itself with peace, help, kindness, tolerance, and so on, forswearing anything even remotely resembling crusades, excommunications, *fatwas*, or *jihads*? A two-*headed* coin, why not?

Against human nature, that'd be. Some people need a God-head to carry into war. (Sigh!)

Robert MacGregor

RESEARCH, MARKET

Seven out of ten say they are. Or aren't

I have never been asked my opinion on anything, by any market research company. Nor have you, I suspect. I believe that all market research is conducted among a closed circle of respondents who are paid to answer the usually silly questions. The same people, all the time, whether it is about baked beans or breast-enlargement, political polling or PMT. Uh, oh. I can hear the market researchers squalling and stamping their feet. They protest. It ain't so. They recruit their respondents on the basis of stratified random sampling (whatever that means) so it is all fair and above board and honest and true and really, really accurate. Is it, it *is, it IS.*

Let's deal first with those pre-election polls which are supposed to tell us how the electorate are going to vote, and have been so hopelessly wrong so often. Am I being unfair? Surely we must allow the pollsters to get it wrong from time to time? Only human, aren't they? Well, no. If polls are so all-firing damned scientific, the researchers ought to get this kind of thing right *every single time.* Getting it wrong even *once* demonstrates to my total satisfaction that market research is a black art, not a science at all.

And then we come to market research which is commissioned by companies who want to find out what prospective customers think of a new product which they are considering foisting on us in exchange for our hard-earned. What the researchers want are *positive* results, and they will turn themselves inside out to construct questions which give them the result they want, so that they can present them to the top management as proof of their diligence and clever analyses. And if the product bombs, the Research Department says, "Well, gee, sorreeeee, the respondents at the time said they *lurrrrved* it. Can't help it if the public they represent have changed their minds, can we?"

However, the biggest problem faced by all market researchers looking for support for a new product is simply this: the public has no opinion on something they have not yet seen, heard, tasted, smelled and touched several times over, and even if you shove it up their noses, they still won't tell the truth. Stop Joe P in the street and ask him what he thinks of … whatever … and he will go into "anything-to-please" mode. In a flash, his mind processes the following thoughts. "What does this clipboard-bearing nuisance want me to say? What will get rid of him most effectively? I know. Tell him that whatever he is touting, I *love* it." And what about in-house interviews, conducted with people who have voluntarily agreed to take part *and* make the interviewer a cup of tea? Surely *they* tell the truth? Did I say voluntarily? Yes, true – but in many, many cases, the respondents are paid for their time. *Paid*. What kind of truth do you suppose they are going to tell *people who pay them?* And the basic problem remains: People just don't want to come across as negative, especially not in their own homes. This is why so many new products which have been researched to within a millimetre of their lives, bomb and then disappear immediately once they hit reality in the open market..

Take radio and TV audience research. Radio in particular has a real battle. Audience research is done on the basis of a diary kept by people who have been recruited to do this, and paid to do it – and many of them are lying. Not maliciously, but because they are filling in the diary according to what they think the research company wants them to say. Do you listen to Radio 4? "Oh, Radio 4, oh yes, Radio 4 is my *favourite*. I *love* the dramas and the, you know, cultural stuff." Craddocks. They actually listen to mindless pop music from mindless pop music radio. Which is fine. They are entitled to listen to any crap they like. But to expect them to tell the truth is an expectation too far.

When it comes to launching a new product, there is only one way to get at the truth. Ask someone with plenty of experience in the field (not a consumer; a *producer*) and rely on his instincts. If he thinks it will bomb, drop it. If not, give it full support. He will be right much more often than expensive research, extensive or not.

The problem is that unless a huge wad of money has been seen to be thrown at some sort of expensive attempt at finding out what the public might or might not like, the product managers will not move a muscle or a brain cell. So, research it is – and expensive research covers a lot of backside if something goes wrong.

S

SAFETY, HEALTH AND
Two but mind your back, sorry, three

How could anyone who claims to be sane think that health and safety is crap? I *don't*. What I despise with passion is the litigation-culture, imported from the USA, which has produced a must-be-risk-free society in Britain, and spawned the Health and Safety Big Brother Revolution. You do not dare do anything which involves five people or more, unless you have done a full Health and Safety Policy Statement, appointed a Health and Safety Manager, a Deputy Manager, an Assistant Deputy Manager and four Just In Case Assistant Deputy Under Managers. And a Sunday Someone Has To Be There Manager. Then you do a Risk Assessment. No, you do several, each one slightly different from the previous one. You file them. You fill in reports in quintuplicate on the most trivial incident, then you eat the report and give yourself up to the Police.

You do all this because if you don't, and something goes wrong, run and keep on running. The Health and Safety Executive will come after you. So will the Local Council. So will the parents, cousins, brothers, uncles, aunts, grandparents and other suddenly interested parties. So will the Police. And then comes the slithering serpentine slime of lawyers, all wanting a piece of the insurance action – you did have an appropriate insurance policy of course? No? You are up to yours in crap. No escape.

Your out-of-control brat runs down a path in a public garden, trips over his own feet, falls, grazes both knees. Not *his* fault. Not *yours*. Blame the garden operators. Sue *someone*. An employee who was fully trained according to Health and Safety guidelines and the Health and Safety Act 1974, loses concentration because, being an idiot, he was trying to light a fag while operating a grab, has his arm broken by a flailing piece of machinery. Not *his* fault. *Yours.* You did not warn him that ... etc.

I have seen successful small businesses close up shop because the burden of complying with Health and Safety requirements was too damned heavy and expensive – and the cost of an insurance policy was just out of the question. I am also seeing, right now, a sad decline in the number of school field-trips in my area, previously organised by teachers aching to show the youngsters what nature looks like close up, but who have decided not to, because the risk to the school and themselves from being sued for even the smallest incident is too great. Swimming lessons? Forget it. Water is involved.

(And what is the only thing that does not require Risk Assessments but needs them most sorely of all? School food, is what. Now that *really* ought to come with a Health and Safety Warning, at least until His Beatitude The Sainted Jamie Oliver's recommendations fully permeate the system).

Health and Safety consultants the length and breadth of the land are growing fat on the proceeds of consultancies for shit-scared organisations of all kinds. We are not a country of innovation any more. It is impossible to innovate without risk, and risk-free thinking is squashing any chance of new ideas. I blame the Blame Culture. So should you. And also blame the lawyers, of course.

SCHLOCK *(see also VULGARITY)*
Gnine gnomes, and six dancing dragons

It's about taste, I suppose. And no, I can't define it any better than many others who have tried. Including, almost certainly, Brian Sewell. (See S for Sewell, Brian.)

Good taste is just sort of *there*, unobtrusively. Bad taste jumps up and down in a clown outfit and shrieks its pitiful message to all and sundry. You can't miss it. It isn't that I set myself up an arbiter of what's tasteful and what's not. But I am of a sometimes delicate disposition and I *am* offended by ducks flying in formation up a wall.

But simple bad taste is just the thin end. All over the world, there are shops and stalls and shambling people with tottering tables, selling stuff of such schlocking awfulness as to make mere bad taste seem quite acceptable. And some people are pleased to display this stuff with pride, in their homes.

Plasterette statuettes of smiling orange cats. Entire lawns full of gnasty gnauseating gnomes. Tat-encrusted primary-coloured leaking plastic bottles of extra-gang-raped olive oil. Ghastly, crumbling pottery Welsh dragons, dressed in national costume, on their hind legs, smiling terrible, unnerving smiles. Carved (with a chainsaw) animals of every kind, with lions that look like hippos which look like trunkless elephants which look like be-trunked giraffes which look like bad replicas of the Eiffel tower. A six-inch high, seated, stuffed gorilla, wearing a vest and underpants, which sings a snatch of yowling song if prodded and wags its stupid schlocky head. And the motorised versions. Dollies which dangle dangerously from dashboards or swing alarmingly and distractingly from rear-view mirrors. Stuffed monkeys which adhere to windows. Nodding doggies on the parcel shelves. Stripes and slashes and streaks of paint, puce or orange or sometimes both, across car bonnets or doors.

Much of this schlock is classed as "souvenirs", and they are brought back from some place far away, so that the bringers-back can remember, fondly, where they have been and what they did there including mooch from shop to shop looking for, and at, schlock to bring back as souvenirs of the time they mooched from shop to shop looking for …

Schlock. There just isn't a better word. It is onomatopoeically, poetically spot on. I know, I have offended you. You have some of these in your home. Or car. You think they are lovely. Well, one man's plastic Jesus which lights up electrically when you touch him is a shrine, and another man's tat. All life is a choice; you have made yours, and I have made mine.

SCHOOLS, BOARDING
Three friendly Rogers, and oooh, matron

I once heard Jeremy Hardy explain that he hadn't been sent to boarding school because his parents actually quite *liked* him. In my case, working on the Hardy principle, I must have been roundly despised by both of my parents, because I was sentenced at the age of six.

There should be no such thing as boarding school, and the fact that they exist at all is testimony to a failed culture where parents have abdicated their responsibilities and handed over their impressionable offspring, *at their most impressionable age*, to massively expensive quasi-foster parents. Now I know that there are some, but only a few, extenuating circumstances. Military or diplomatic personnel, for example, posted to The Arsl of N'Whir in the Emirate of Dosh, where schools are simply not available. Or at least not sufficiently English-speaking to give little Tristan or Isolde an education worth having. There's a need to cater for desperately sad youngsters who have lost a parent, or have been orphaned and left in the care of grandparents or aunts and uncles who simply cannot cope. There's a case for weekly boarding schools for the children of farming families who live too far away from schools to make the daily school-run practical. And so on. In all *but* those and similar circumstances, parents ought to have enough love for, and connection with, their children to want, *deeply want* to have them educated at a school as close to home as possible so that they can *come home* at the end of the school day.

When I consider what's been going on in Britain for aeons, with moneyed but mad mothers and fathers finally going close to bankruptcy in order to send their youngsters to Eton, Harrow, Winchester, Rugby, Roedean, and all the rest of the English Public Schools, I despair. Public Schools means *private* schools, as we know, in that deliberately misleading and perverse British way. And this public boarding school system produces at the end of the process some of the most disturbed, unbalanced and frightening people on the face of the Earth. Right now, we have a Prime Minister and an Opposition leader who went to Eton

(Boarding) School. Double whammy, there. (Then went on to be lawyers. Quadruple whammy.) Paradoxically, most of the parents of children who are sentenced to boarding school have great wads of wedge, and live in very comfortable, large homes, usually close enough to a selection of schools to be able to make a day-school choice.

Still, they seem to believe that an education in England is not properly complete without the boarding school ethos, whether or not this includes experience of homosexuality, discomfort, homesickness, horrible food, and bullying.

The formal educational side of things might well be wonderful, but what a price there is to pay in the stunted emotional development of too many of the boarded offspring.

In many cases, and I know of one personally, there was absolutely no need to send young James and Jenny to a boarding school miles from home. Problem was, Mummeigh had gorn there, y'see? Syeeoh, hev to keep arp the famileigh tradition. If the children turn out the way mummeigh did, dysfunction is staring them all in the face.

SEWELL, BRIAN
Six strangled vowels, seven on a good day

As someone once remarked, and I wish I had thought of it, he is the only person who makes the Queen sound common. And his ability to turn his mouth into something resembling a constipated cat's arsehole is prodigious. Hw h gts nythng ut f t I dnt knw. *And* he is s-o-o-o disapproving.

The longer he talks, the tighter his lips become pursed, as though he has inadvertently discovered the reverse of a botox treatment and something is sucking his mouth-parts inwards towards his tonsils. One day he is going to swallow them. His lips, that is. Aside from the tortuously extruded, strangled sounds he makes, his accent is such that it is frequently quite difficult to understand him. In centuries to come, ancient videotapes of his appearances on TV will be discovered, and

mwwmm, spuuuum fwawl ngh grwwwwwwn, yerlll mwerlll.

paleo-linguists will drive themselves nuts trying to work out what the hell language he was speaking.

Recently, a voice suspiciously like Brn Swl's has been heard doing a particularly dumb voice-over for a car commercial on TV. I suppose it could have been the man himself – he is almost certainly no more

Robert MacGregor

embarrassed by having money thrust at him than any of us, but I have not the slightest idea what he was saying. What I heard was *muwwmm, spuuuum fwawl ngh gruwwwwwn yerlll mwerlll*. I'm sure that was it.

But can he write? A storm. He is vastly knowledgeable, insightful, and sometimes very, very funny. In his hands, the pen is truly mightier than the s(poken)word. But he must stop talking in public. People are getting very frightened.

SHAG, SHAGGING
Go on, give us one, or three if you're hard enough

I don't know where this use of "shag" comes from, when its other meanings (a bird related to the cormorant, pipe tobacco, a rug, and a small delicious fish) are more than enough for any four letter word to cope with. But its use to mean, well, you know what it means, just strikes me as being uncommonly coarse and down there in the chav yob-knob world.

It appears that the F-word is now absolutely essential in certain circles in order to make oneself understood and it falls out of mouths without passing through brains. Also dribbles off fingers onto keyboards, using the same brain-free short-cut. If the F-word were to be surgically removed from Jamie Oliver, Gordon Ramsay or Janet Street Porter they would be rendered almost incapable of speech at all. Already, what we hear once the F-checker has done its work on their public utterances is "beep the beeping well beep and beep that". Same goes for writers galore. The length of their pieces would be reduced by about a third if the F-word were to be excised. But am I repressed and self conscious about using it? Fuck, no. No fucking way. I am just bored by it.

The F-word is severely over-used, to the point where it is starting to lose its force and its meaning – like saying "duck" repeatedly until it is just a noise. Fuck no longer automatically refers to sexual activity, so it had to be replaced. But "shag"? Replacing "fuck" with "shag" has, for me, even worse connotations of every kind of sex devoid of affection, never mind love. It speaks of porking, ramming, bulling, thrusting copulation carried out as fast as possible in dark alleys, with no intention other than the slaking of cravings and getting off of rocks. It is chav-yob language, born of football out of dumbed-down-to-death.

You will know by now that I am fairly uninhibited. But I *have* to draw the line somewhere, and I draw it at the use of yob language by people who ought to have better vocabularies at their disposal, and generally do. However, I know that it will not be long before the "s" word fully takes the place of its "f" brother in verbal crime. Get the shag off my lawn. Who the shag do you think you are? I am shagging well fed up with you, you, you, you, *SHAG*. Yoo shag 'oo yoo shaggin' well loike, Janet. And so forth.

While I am having at this, let me deal with "bollocks", too. Same problem as "fuck" – it is just a noise these days. But it is a singularly expressive and colourful noise, and something that sounds like "bollocks", I decided, could do a similar job for me, without having to resort to a word which is repeated ad nauseam all over the place. Hence the made-up look-alike words you have come across from time to time. *Such* fun.

There are two lovely supporting roles in "Love, actually", and they are charmingly played by a pair of actors who are very, very good. Martin Freeman and Joanna Page. They play stand-ins in a porn movie, and they handle the absurd things they are asked to do with a graceful innocence and insouciance. Throughout the movie they are seen to be shy and very proper. Lovely bit of writing by Richard Curtis. But then right at the end, when they realise that they are in love and get engaged, the nice young man is heard to say that he "might actually get a shag at last". Ruined. Gratuitous verbal violence.

By the way, my wife dislikes hearing "shag" as much as I do – but she has her own favourite hate-word. Pimple. I have no idea why. Nor, she says, does she. But one thing I can guarantee. She will never, ever, be caught in front of the bathroom mirror saying, "Oh, God, shag this for a joke – I've got a shagging pimple again!"

SHARKS

Eight rows of teeth, at eighty mph

I am *almost* a tree-hugger. Very committed to the environment, green as grass, all that. Love the sea and all its fishes, and get very upset when I hear that some species are being fished so viciously that we are eating them into extinction. So I am not surprised when certain other fish want to take revenge on us, and there you have your sharks, roaming the oceans with vengeance on their primitive minds, possibly.

No, perhaps not. At least I don't *think* so. They are just permanently out to lunch, and anything that moves is main-course. It's what they do. But holy *pisces*, is there anything so ferociously horrifying as being attacked by a Great White, or even a Medium Grey? There are plenty of land-creatures whose appetites and general demeanour are just as terrifying, but bar a few, you see or hear them coming and you can, with half-decent luck, get the screaming hell out of there and hide up a tree. With sharks, you are got at from below by a silent torpedo with teeth. The next thing you know is that you are no longer capable of knowing anything, or that your leg/arm has become shark-snack. This is

not fair.

Are sharks not acquainted with the Rules of Engagement or the Geneva Code? Shouldn't they have evolved to roar or hoot or something? Blow a few bubbles? Whales do it, and they do not eat anything larger than a prawn. We are into snake territory here, with sharks. The same sort of eye full of bale, the same sort of face indicating permanent ill-temper.

We are told that the total number of shark attacks worldwide, per annum, is small. A heck of a lot less than people running into the badly lit bums of large trucks, for example (see T for Trucks, below). But I never buy this argument, any more than I am convinced that flying is by far the safest form of transport. That's all statistical futtocks. In the real world, you are highly unlikely to walk away from an air crash and you are equally unlikely to paddle away from a shark attack.

SIDE-LIGHTS, DRIVING ON
Two pinpoints, three ex-pedestrians

This book, in case you had not noticed, is liberally peppered with vehicle-and-driver stuff. There is just *so* much crap associated with it all.

Here's one of my greatest problems in this category: people who are stupid and inconsiderate enough to insist on driving in the gloom and sometimes actually in the *dark*, with nothing showing but silly piss-willy side or parking lights. It is, again, a singularly British thing, this crass idiocy, and if I could get a law passed tomorrow, it would be to force every driver of any vehicle to use dimmed headlights at any time when it penetrates the recesses of the driving mind that lights are needed. Hang on. You say that there is already a law on the statute books to this effect? Has anyone told the Police?

Headlights have a twin purpose. They are to see by – and to *be seen* by, from the *front* of the car. But there is some mysteriously still-alive British motoring folk-lore which gives far too many drivers the belief that it is OK to drive on lights which are called either side lights, or parking lights. *That* would be a clue, wouldn't it? They are there to indicate to passing traffic that a car is *parked*, and that the side of the car is approximately *here*, so watch out. To move at any speed with nothing but those pinpricks showing is almost unbelievably foolish. "Oh, but my *tail-lights* are on – I can be seen from behind me, can't I?" From behind, yes, but do you assume that a moving car is *only seen from behind?*

During The War, The Blackout required every motorist to drive about peering into the murk. Vehicle lights were dim to the point of invisibility, to confuse the Nazis/Boches. But now, sixty years after The War, people are still driving as though There Is A War On. And this is not confined to superannuated codgers who got into the habit and never lost it. *Much* younger people are doing it, and it has to stop.

I checked with an auto-electrical engineer to see if, by some strange age-related degeneration or genetic malfunction, older or any vehicle-owners believe that using their headlamps, even on "dim", wears them out. His answer: "Yes, I suppose that, over a very long time – several years – the life of headlamps is reduced by a bit if they are used a lot, but tyres, clutches, brakes and much else wear out a lot faster and no-one suggests that *their* use should be cut down. And even if headlamps do wear out, it costs a couple of quid to replace them, that's all". Clear?

I spoke to a friend who insists on driving on side-lights, and his reasoning is so maddeningly and pathetically English that I wanted to shake him. "It's only polite," he mumbled, "not to dazzle oncoming drivers with headlights when we can still see each other". But, apparently, by this logic, it's perfectly OK to dazzle when it's dark. Such garbage.

In all the Scandahoovian countries (think Ikea, Carlsberg and Gravad Lax) new cars have been fitted for years with systems which automatically turn on dimmed headlamps with the ignition. Saabs and Volvos are properly and sensibly visible at all times as a result. From the front. They are called Daytime Running Lights, or DRL's and the same is true now of all vehicles made in the USA for use on American and Canadian roads. Is this because those countries are somehow darker and gloomier than Britain? Take a drive around Manchester or Birmingham or not very bright Brighton on a wet winter evening, and you will rapidly understand that we do gloom and dark/murk as well if not better than anyone in the Northern Hemisphere. World.

What's the bottom line? Life-saving, is what. A car approaching a pedestrian crossing at 30 mph can be seen five times further away, even in broad daylight, than a car showing no lights, *or* side-lights. Old, very young, disabled or nervous people need all the help they can get to avoid being mashed by some jerk who does not see them hovering at the roadside at a zebra crossing, or halfway across the road – and, more critically, whom *they* never see coming either.

Have a look next time you drive – you will pick up an oncoming properly lit car much, much further away than one driven without lights, or on parking-lights by some dim dolt. In the evenings, at dusk, this is even more important.

So, please. If you ignore and disagree with everything else in this book, take this on board. If you think you need vehicle lights on *at all*, switch on dimmed headlights. Please.

SMOKING
Millions of fried brains, ten million burned lungs

I disapprove of smoking. *Disapprove?* I despise and detest this disgusting habit whereby grown men and women revert to childhood and have to have their dummies back. Waaaaa! I have nothing to say about the disease implications of smoking that has not been said already.

There will only, ever be one way, or one combination of ways, to stop people, including those who whinge their pathetic way through every excuse because they really, *really wanna* quit, but they just can't, sob, can't. Make every packet of cigarettes cost £20 retail. Make that £30. Actually, no, let's go the whole hog. Having put up the price, let us so order things that cigarettes can only be obtained with a Smoking Permit, which can only be obtained *in person* from a Government department in, say, Penzance, if you live in Paisley and in Dundee if you live in Devon, after filling in a thirty-seven page form, not available on the Internet, and against a payment of, say, £500. The permit would be valid for six months and would have to be renewed. And then ban smoking everywhere but inside the privacy of the smoker's reeking home – and inside means inside, not in the garden. Ban it *everywhere* else.

And if parents insist on smoking in a house where there are children, irrespective of age, exile them to Zimbabwe. There's lots of tobacco there. And they will love Robert Mugabe, who has about the same amount of feeling for his fellow humans as smokers do for theirs.

Sooner or later we will all realise that setting fire to poisonous leaves, inhaling the smoke, exhaling it, and then forcing others to inhale the fetid end-product is unbearably dumb, irresponsible, antisocial, uncaring and dangerous. There is not one other human activity where the action of a minority of people, doing something for pleasure *and for no other purpose*, causes such a horrible knock-on effect. Think about it.

SNAKES
Five nightmares and two fangs

If ever you wanted proof positive that evolution has always been a haphazard business, and that no-one has *ever* been in charge, Snakes 'R It.

I was once driving through a very arid moonscape-like area in Africa, in a small open car. Something to do with a TV commercial. I stopped on a valley floor to admire the view, and no sooner had I come to a stop than I happened to move my head a quarter-turn to the right. My face, with the window down in the low-slung sporty number I had been asked to drive, was about two feet off the deck. So was the head of a very large, and I mean *very* large black cobra, looking straight at me from about a foot away. I remember nothing of the next minute or two, until I stopped the car at the top of the hill and staggered out, my eyes starting out on stalks from my dead-white face.

"What's that *smell*, for God's sake?" said a member of the film crew as I tottered towards him. Do I need to explain?

I can't take any more crap

Every living thing has its place on the Great Food Chain. With us on top. No, actually, if you include what happens *after* death, the *really* top organisms are the bacteria which turn us back into dust via lunch. But barring that, every living thing has four objectives and only four. To become, to continue to be, to reproduce, and then to die. No question. And while continuing to be, to make themselves available as nourishment for something else. Now where the hell do snakes fit into this? What, aside from some confused raptors such as very mean eagles which will attack and eat anything, and other snakes, eats snakes? *They* do the eating. And the *way* they do it. Gheeagh!

Being limbless (good bit of Creative design, that) they have to poison their prey in the most vile and terrifying way, unhook their jaws and swallow the whole thing, whole. It is terminally disgusting. It takes undiscerning wildlife lunatics and unhinged herpetologists to want to watch this.

Of all animals, snakes are not only the meanest and most ill-tempered; they look that way, all the time. Snakes have only one facial expression. Terminally pissed off. Even when they have just swallowed a whole pig, whole, they look dyspeptic and annoyed. Mind you, the dyspepsia I can understand. *I'd* be pretty aggravated via the stomach department if I had swallowed a pig, whole.

Despite (or as a result of?) snakes' permanent bad temper, and their one-expression featureless faces, there are people who actually keep snakes as pets. I don't know about you, but I have very basic pet requirements, viz., that pets should, preferably, be hairy or furry rather than scaly, and have the ability to show at least a *small* range of emotions, mostly pleasure at the attention I give them, of course. But that is far too much to ask of a snake. It never gives a damn. You just never know whether it is pleased to see you, or whether it is going to rear up and bite your face off.

In Southern Africa they have, and oh Jaysus, I hate even writing this, spitting cobras which can eject venom through their fangs into your face from fifty yards. And there are people who go looking for them. Certifiable, of course. Out in the community but should not be.

Snakes have no redeeming features. Oh, there are herpo-ginks who say that some of them are beautifully marked and coloured. Great. Lovely. As far as I am concerned, the only redeeming part of *that* feature is that it makes them more visible further away so I can run like buggery as soon as I spot one.

SPAM
Nine hundred deleted, ten bulk expletives

I am not very fond of the real thing either. I have never discovered what it is actually made of. Says what it is on the tin, you say? And that would be …? I have never had the courage to look.

But, oh, the computerised version. To describe this electronic mass sodomy by the same name is very sad. I appreciate that we are all bombarded from every angle every day by advertising for products and services we are never likely to want to buy, and indeed, if you think the way I do, you frequently take affirmative action positively to *avoid* any product where you feel that you have been swamped and force-fed all in one.

But when we have to put up with this stuff being sent un-invited into our homes by gonad-free cowards who disguise their identities with coded garbage so that blocking their subsequent excreta from our screens becomes impossible, then I really, *really* want someone to invent molecular transubstantiation so that I can inject myself into the telephone line and emerge at the other end with a machete and behead the bastards.

I have all kinds of anti-crap filters and firewalls designed to stop this stuff from getting through to me. Great. But the price is that all these blocking mechanisms cause my computer to get indigestion, whereupon it burps and hiccoughs while slowing down to a crawl, throwing up endless windows on top of my working documents to tell me what a great job it is doing. Can't win.

SPEAKERS, LOUD, QUADRAPHONIC
Sorry, was that five, or nine? Can't hear you

How many ears do you have? Me, it's two. The good thing about ears, pairs of, one each side of the head more or less, is that they can pick up sounds from every angle and direction and the brain tells us where to concentrate our attention. So, provided we can mimic the stereo-effect of left-to-right input to our heads, and use two speakers, we are there. Job done. Millions of years of evolutionary ear-conditioning.

But not if you are a motorised hi-fi-geek chav-yob, whereupon you cannot exist without a very loud speaker in each corner of your doped-up Fiesta. The main reason for this is simple enough.

If you are the kind of quasi-human who needs blasting, ear-bleedingly pulsating, yowling "music" to take the place of what would otherwise be conversation, you fit your car with quadraphonic sound, so that neither you nor any of your passengers need to try to speak. If you do try, what emerges is a cacophony of unintelligible glottal gasps and blurps anyway, so why bother? Better to drown everything in the heavy mental yangings of The Slopes, or The Doiks or … or.

But this multi-polluting is not confined to cars. I visited a relatively close relative the other day, for the first time in years. New house, new car, new this, new that. New wife too. Beaming with pride, he ushered me into his new living area, to demo his new hi-fi gear. He put on a new CD by … by … I forget, but ghastly. Then he got clearance from Ground Control and pushed several buttons which caused immediate lift-off and instant insanity on my part, as *screeowl boom boom gadoing blam-blamm* issued from, wait for it, *six* speakers positioned around the room.

Sexaphonic? Would that be right? I saw his smiling lips moving in what I assumed to be a proud speech about how a-m-a-a-a-a-zing this was, yeah? But I hit him with his new standard lamp anyway.

SPITTING
Four gobs and a hawk

In some cultures, people go about spitting with abandon. It's just what they do, and everyone does it. It's the law. You have to spit every few minutes or you get arrested.

But here in so-called civilised Western society, there is no excuse for the amount of spitting that goes on. Naturally, it all starts with sports stars, most of whom seem to find it essential to evacuate all possible fluids from every nook and cranny of their upper digestive and respiratory tracts, and they spit as often as they can. For the most part, its fooballers. It goes with the whole ethos of the game. And, sadly, it's the stereotypical shave-heads with two-day beard-growths and snouty noses who are the worst culprits. The few who are more, shall we say, refined, are never seen to gob. I have never, for example, seen Gary Lineker do it.

Some rugby players are guilty. But I have never seen rowers do it. Some tennis players, even at Wimbledon, are seen to be doing it, but discreetly, into a bucket, I think. To their credit, the TV producers of sports programmes watch for the first signs of a roiling of the throat muscles and a pursing of the lips, and cut away as fast as they can. Sometimes not fast enough, and given the closeness of the close-up, we are treated to a … to a … never mind. You have the picture in more ways than one. Athletes are seen to do it. Swimmers are doing it all the time, but you don't see it. They have the perfect excuse and the perfect camouflage. I wonder what else they do in the water.

So, the foopalling role-models spit and are seen to spit. Therefore it is OK for those who watch these creatures, to follow suit. Walk along the pavement of any city these days, and before you have covered a hundred yards, you will see some mannerless cretin ejecting a huge glob of phlegm. Ride the London Tube, and watch them going *gggggghhhhhaarg-blab* onto the tracks and platforms. Sometimes, in the carriages.

If bird 'flu ever does flap its way into Britain, and if TB continues its unwelcome return we are all in trouble if the world's great spitters are allowed to go unchecked and we have to negotiate our way around gobs of spittle all over the place. Disgusting? Uncivilised? Dangerous? Yes, yes, and yes. Shiny, viscous little signs of our times, though.

While I am on the unpleasant subject of the public evacuation of bodily fluids from the head, let me deal swiftly with tissue-free nose-blowing. In the un-developing world, blowing of noses happens without tissues or handkerchiefs, because there are none, and it is culturally *de rigeur*, but everywhere else, there is no excuse for the laying of a finger along one nostril while ejecting a blob of snot from the other, onto pavements and playing fields. Especially playing fields. Recently, an otherwise delightful and very good Cypriot called Bhadwhatsit or something, impressed at Wimbeldon, and very rudely put Britain's Great Scottish Hope out of the men's singles. But even more uncouthly, he was an open-nose-blower. Onto the centre-court greensward. He is bound to be back next year. I hope someone gets to him and teaches him some basic manners. And gives him a few tissues. Yeeeerrrgh.

STREE' POR'AH, JANI'
Nine. Twelve. Piersmorgan level

Jan'i' phneep ortah. Fark. Farque. Pharque. Farkity farkity fark fark. Farkinell.

And why does she need so many teeth? What? I don't have to watch her or read her stuff? Quite right – but she is all over the place, unavoidable. Give me a break.

STUBBLE, DESIGNER
Five o'clock shadows and several ladyboys

Ah, please, for the sake of all the gods. I know that the pimply nerds who work in advertising agencies will stop at nothing to create something "new and arresting", something to shock the poor benumbed consumer into parting with yet more cash, but ... *designer stubble*?

You know the sort of thing. Some vacant-eyed, slack-lipped scowling bestubbled modewl (of course *male* – were you thinking stubble on a bimbette? Not yet – but I am sure they are working on it) is actually told not to shave for a couple of days, so that he can present a picture of dissolute don't-care he-manliness which is supposed to be so

213

very attractive to the opposite, or even the same, sex. In fact the poor slob just looks exactly the way he looks – unshaven, slightly dirty and uncaring about his personal appearance. Or is it that the male foto-modewls currently being used are so androgynous, so unisex of face that the only way for the public to tell that they are looking at something vaguely male, *wearing* something vaguely male, is to have it grow facial hair, but only just enough?

Is this stubble supposed to sell the product with which his unappetising face is associated? No-one from the retailer, and certainly no-one from the advertising agency ever seems to walk around the shop to have a look at the average potential buyer. Most normal men come in two varieties. Clean shaven or properly bearded. Nothing in between, except on a Sunday morning when we can't be arsed, our faces need a rest and why would we be out shopping anyway? And the females/males who are shopping for/with them? They would start hammering their partners with umbrellas and handbags if they even thought about leaving home deliberately stubble-faced.

Where did this "designer-stubble" garbage come from? Will someone please kick the advertising dickheads and tell them that the real world is crammed with decent-looking, incontestably *male* males who do not go about unshaven in order to establish their machismo, so please use them instead of these bestubbled numpties.

STUPIDITY, GENERAL LEVELS OF
IQ at 40 and falling

Time for a summary. Sort of.

We do ourselves no favours, really we don't. So many of us behave as though we excreted our brains the last time we moved our bowels, and we deserve everything that the sucker-players of the world throw at us. Some of what follows has inspired me to give them the full treatment as you have noticed, but I can't resist having another poke at some of them.

- We set fire to leaves containing cancer-causing chemicals, and we suck the smoke into our lungs. We then get abusive when we are told that our second-hand smoke is killing others.
- We drink bladder-bursting amounts of booze and wonder why our livers pack in the uneven battle.
- We watch crap being shovelled at us and our children by the hour on television and then slump even lower in intelligence as our levels of education and cultural awareness plummet.
- We buy tit 'n bum-loid "newspapers" which we "read" after looking at page three with wrist-action to match, and we allow the people who publish these flat bog-rolls to poke their noses right up the public arse, destroy lives and behave without morality or decency, but with icy *sang froid* and impunity.
- We eat fatty, sugary, chemically dangerous stuff which ought to go directly into the garbage bin rather than into our stomachs. Then we get sick and fat, and we wonder why.
- We close and then sell off school sports fields and encourage our children to spend more and more time in front of computers, getting fatter by the day as they play games which call for no intellect and offer no exercise at all.
- We elect some of the most ambitious but useless people to every representative body in the land, and we watch as they "lead" us to ever lower levels of achievement.
- We allow a legal system to flourish and batten on our misfortune, and we watch as the system gets heavier, greedier and more arthritic with each passing year, with justice increasingly a rarity in our lives and only available to the very rich.
- We acclaim and worship football players, pay them lottery-jackpot sized salaries every week, fail utterly to realise how terminally vile some of them are, and permit our children to ape them as role models.
- We glorify some of the most cretinous gobshites on the planet as celebrities, and the people to whom we do this homage tell

us everything we need to know about ourselves.

- We see barely-competent bosses of industry and commerce being paid obscene amounts of money, and believe, wrongly, that we can do nothing about it.
- We wallow in an environment which is poisoning us by the minute, and then, when we are presented with opportunities to clean up the Earth and our act, we tell ourselves, "Tomorrow, maybe".
- We shrug as people are gunned down in our streets by brainless thugs and we pretend that by making hand-guns illegal, we have solved the problem.
- We are allowed to vote in local government elections – that's *local,* as in *local,* as in our back-yards and we vote according to the party the most publicity-successful candidate belongs to, when the leaders and the rest of the governing party are losing it, and the opposition leaders are waiting in the wings to do the same.

And a lot more. We no longer to deserve to live in a decent, tolerant, broadly liberal and more-or-less easy-going country. We abuse its benevolence every damned day. We are stupidly stupid. I think we are crap. I am having a bad brain day. I'll be better in a minute.

SUPER-MARKETS, HYPER-SIMILAR, AND
Aisle seven, no, nine, no, out of ...

It is not about price. Sooper prices are often higher than the local shops'. It is not about pleasure or fun-shopping. *God* no. It is not really about choice either – ask any honest supermarket operator, if you can find one, and he will tell you that the vast majority of his customers buy almost exactly the same basket of products week in and week out. So who, exactly, is making what choice? And as for "helping you to spend less", this ought to be reported to the Trading Standards Authority.

I can't take any more crap

What every SM wants you and me to do is spend *more*, every time, and that's how they *really* go about their business. "helping you to spend less" is also a terrible piece of rubbish English, but what can one expect?

No – it is about convenience. That is the reason why 99.9 percent of those who use SM's, use them. How do I know? I do it. So do you. It's about being able to park in one place, buy everything in one place, load it into a car (a *car*, note, not a bus or train) and bugger smartly off. Or as smartly as the queue at the checkout allows you. I think it's crap, but do I use my local SM regularly? 'Course I do. But I know *why,* and it has nothing *whatsoever* to do with the messages which the SM chains (worrying image, but let's move on) thrust at us from every medium. I am hooked on the idea of getting there, doing it as fast as I can, and getting out, as the Bishop may have said. I also use local shops as often as I can, but the problem in our over-crowded country is *parking* in the towns and villages. Convenience, you see, convenience. Overall, it is a sorry experience. And what price convenience when …

- There are always mooching, indecisive shoppers with trolleys parked sideways across the isles while they peer, open-mouthed, at the wrong shelf for the wrong product. Funny, isn't it, how some people use their mouths for looking?
- The trolleys have wheels operated individually by mischievous aliens so they go where they want, not where you and I do.
- There are always undisciplined brats shouting, screaming, bawling and throwing things, until they are old enough to run everywhere, while their idiot parents look blank and do nothing.
- There are always huge crowds of huge people moving in all directions.
- There are never enough checkouts open at busy times, and never enough checkouts
- Too many of the checkout staff are sulky, blotchy teens who are not allowed to allow us to buy a bottle of wine, so they have to call a proper person to handle this, and cause mouth-

frothing delays in the queue.

- There is always some brain-dead berk behind us, not looking at anything much, so that he/she repeatedly runs her trolley into our Achilles tendons, with a trolley designed (designed!) to have a hard steel bar at exactly the right height for the infliction of this agony.
- The product you want (because it is a BOGOF) has run out, of course, precisely because it is a BOGOF.
- The staff are encouraged to switch product lines about, so that they are no longer where we are used to finding them.
- When it is pouring with rain, there are too few trolleys in the covered trolley park.
- When the store is at its busiest, that's the time store staff will batter their way through the store with two-story pallet-loads of produce and position them right where you are, having run over five entire families en route.
- The fresh produce is perfectly shaped, perfectly the right colour, and perfectly flavour-free.
- Special offers which get us loyalty points when we spend £1 always cost 99p so you have to buy two of them to "save" money. This is called "helping you to spend less".
- SM Shopping bags are a special kind which breeds in the boot of our cars, so our kitchens are always full of the things.
- Suppliers are being shafted on price and payment – and eventually some of them go out of business.

You know the worst thing about all this? I hate the fact that I hate myself for having to hate the SM's.

T

TABLOIDS (A.K.A. Titnarseloids, Boobanbumloids)
Ten noses up your arse, and you haven't been introduced

There have always been ways to tell when a civilisation is on the way out. The Romans started to be beastly to beasts and other beings, binge-drink and acquire sexually transmitted diseases en masse. (Sounds uncomfortably familiar, don't you think?) Various South and Central American civilisations ending in "-ec" went on a blood spree and sacrificed themselves into oblivion. The Third Reich went power-crazy and shot itself in the bunker. The Soviet Union broke when a wall fell on it.

So it is with us, in the New West. There are signs. Every Western country which is pleased with itself, and that's about all of them, now has a high-smelling stable of low-brow "news"-papers all of which are the printed equivalent of the Circus Maximus on a thumbs-down day, appealing to base lusts, prurient voyeurism and the lowest possible level of intellect. Don't argue – that's exactly what they *themselves* say they do, and they are proud of it. And they have become the voice of the nation's people, the arbiters of what will interest the public, utterly incapable of seeing the difference between things of interest and what they want the public to be interested in. Personal tragedy and privacy are concepts which they do not understand and if they did they would not care about. They have become so immune to criticism, so willing to pay any fine for what they might have done and been found guilty of, that they are completely out of control. In a word, they simply don't give a shit. And until we stop taking the tabloids, we won't get better and neither will they.

But should we be so critical of them? Are they not, for all their lack of decency and humanity, very good at smelling out corruption in the political world and elsewhere, and exposing it? They are, after all the famous fourth estate, a bastion of our democracy, yes? Sometimes, maybe, but does that permit them the kind of carte blanche they give themselves to do all this whatever the price paid in intrusion into the lives of those who do not seek intrusion? That does not, of course, include the attention-seekers who go to a lot of trouble to bare their backsides and bend over so that the titnbumloid reporters have an easier job of shoving their noses up the anuses of the aforementioned me-me-meeeeeee-ers.

So, what's to be done? Easy enough. Pass a law which gives anyone the right to sue any publication that publishes anything they did not wish to have published unless they have been convicted in a court of law, or unless a judge (one of the more intelligent ones) has made an order permitting publication in the public interest. Takes too long to get a judge to make an order on a subject destined for "today's" 'paper? Tough. Leave it out, then. And if the editor of the offending publication is found guilty, he or she goes to jail for at least a year without passing "Go", without collecting any fancy lawyers en route. Period. That will concentrate their tiny minds.

This will mean that certain bent politicians and others might get away with some stuff, but it's a decent enough price to pay for curbing the excesses of the some of the arsehole sniffers who pass for reporters on these titnarse publications. The job of rooting out corruption belongs to the Police, anyway. Or should. If the Police are not doing their job, then put several pounds of dynamite up the bums of the Chiefs of Police and get thing changed.

When our so-called civilisation ends and all of us have been vaporised by MAD, our dead city streets will whisper the sounds of Daily Titnarse sheets blowing this way and that, that way and this. Paper monuments to the last days of dying.

TARGETS
Four 'stars' and three lists

How did this appalling stuff start? No, don't tell me. Some overpaid and underemployed paper-shuffler in Whitehall decided that every service rendered unto mankind by mankind's Government should be rated, weighed, measured, graded, and generally subjected to dehumanising scrutiny. None of which the institutions in question would not work out for themselves. Grading? *De*grading.

The Whitehall (progressively becoming Greyhall) mandarins and their politician bosses do not appear to have the intelligence to see that the creation of these false-competitive lists and grades cannot even come into existence without a parallel growth of yet more pen-shufflers and paper-pushers to inspect and impose opinions, enter numbers and produce the analyses. Or perhaps I do the mandarins and the politicians an injustice. Perhaps they see only too well that as Britain progressively loses its will to live as an industrial nation, the only way to maintain high levels of "employment" is to recruit more and more people whom they can mould into only slightly less powerful versions of themselves. Yes, that has to be it.

The saddest thing about all this? We, the gullible public buy into it *en masse*. Wearing our Ralph Lauren or "I'm with stupid" T-shirts respectively, we scour the lists of top-rated schools to see where we ought to be sending our Damiens and Antonias, our Kevins and Sharons We look in amazement at the star-rating given to our local hospital, and we think, "Oh, good. The only hospital for fifty miles has just been awarded another star. Phew!" Or, "Oh, God, the only hospital for fifty miles has just been downgraded because too many patients who set foot there are carried out in a box having succumbed to MRSA". What can we do in either eventuality? Nada. If you are an NHS sufferer, particularly in the rural areas there is no such thing as being able to *choose* a hospital. You have a hospital which serves the area in which you live. That's where you have to go. Period. You *may* have another NHS outfit about the same distance away, but in your case, *that* non-alternative is not equipped with the MRI scanner which is the only diagnostic apparatus capable of telling you and the medics what part of your body is not working. Some choice. So what's the point of targets which are supposed to point us all in the right direction in order to make choices? Crap, isn't it?

Robert MacGregor

TAUTOLOGY
Repeat again, several times

I can be brief about this. I am edging into Truss–Humphrys territory here, and I don't want to. Too scary. But something has happened to the way we use our language these days. Education, education, education is a dead lame duck.

Repeat again. Return back. I'll start with you first. Reverse back. Revert back. Return back. Regain back. Proceed onwards. Droop down. Repeat again. Join together. Combine together. First invented. Raise up. Cook up or off. Reduce down. Transfer over. Meet up with. An assassination attempt on someone's life. Not to mention completely, absolutely, entirely unique.

Endless. But, as with so much else that debases our great language, there is nothing be done, no end-objective, no final solution, no declared purpose, no etc., etc. Verbal garbage. Where's the skip?

TELEVISION
One channel five hundred times

This has merited a whole section all to itself, so take a breath and the plunge.

I am happy to say that I do not belong to that tight-ass flock of holier-than-thou "we-do-not-have-a-television-in-our-house" twerps. I watch TV, and I watch a fair amount, because it is a brilliant medium of communication and I love some of it. But there is also a lot of crap. In no particular order:

Unreality TV
Do the commissioning editors not understand that life is already full of more than enough reality which pokes us in the eye a hundred times a day, and the *last* thing we need if we have any intelligence or discernment is more of the same on TV? Oh, but of course – I have answered my own question, haven't I? *Intelligence and discernment.* No

222

S'almost as good as watching 'em on TV, innit?"

call for it these days, squire. But it's what people want, we are told by the TV channels. The uncomfortable fact is that people will "want" anything that is thrown at them if you throw it gently enough and wrap it in candyfloss. After that, they are addicted, just as heroin addicts are addicted to heroin. Hence Big Brother, etc etc. Cold turkey required.

Children let loose on cameras and editing software
Watching a really well-made documentary is a major delight. But at the other end of the scale of competence are programmes made by directors whose brains have clearly been addled by too much nose-candy or sheer shrieking boredom, and who allow camerapersons and editors, also bored out of their trees, free reign to do what ever fancy takes them.

So – upside down. Forty-five-degree angles. Jumpy hand-held follow-the-action shots taken by a cameraman with St. Vitus' dance.

Eye-wateringly fast pans this way and that, and back again, designed, I
assume to "add reality" to the scene. Adds exactly nothing. And my
worst, currently very much in fashion; the out-of-focus shot which
either stays that way, or only very gradually comes into focus. The
human eye and brain have evolved to see things *the way they are*, and
abhors things which are out of focus. So, when faced with these utterly
unnecessarily blurred images, the eye/brain combo tries fruitlessly to
correct them resulting in a horrible headache, because it can't be done.
This is a problem unique to me? No. I have asked a lot of people about
this – in the age range from ten to death – and they all say the same
thing. It's a nuisance and adds nothing to the programme. So just stop it,
OK? Use the damned camera lens the way it was designed to be used.
To bring as much as possible into sharp focus *and keep it there*.

And does it end there? No. Editing either film or video is a digitised
doddle now, compared to the old methods which involved razor blades
and glue, and thank God for that.

But what in the same God's name persuades directors and editors
that transitions from one scene to another have to be carried out with
irritating flashes, whirling circles and animated squares, discothèque-type
strobe effects and a lot else, all doing nothing other than give bored
seventeen-year-old editors something to play with? Drives some viewers
mad? Too bad. Modden, innit, so we are expected to live with it.

Needless music
Recently there has been a sharp decline from bad to dreadful in the
music used in all kinds of TV programmes; a talentless madman is let
loose on a high-pitched synthesiser designed for very small children.

The result is an endless loop of tuneless, rhythmless eedles and
deedles which do nothing for the visual at all. No, that's not right. They
certainly *do* do something. They make the end result so maddeningly
irritating that it all becomes un-watchable – so I stop watching.

Where is it written that all programmes, with vanishingly few
exceptions, must have music as part of the sound-track? Why is it not
good enough that the natural sound of whatever is going on does a
perfectly good job of enhancing the story and adding to the atmosphere?

Why is it not good enough that silence can often do exactly the same thing, while allowing the images to carry the day?

I am not suggesting that there should *never* be music with video-imagery – some of the best movies of all time have used music to great effect to add tension, or exaggerate comedy – but there are times when the directors of TV programmes fill the silence with truly, excruciatingly awful sounds. If there is a visual passage where the natural sounds of whatever is going on are either missing or not good enough, and commentary is *de trop*, then let the producers have some well-chosen but discreet music to go with it by all means, but only if they really, *really* have to. Well-chosen and well-played. Not hard to find. Easier and cheaper than paying some plonker to go *tink tink tink wooooo doink plonk wheeeee*. Unfortunately, money, or, more accurately, lack thereof in the production budget, sometimes plays a part in this – so the director is forced, having decided to use music for no good reason, to rely on computer-generated whallocks which is so often a series of repeated phrases which go *ploing ploing doingggg feedle teedle ploing eedle tweedle whang teedle plang*. And then they start again. It makes the kind of music which accompanies Japanese kabuki sound blissfully melodic by comparison, and if you have ever seen a kabuki, you will understand. If you haven't, don't. It will shorten your life.

Recently, polymath but strange Dr Jonathan Miller did a series on atheism. Brilliant. But some producer-idiot decided that the few scenes which did not require Dr Miller to be speaking, *did* require the silence to be filled with … something. So they hired a tone-deaf robot, put it in a room with something sounding vaguely like a xylophone, and the result was a desperately annoying and pointless *tinga tinga tinga tonga tinga tinga tonga* repeated umpteen times. A drama on the building of the Titanic? Epic. But, throughout, *zinga zonga zoinga zanga zinga zanga,* on and on.

Somebody please grab these people by the … by the … whatever is handy, and drum it into them that if they have good, well-edited visual material, a script written by someone who knows how to match words to those pictures, and a pleasant voice which delivers them when words are called for – that's enough. Less is more. Don't add anything. Especially don't add music.

Wildlife clichés (And they abound like wildebeest)
Starting with time-lapse clouds
When someone discovered, decades ago, that you could leave a camera locked down somewhere, point it at the sky, and take an exposure every few seconds, lo and behold when you played it back at normal speed the clouds moved at mighty speed across the scene producing an effect of clouds moving across the scene at mighty speeds. Great. Interesting, the first seven hundred times. But watch any wildlife or nature doccy, and they'll be there, scudding furiously. They have even started to stack up in dramas. Enough! Enough!

"Safety in numbers"
A predator is shown predating, while a swarm/herd/flock/lots-and-lots of whatevers stick close together, "because there is safety in numbers". No wildlife documentary is complete without this phrase being used several times, with fish, birds, antelope, ants, anything that moves in swarms/herds/flocks etc, etc. Just listen next time Saint David Attenborough or Bill Very Oddie is drawing your attention to the plight of the lesser-breasted tit or the blue-ballacked bandicoot. He'll tell you that there are so few of these left in the wild that they *cannot depend on safety in numbers any more.* Just to make sure he gets the phrase in.

Sunrises and sunsets
In quick-mo. In blazing colour (orange). In muted tones (orange). In every corner of the world (still orange). But hello, here's one in black and white! Adjust your set! No, don't adjust your set. It's a director who is searching for a special effect, and has 2,584 sunset shots taken by a deranged cameraman in Namibia, so let's bugger about with that.

The four seasons of every living thing
There is only one theme to all wildlife documentaries: winter, with nothing to eat, but here comes spring, with speeded up footage of stuff sprouting and doing that crazy waving-about thing that sprouting things do, then summer where everything goes brown, and then autumn when something else happens, but by then I am too bored to care.

226

Devour, doink and die
Woody Allen famously said that nature was just one big restaurant, but what he omitted to go on to say was that nature, being what it is, all things have a super-simple philosophy. I eat, therefore I am. And when I am not eating I am looking for something to roger or something that will roger me. Every wildlife documentary is about these two things and not a lot else. Blowfish, antelope, fruit flies, newts, anything.

Moving on, now, from wildlife.

"Could it be …?"
This non-question question is in every script for every documentary ever made about anything. You know damned well that it could, and will, and they are about to show and tell you. Could it be that this fossil will turn out to be a Borosorus from the Pre-Phrenetic period? Yes, of course it will. Could it be that this piece of shapeless metal unearthed from a slag-heap in Doncaster was the actual screwdriver used by Stephenson or Brunel? Yes it could. Could it be that the shameless over-use of this phrase to keep me in a state of somnolent non-suspense is starting to drive me nuts? Yes it could.

Dramas a mile too long
I am all for authenticity. I am also in favour of allowing time for characters to develop so they become credible. But when Channel 4 and Beeb Two rear back and let fly with two hours at a sitting, all of it in period costume and with evidence of horses having crapped authentically in the otherwise miraculously clear streets, I can't take it.

Especially I can't take tediously long scenes between two characters whose every secret was out in the first ten minutes and who are now allowed, nay, *forced* to drip-feed us with every kind of extraneous information, utterly devoid of action beyond the occasional raised eyebrow or pout. Absolutely *nothing* on TV should be longer that an hour, no matter what.

Robert MacGregor

Appallingly bad voice-over deliveries
There are far too many who plonk. What's plonking? Technical term which is furiously hard to illustrate in writing because you have to hear it to understand fully. But here's my best shot. If you read a script aloud, and consistently put the emphasis either on the wrong part of a word or on the wrong word in a phrase or sentence, you are plonking. It happens all the time. Young trainee news reporters, crouching fearlessly in a gunfight between this lot of Iraqis and that lot of Iraqis ruin everything by plonking their commentary. You would think that the producers or someone who does not have a tin ear would hear it and get it corrected, but, no. They don't hear it. Or if they hear it, they don't care. And if they care, they can't be arsed to ask the plonker to read it again, only this time with the emphases in the right places, please. So here he goes again, plonking away so that the sense of what he is trying to say is lost because it is like trying to concentrate on counting to twenty while some fool within earshot is saying three, nine, seventeen, fifty, eight.

Enough about TV. So much room for improvement. But would you like to know if I have a gold standard by which I judge all TV production? Yes, you would. It's the West Wing (with ER a close second). It's really crappy that they are American and that we in Britain have never come up with anything even remotely as good, but there it is. The West Wing has the best scripts, casting, acting and direction on TV anywhere. No fancy, flashing, distracting graphics. No silly camerawork. They just let some of the world's best actors get on with telling the story, point the cameras and the mic's at them, and that's it. The only thing that could in any way be called fancy is the hand-held camera which goes backwards while the actors walk in every possible direction, at speed, towards that camera – which manages to keep its distance. Just brilliant. They use a similar technique on ER of course. American too. Sigh !

God, what is going to replace the West Wing? Will anything ever be as good? What am I going to do? I will stop watching TV. Possibly.

TIPPING
Ten percent and nothing gained

First, let's get past those thieving restaurateurs who add ten or fifteen percent to the bill as a "voluntary gratuity" and hope that you won't notice – then expect you to add something to the total by way of a tip (to themselves; the waiters never see a penny). They should all go bust, immediately, and choke on their left-over *beouf a la mode voleur a la sauce brigand*.

Bit careful here. Like so many parents, I have children who have made holiday money, must-have-brand cash and Uni beer-swill moolah by waiting table in restaurants, paid just at the minimum wage, and they depend heavily on the generosity of the customers to leave tips. So I tend, when I have been served by some clearly part-time young thing, to feel enough sympathy to leave a bit extra. But I really detest this blackmail. Why do we feel this compulsion to tip waiters, hairdressers and cab drivers when what they do is what they do, and make a living out of it?

Ah, but it's about showing one's gratitude for extra good service, is it? Well, I say clattocks to that. All service, rendered by anyone rendering it, ought to be as good as possible, always, and if it falls below par, far from *not leaving* a tip, the right thing to do is *deduct* from the bill whatever percentage one feels appropriate to the circumstances, for *failure* to provide proper service.

I once had to take a mini-cab in London. It only happened once. I am a fast learner. The driver who was, possibly, totally familiar with Tblisi or perhaps Islamabad, was as lost in London as I was. He took us both for a ride. Especially me, when it came to paying the fare. I paid the fare, exactly to the penny. "Nawtip?" he snarled. Naw. I tipped myself out of the car, while the rain tipped down, to find that the un-tipped gentleman from Vilnius or Calcutta was now advancing upon me with menaces.

Adrenalin took over and I hit him with a torrent of abuse, turned, and stalked meaningfully away. I very nearly hit him, period. As I departed, I did have that twitching feeling between the shoulder-blades, expecting a sharp implement between them at any moment, and none came of course. I heard him drive tipless into the night.

TRUCKS
Twenty-six wheels and ten four letter axles

Oh, come on, I can't seriously think *trucks* are crap. Truck *drivers*, maybe. But the actual trucks?

Driving on almost any roads these days brings us into the unwelcome proximity of massive pantechnicons, artic's and other road monsters. Here's my first beef: The backs of these massive machines are, well, massive. It's like coming up behind a block of flats which is doing seventy mph-plus. Bad enough right there. But if it happens to be raining or dark or both, and in Britain that is a lot of the time, you are involuntarily in the vestibule of the block before you know, because the tail-lights of the road-monster are tiny little wimpish pinpricks, suitable only for a bicycle. You just don't see them until you are far too close behind.

You don't believe me? Go, then, pick up your little measuring tape, sidle up behind a parked truck as I did and measure the rear-light assembly. Then do the same for almost any reasonably modern car, and you will see what I mean. And check it out next time you are driving behind any truck, anywhere. There seems to be a rule at play here: the larger the vehicle, the smaller the tail-lights and vice versa. The trucks hide their mega-bushels behind puny little lights, far, *far* too small in comparison with their size, and it makes no sense whatsoever. Some cars go OTT of course, with great baboon-bum confabulations of red and yellow, but at least when they are on, they are ON, and you can see them a long way off.

Truck manufacturers all appear to buy their tail-light assemblies from Smallprick Light Assemblies in Slough, and clap them onto the back of their thundering monstrous great road-beasts. Nice and cheap.

"Free trucking roadside rinse? Nothing like it."

This is what they have done for decades, so why change things now? Trucks made in Sweden, France, Germany, Japan, anywhere. The manufacturers *all* buy their tail-light assemblies from Smallpricks, it seems.

That's it? My only beef about trucks? Not by a long vehicle. No matter how cleverly the road-makers have made cambers and drains, rain causes water to lie on the surface. Truck tyres, never less than four feet in diameter and about two feet wide, throw out huge gouts of water and make driving either behind or alongside them a lottery. Even the most efficient windscreen wipers cannot cope with the sheer volume of spray which clatters into your windscreen, and for a few vital seconds, you are literally driving blind. It is frightening.

Why do *all* truck wheels not have skirts or deflectors which reach almost to the ground, so that the spray is caught before it lashes out at other vehicles? I have it on very reliable authority that there is indeed a law which requires spray suppression on truck wheel arches. Law there may be. Law enforcement there isn't. Same thing with driving on parking lights, as you will remember.

I am not in favour of any more nannying from Government. Enough, already. But as roads get busier, as trucks get more numerous, bigger and faster – and the weather, thanks to global heating, gets worse and wetter – the only way to force truck-makers to understand is to Enforce the Law. And amend it to make the fines for non-compliance really draconian. Pity, but that's the only thing that will work. Unless the truck-*users* get a rush of brains to the head, of course, and insist on … But no. Dream on.

ULCERS, STOMACH
Four jars of acid but no stress

Say hello to Helicobacter Pylori. It seems that anyone brought up in deprived circumstances in, say, a colonial country or in post-war Europe could have acquired this nasty little bacterio-beast which thrives in the Martian environment of the human stomach. *Thrives*, mind you, where absolutely *nothing* ought to. The whole evolutionary purpose of the stomach is to break down and reduce everything to dead mush. But a brave, mad Australian medic proved otherwise. By infecting himself with this bacterium, he showed that if you have H Pylori in your stomach this ghastly little colony can be a serious cause of stomach ulcers because it positively loves acid, and the more acid the acid, the more they like it. And it's *hydrochloric* acid, which the stomach produces in industrial quantities. But if the levels or concentration of stomach acid go beyond the merely catastrophic, even the stomach lining, normally up for any kind of punishment, rebels and comes over all craters. In my case, no-one understands why I was H-Pylori-positive, but I was, hence ulcers hence endoscopy (see under "E")

The cure? Anti-biotics in a special cocktail which kills the H-Pylori, some pills to help control the acid levels, and bye-bye ulcers. Stomach returns to relative peace, to its job of mulching, munching and mushing.

But do the ulcers go away permanently at this point? Do they hell. It seems that once a stomach has been ulcerated, and looks like the surface of the moon only inside out, it will, for life, have a tendency to erupt even when non-H-Pylori circumstances prevail. Stress, over-consumption of booze, curries, white wine, coffee, fags and aspirin will all tend to bring ulcers back. In my case, I could and did eliminate fags

233

"Helicopter Backers? Who needs 'em? Let 'im 'ave it, boys."

and aspirin, because I have never used either, but I rather left myself open to attack as far as the rest of the list is concerned.

But why does the ulceration make an unwelcome return at all? It seems that the sensitive, scarred areas of the stomach are still subject to acid-attack if the acid goes beyond a certain concentration. H-Pylori was the original cause of the problem, but even when it has been beaten to death, the stomach is left vulnerable. Anything that adds to the acid or aggravates the lining and the balloon goes up. Or that's how it feels, anyway.

No, no, says the medico-pharmaceutical complex. These days we have *Omeomyocyranopicassopetronitroglycerine* (I could swear that's what it says on the tin, but the writing is very small) which keeps acid production under control, so no more ulcers. So, really? So where does mine come from? How come, now that I live a completely stress-free life (having off-loaded all my stresses into this book) and now that I eat *terribly* sensibly, I still get ulcer-pains? Huh? *Huh?* Helpfully, my GP says he doesn't know. Turns out there's quite a lot he doesn't know.

UMBRELLAS
Three showers and two soaked heads

The design for these things has not changed since 1554 or something. They still consist of stupid bendy spines which boing and splang at will. They are attached to the main pole thing with the nambiest pambiest little wire hinges which are classics of built-in obsolescence, making it a dead cert that the first time you expose this piece of pre-Victorian flimsiness to a gust of wind, it eats itself after turning inside out. Look for the nearest bin.

Given the advances in all sorts of bendy and stretchy materials usually associated with space travel, you would think, would you not, that something which performs roughly the same function as these ancient hangovers could have been perfected by now. Something without splines or ribs or dinky little connecting pieces. Something functional and robust yet elegant, like Lesley Garrett.

I have seen some umbrellas with peculiar over-the-top straps attached from here to there, which are supposed to stop the inside-out thing happening, but I have also seen plenty of *those* in skips and bins. They work in a gentle breeze – no prob, but live where I do, watch the gulls crouching behind hedges, and the thing is useless. Aside from which, these be-strapped versions look so damned *stupid*.

The whole thing is a conspiracy. I am convinced that International Universal Umbrellas plc have cornered the market, bought up any new ideas, shelved the patents and now rake in huge profits from repeat sales to rained-upon mugs like you and me who are forced to buy their delicate wares. My grandchildren will still be poking people in the eye, or being poked, and bellowing with rage as yet another dinky gamp destroys itself at exactly the wrong moment. As for the telescopic kind which is supposed to fit into handbags and brief-cases, the engineering which goes into them is of such intricacy that they explode into bits at the second use, max. Or, as happened to me recently, deploy unwanted in a crowd, forcing metal spikes up outraged backsides.

All in all, I prefer a large-brimmed hat. Except I look so stupid in a hat. I do not have a hat-face. I don't know what that means. Except that I have to carry an umbrella.

UMPIRING, CRICKET, TEST MATCHES, BAD
Five for two but maybe that should be four

You can skip this item if you like. You may well have as much interest in cricket as I do in football.

I am a cricket madman. Way beyond fanatic. Love the game, always have, always will. Glued to the box during test matches between any two teams. Lose weight, get bum-blisters, bleary-eyed. Grounds for divorce, probably – but we have a deal. I don't complain about the amount of time my dearest spends on and with horses. And she leaves me to my cricket, aside from the occasional head-around-the-corner and "have they scored any goals, yet, darling?"

However, these days, I find myself shouting at the TV set, demented at yet another umpiring decision of such obvious wrongness that I have suggested in a letter to the International Cricket Council that the score sheets have an entry which says "*Given* out, bowled Bowler". Stony silence. Of course. And bad decisions go both ways. There have been just as many batsmen who stayed at the crease, smirking at the fielding side while knowing damned well that they ought to be taking an early shower, having been given "not out".

None of this matters much down at village green level or, even county games. But in international one-day matches and tests, with a lot at stake, it is utterly comical to rely on the human eye being right more than about two-thirds of the time, when the technology is there to make sure people seldom, if ever, get around the rules. I don't blame the umpires. They do a great job, develop fallen arches, chronic lordosis and ulcers, and are vilified when they get a decision wrong.

But these days, there are third umpires who can rule on close calls such as run-outs, stumpings, or boundaries, by using video technology and ultra slo-mo to see what actually happened, and on some other stuff about which the on-field ump's are not sure. But the use of technology stops short of the two most common areas of doubt any cricketer has to face — leg-before-wicket and caught-behind decisions (the latter usually involving the batsman's glove or his elbow). As far as LBW is concerned, we have Hawk-eye now, which makes it clear beyond any doubt that the batsman either did put his foot in it, or didn't. And we have the Snickometer to put beyond doubt whether the batsman touched the ball with his bat or gloves and not his ear or his arse. Why should test batsmen have to depend on umpires who have about three nanoseconds to decide whether or not a ball delivered at close to 100 mph by Brett Lee or Shoaib Akhtar, did anything other than go from here to there? Or when the Sri Lankan with the impossible name, who throws the ball, or Shane Warne, who doesn't, are making the ball change direction by ninety degrees off the pitch?

So, lets have that simple change to the system which applies only at international games, and which is now being discussed, at last. I say that the batsman should have three chances in his innings to counter-appeal if he thinks that he has been "given out". All he has to do is make the "TV" sign the way the umpires do. If the video says he is out, he is out. If not, not. And give the fielding side three chances to appeal when they think an umpire has got it wrong.

This will hold up the game? That's like suggesting to a hearse-driver that driving at half of one mph faster will ruin the gravity of the situation. Cricket is played a decorous pace. Another minute or two here and there will make not the slightest difference.

But the International Cricket Council have (one hopes only for the time being) decided that using obvious and available technology would be "against the spirit of the game". I see. Just like wearing helmets, or allowing a Sri-Lankan star wicket-taker to throw, or, for that matter, using technology to help decide on run-outs and boundaries, which they already do. Yes, all against the spirit. Must stop all this immediately. That's *it* about cricket. I promise.

Hang on – not quite it. When cricket went the way of football and turned cash-grabby professional all those years ago, my Dad was heard to mutter that it would all end in tears one day. End, I don't know – but when Australian umpire Darrell Hair can make a terrible mistake, clearly demonstrate bias, dissolve a test match in mid–flow, create a storm of outrage, demand a fat lump of cash to go away, and then retract his demand because he says he was upset, The End is Nigh. The first shot in the battle to replace all umpires with all-seeing technology has been fired. You read it here first, OK?

UNDERGROUND, LONDON, THE
One, but mind the gap, heading for two

I have done my time. I lived in London for years, balanced its unique cultural richness against its rank over-populated dirty rawness, came out about even, and left.

I know that part of my dislike of London is down to having grown a little older and less tolerant but almost everything one has to do in London is made unpleasant by horrific prices, pollution of both air and ear, congested decongestion zones, rude and surly shop assistants, nowhere to park, and the press of under-washed bodies everywhere. And an underground system which is the railway line to and from Hell.

Because using a car is simply out of the question, and buses are simply very large cars which are just as traffic-bound as anything else, the Tube is the only way to get anywhere unless you happen to be very wealthy, have lots of time and can afford to take a taxi (but which is, in any case – see above, re traffic). Unless you are prepared to walk. With a large suitcase. Walk through the park? There's a drunk pissing against a tree, and a couple going at it like knives in full pudendum. You get run over by a runner, jostled by a crowd of Eastern gawkers who can't see where they are going because their eyes are clapped to cameras. You are accosted by panhandlers. And as you step out of the way, you step into a steaming pile of poodle-shit deposited by one of the only two breeds of dog in London. Mincing French toys with nightmare wool-do's, and menacing down-at-haunch Alsatians, hungrily slinking. Oh, and there are some demented-looking Weimariners, being pulled along by equally demented owners. I don't care what anyone says. Dogs should not have blue eyes. They just shouldn't.

So, to the un-lovely London Underground. Let's not talk about bombers, OK? Let's assume in true Brit style that everything is normal and we are just jolly well getting on with it, Johnny Mad Muslim notwithstanding. There is a seven-foot gent in a tank-top alongside me, while the backpack on a backpacker from Belorus pushes me until my face almost buries itself in a naked armpit the size of a dustbin lid. The armpit boasts a bush like a buddleia, and smells like the core of the cauldron of Hades. As the train nears my destination, it empties, and a crowd of young slobs occupies the carriage, their filthy trainers on the seats, their gobs of spittle soon shining brightly on the floor. Further down the carriage is a drunk madman, shouting, waving, swearing, crying. Then he projectile vomits copiously, and with enthusiasm. The smell made me long for the armpit which left the train some stations back. And that's on a good day. If you happen to have a meeting either first thing or last, you are caught in the crush-hour, which is enough to make strong people faint. If the weather happens to be summery, the Tube from one end to the other is a fetid swamp of immobile air straight from a condemned Turkish bath. There are people who do this twice a day, every week-day. London, the Masochism capital of the world.

The Tube is outrageously expensive. A return trip within Zone One (i.e., a couple of miles at most) costs £4.00. Steeply upwards from there, of course. Buy a Day-Pass or whatever the damned thing is called? Great. But *that* assumes you are going to make several tube journeys on the same day, and you may not want to do that after your first journey, having had enough, or because your plans have changed. The ticket machines work when they feel like it, and the queues at ticket-booths are always blocked by someone who is ninety-three, deaf and from Turkmenistan, buying a devastatingly complicated season ticket which involves the ticket clerk in Einsteinian calculations and re-calculations.

Now, to the platform. With a heavy case, which first has to be squeezed through a turnstile exactly two inches too narrow, so you have to beg a surly attendant to open a special gate, which he does with the most ill of grace. You are through – but your case has to be humped up and down steps every few yards, dislocating your shoulder while you pick up stiletto-stares and rude snarls from Londoners who are, in true Euro fashion, learning fast how to be even more unpleasant than Parisians, which takes a lot of doing.

The platform, at last. It is a warmish day. Down here in Dante's District and Circle Inferno, the temperature and humidity are up in the nineties, and you are gasping. Alongside you is a slattern who has a streaming cold, and her task today is to infect as many people as possible, including you. You try to stop breathing. The train arrives, and it is sardine-time, and bodies that you would prefer not to be *anywhere near you*, are touching you with intimacy. There is no air-conditioning. Why would there be, on underground trains which were built when Queen Vic was alive? The trains, which are noisy and unstable, stop between stations for very long minutes (hours sometimes) for no reason that the staff are prepared to disclose, inducing claustrophobia, irritation, perspiration, and consternation.

Will the London Underground ever offer a remotely pleasant experience? By 2012, when London is the massively expensive home to the massively expensive Olympic Games, something will have to have been done. Maybe. But that's years away. I'll still be walking, if and when I absolutely have to go to London, which I will avoid with determination.

UNITED NATIONS ORGANISATION, THE
Seven hundred thousand drones, but that was yesterday

The United Nations building in New York lifts its blunt phallic presence into the Manhattan skyline in a massive sexual gesture of disrespect and disdain for the world and all its works. It is one of the world's largest bureaucracies, if not *the* largest, sucking down vast sums of money and providing work-experience for thousands of people who cannot be given anything better to do in their home countries. The UNO is a monument to the *dis*-unity of nations, powerless since its inception to stop the scores of dirty little wars which Churchill, naturally, foresaw and which he knew could never be stopped by something as distant from reality as the UNO. But, *faute de mieux*, he encouraged the UN in much the same way as politicians encourage community service. Waste of time, but politically correct. The League of Nations by another name, Churchill thought, and the League had also been a waste of time, money and space. *Vide* Hitler, Stalin, Hirohito, etc., etc.

If national knowledge of right from wrong had been qualifying factors for membership of the so-called Security Council, most of its permanent members should have been permanently excluded, starting with the Soviet Union/Russia and China which lead the charge into bloody infamy and hypocrisy. A body which ought to exist in order to provide a forum for nations with ideas and internationally moral stature, has become simply a talking and boasting-shop where size matters above all else. And where the top man (it is always a man) is appointed according to some mystical formula where the continents take turns to find some grey nonentity, ensure that he has not actually been caught doing what he shouldn't, and propel him into a job which ought to be bigger than his capabilities but never is.

But it is not all bad. Away from New York there are agencies of the UN which do quiet and good work on behalf of the worlds poor, the uneducated, the starving and the dispossessed. UNHCR, UNICEF, and others. These agencies, centred in Geneva and elsewhere, work in spite of the UN not because of it. As agencies for good works, they work. Ironically, the UN's good guys could do their work under almost any international banner, whether the UN existed or not, and conversations with their operational staff make it clear that they have no respect for the dead hand and dead heads in Manhattan.

Poor Kofi Annan, his predecessors and successors were, are and will be Secretaries General of the most comprehensively useless body ever. Dis-united nations. Untied nations. But why single out the S-G? Because he gives every impression of being *in charge* of a political madhouse in New York City, standing there in his distinguished grey hair and his distinguished grey suit, hoping against hope that no-one notices that he also has pale-grey ambitions because he cannot have anything else. Or perhaps he is just plain tired of the whole damned charade, having taken the S-G's chair at a time when he thought he might be able to stop the political lunatics who run most of the world's countries from looking for even more fiendish ways to clobber the living poop out of their neighbours or others, and now realises that he has been wasting his time and everyone's money – including yours.

A pox on the UNO. As a political phenomenon the UN is a bad joke, badly told.

UNITED STATES, CITIZENS, WRONG KIND OF
O-o-oh say can you three or several hundred thousand?

My oldest and dearest friend is an American. I love him to pieces and have done for thirty years. He is the *right* kind of American – a clever, kind, gentle, funny atheist married forever to a devout Jew (as the Yanks would say, "go figure") who mirrors my hatred of everything so many of his countrymen are getting so hopelessly wrong. Getting wrong, and showing no signs of understanding, with a view to a bit of, shall we say, reconsideration. Starting with the election (by a system which defies belief) of a president who is, beyond a peradventure, by Forest Gump out of Daisy Duck, with his finger on the nucular (as he pronounces it) button, worked from behind by some of the most deeply worrying presidential aides and advisors ever to strut the White House corridors.

George W Bush cannot help the fact that he is several syllables short of a word, with a silly walk which not even John Cleese could replicate, and a shocking and awesome ability to put the emphasis in the wrong place on such words as he does utter, rendering even his most important

The Usual Suspects

statements devoid of credibility and filled with hilarity. What *could* have been helped was the way millions of Americans voted for this man. But they did.

Would that it stopped there. But no – the United States compounds all its errors by being determined to use force of arms to compel the rest of the world to live in its own image. Strange really, because the job has been done already, by American world-colonisation through the spread of the American language (closely related to English, but not the same), the ubiquity of American products from McBurgers to Microballs, and the total Americanisation of popular music. As has been observed, we are all Americans now, with no more than matters of degree making us more or less so. But this is not good enough for a country with positively Roman delusions of grandeur, with an army which craves the maximum number of live targets, because training isn't the same when adrenalin-pumped marines have to shoot at cardboard cut-outs in the Nevada desert. And the US of A has an oilo-holic's thirst for fuel which, irritatingly, still persists in lying under ground which belongs to someone else.

Most Americans, bless them, have an evangelist's belief in the rightness of their cause, their God and their culture. So, of course do far too many Muslims, which turns out extremists including self-exploding fanatics who, far from believing that their lives are *without* value, consider that giving up their most valuable possession to their cause is the highest form of giving, but that's another story. Americans on the other hand nurse no such illusions; life is for hanging onto. Americans do not become suicide bombers, do they? No? In Iraq, at the time of writing this, well over 2,000 Americans have had their lives taken away in the cause of the American Way. Could it not be argued that they became suicide-soldiers as soon as they joined the armed forces? While it is true that they don't usually kill innocent civilians at the same time as they give up their own lives, they do so on a delayed basis, and without the same *immediately* murderous intent. The results are very much the same. But soldiers don't join the army in order to be killed, you say, whereas suicidal fanatics become bombs precisely for that purpose. Well, OK.

Where was I? Americans, wrong kind. Marble-in-the-mouth crop-headed Texan generals or admirals, practising murder on the English language before putting those skills into effect wherever people disagree with them. Massively overweight men and women in the cities all over the USA (it is *always* in the cities, have you noticed?) hauling their elephantine arses from McMuck to Pancake A-Go-Go and back again. Born-again mostly Southern-state Jesus-naggers who refuse to understand that a lot of people *just don't want* the teachings of Christianity or anything else crammed down their throats, and least of all do they want a Government which seems to believe in obligatory Christian religious fervour for all.

Idiots who drive immense SUVs in the cities (never shifting into four-wheel drive, ever) sucking down petrol in greedy gulps and issuing great belching farts of CO_2, making more of a mess of the Earth's atmosphere than any other nation, except perhaps China, and refusing to 'fess up to it.

A uniquely American breed of excruciatingly badly dressed and (again) over-flowingly fat blue-rinsed tourist-women of an age which ought to have brought at least some wisdom and modesty, but hasn't, talking at a shout to everyone while wobbling acres of cellulite visible below horrible floral Bermuda shorts create huge offence and disgust all over the world.

And yet, and yet. The very fact that I have to describe some Americans as the *wrong* kind automatically indicates that there are Americans very much of the *right* kind too. And, thankfully, that's the vast majority. The right kind are energetic, intelligent, articulate, amusing, sensitive, tolerant, kind and generous to a fault. And hugely successful too.

While their wrong-kind crop-head militarist *compadres* are waving bombs, the right kind believe that everyone ought to have the right to any kind of democracy *they* feel is right for them, and the Good Americans are brow-furrowed in anxiety to persuade rather than blast into submission. I admire them. And I suppose that without their armed forces the entire Western world would have spent the past seventy years first under Nazi Holocaustism and then under Soviet Communism. Yes, they had to chuck a few a bombs to achieve that for us, but you get the point. And if, heaven forefend, something like a Hitler or a Stalin were to emerge from the sewers again, the Americans would be there to push them back down – again. We have to pay a price for that. The wrong kind of Americans are making us do it.

VANDALS
Ten ASBOs and nine cautions

You have to catch them first, of course. Vandals are cowards, so having destroyed or defaced in the dark, they slide away like the snakes they are, and they are seldom caught. If they *are* caught the law tells them what awfully naughty fellows they have been, and they *really* mustn't do it again, OK? Now go away and have a nice cup of tea with your Mum.

I suppose that pointless behaviour has a point. It is one of the many physical manifestations of a civilisation in steep decline and ranks alongside cage-fighting for sheer stupid action for its own sake. When a *soi-disant* civilisation reaches a point where the pent-up energy of young men in particular (but young women are in there too, with saddening increase) has no outlet and seeks none of any value, a lashing-out at anything within reach is utterly predictable. And between this behaviour and a solution to it stand the indignantly quivering ranks of the Politically Correct, for whom firm action is the equivalent of legalised Sodom and Gomorrah. The Prime Minister has now decided that, you know, enough is enough, really it is, and yobs must be de-yobbed, you know, by tomorrow morning. Fat chance. It has all gone too far. Vandals are here to stay, so lock up your statues, don't bother planting any municipal flower beds, and stop wasting money cleaning up graffiti which will simply re-appear the next day.

The only thing that would start to make a difference? An invasion of these islands, requiring full mobilisation of everyone over the age of twelve. Ten. Do you think we could come clean with George Dubya, tell him how much we despise him, and make him so cross that he decides we are ripe for a regime-change?

Robert MacGregor

VANS, WHITE
Three feet from my bum, two fingers in the air

Much has been said and written about White Van and the Man. As with so many urban myths, it has a strong root in reality, even if it means tarring every driver of every van with the same brush. Which I would love to do.

There was a time when delivery vans were dear old things, painted a bland green, vastly underpowered and driven by gentle men of a certain age, wearing aprons, moustaches and friendly if vacant smiles. You came up behind them as they laboured along the straight, doing about forty mph, and a shirt-sleeved arm (buttoned to the wrist in all weathers) would wave you past. When did all this change? I have no idea when the van-making world decided that Van-man could have any colour he wanted as long as it was white, but here's something I do know: somewhere in the late seventies, the van-makers started to put seriously powerful engines into these vehicles. Muscular diesels with exhaust pipes pointing jauntily sideways, eight gears, go-faster tyres, the lot.

Suddenly, the old delivery van was replaced by horribly fast turbo-charged snorting white juggernauts, capable not only of staying ahead of you on hills up and down, but of overtaking you when you are doing a naughty ninety on the M-way.

And the drivers. Oh, dear. Many are shaven-headed, pig-nosed, tank-topped, dark-glassed, with a lot of hair sprouting from everywhere, large beefy arms circled around steering wheels, aggression and mayhem written all over their faces. Behind you? *Right* behind you, filling your rear-view mirror with white fury and you with abject terror, as you try everything to get his nose out of your anus. In front of you? Overtake, if you dare, and you will, in three nanoseconds, be re-over-taken in a cloud of diesel fumes, dust and abuse involving the driver's use of gestures which accuse you of automotively playing with yourself. Find your path blocked in a city street by a white van parked slap in the middle of the road while the man ambles to and fro carrying a light-bulb at a time? Just sit there, OK? Don't even *think* about complaining and never, *ever* toot your horn. You will wake up in hospital.

I say round them up, put them in the army and let them drive tanks. They are so pumped up with bad-tempered aggression and adrenalin that they will frighten the living piddle out of any opposing force. But you will have to paint the tanks white.

VASECTOMY
Two but one time only, thanks

Been there. Had that done. But the memory lingers, and the tears still come to the eyes. Had it done *why?* Because then-wife was told she had been on the pill for far too long, and I never have and never will use a condom. I would rather refrain than have to pull a rubber stocking mask over the head of ... the head of ... and turn the activity into sexual bog-snorkelling. No. So, no un-safe sex please, we already had three sons and the puking, full nappy, shrieking colic, sleepless nights, etc., etc., would not be seeing us again. Only solution – into the surgery for the reproductive plumbing to be re-arranged. Hmmm. Well, OK. Fine.

Local anaesthetic of course. Helpful ball-surgeon positions large magnifying mirror so that I cannot help seeing what's going on, and before I could say spermogenesis there were pale beige pipelettes emerging from my numbed scrote, to be snipped and tied and put back. Yi-i-i-i-i-i-kes!

Couple of stitches, and out of there, legs more than slightly akimbo. Manhood-minus. Hateful. But in the interests of marital peace and occasional ... occasional ... you know, job done.

Time to get my own back, if you see what I mean. Three months, I was told, before the last of the wrigglies would expire out of boredom and nowhere to go, and then back to the surgery for a test to see if it had all worked. Whether part of me had *stopped* working. Prune-faced receptionist hands me a small glass jar – about the same size and shape as those which hold breakfast jams in hotels and guesthouses at the cheaper

end of the market. Into which to … to … provide a specimen. In a small cubicle along a corridor which smelled faintly of bleach. Worked out why, eventually. Have you noticed? Selection of magazines of a certain kind on a shelf. Box of tissues. Am I getting too graphic for you?

But instead of … of … um… I emptied a carefully prepared small bottle of wallpaper paste into the jam-jar, and it looks exactly like, well, like the stuff I was supposed to … to … have produced. Only, I filled it to the brim. Anatomically impossible, I am told, if the real thing had … had. Walked to the reception desk, took a label, printed my name, stuck it on the jar, and marched out.

I was asked, stiffly, if you will excuse the Freudian, to come and re-take the test properly a week or so later. Blanks. Ever since. But there is a scar, both mental and physical. The slightest inadvertent knock to the affected area, and it is like being kicked by a horse. Impossibly over-sensitive. I have been told I ought to have it looked at, entailing another operation, to remove scar tissue. No, no. Mentally, that's an even deeper scar. Ain't going there. Vasecto-not-me, sunshine.

VATICAN, THE
Twelve Hail Mary's and is the Pope Catholic?

I don't want to offend any Catholics who might have bought this tract of mine, but if I am going to take a pop at the Vatican, I can hardly avoid that, can I? So, here goes. Sorry.

The most predictable thing that has happened so far in this still-young century was the election of Cardinal Rottwelier to the Papery. Rottzinger. Ratzonger. Ratzinger. At a time when all the old-style Christian churches worldwide are losing their grip and their congregations to new-style Jesusmatazz, the last thing a centuries-old power-house is going to do is liberalise, even if liberalisation is the only way to secure a future, because that's the beginning of the end. When you have hold of a population by something sensitive, relaxing your grip is asking for trouble. Having put up with the ache of pressure on sensitive points for aeons, any slackening the grippee feels is an invitation to have a grab at the gripper themselves, and those who control the Catholic church know this only too well.

So, retain the grip and issue diktats and appropriately named "bulls". No condoms in a world dying of HIV. No condoms, either, in places where any more population growth will result in certain population death. No terminations for hopeless teenagers pregnant out of ignorance or rape. Might be killing a Mozart, or an Einstein or a Picasso. Might also be killing a Hitler, Stalin or Idi Amin. Well, that's life. Life's rules laid down by people who never get laid. Life at any price in a world where Catholics greet the death of millions with resignation, but cannot accept the cessation of life before birth. It's just one weapon in the great catholic Catholic armoury which keeps power where it has been for centuries – in the Vatican.

If you have enormous power, the last thing you are inclined to do is give that power away. Not natural. So, the Vatican clings on. Incapable of realising that a more realistic and more humane approach to the human need for religious faith would grow their church instead of killing it slowly. *Habemus papam*. "We do indeed have a Pope, but he is losing his Church". That's how a once-devoted Catholic put it to me recently, after the recent election of Benedict XVI. *His* words, OK? Not mine. I'm an atheist, remember. I don't really care that much.

VEGANS
Eighteen pimples and a case of nuts

It's hard to despise vegans, really. They are harmless enough – but what the hell, the qualifications for getting into this book do not depend on being violent or harmful. Just being annoying is enough.

I am married to a vegetarian. Nothing with a face passes into hers. Good. Forces me to eat healthy stuff and stay regular. I sneak the occasional piggy, fishy, chicky or cowy part into the diet from time to time and, boy, do I enjoy it. But no complaints, really, other than having it suggested that I really ought to read barmy articles in veggie magazines which claim that unless I stop even *thinking* about eating meat, I will turn all over blue and my gonads will shrivel.

But vegans are something else. For a start, they always look as though they need a square meal, which of course they do. However, what they do in the privacy of their own homes and kitchens is up to them and I don't care, but look what happens if a dinner party happens by mistake to include a vegan nut-job. Eggs, no. Cheese, no, butter, yoghurt, milk, no. Nothing that was even *looked at* by an animal of any kind. Cooking for such people is impossibly hard, so if a vegan happens along, they get a plate full of lettuce, a carrot or two, three brazil nuts and a glass of water. And a great deal of joshing from everyone else. I jest. I have actually done stuff with lentils, onions and beans. But I badly wanted to sneak some beef-stock into the mix. I didn't, but if I had, would they have known? Would I have lied if asked? Hur, hur.

But here's the ultimate. We had some visitors not long ago, and they turned out to be members of a sect which was not only vegan, but believed that eating onion or garlic was an affront to their gods, on account of bad breath during prayers, I think they said. To this they added a health-driven abhorrence of salt. Now I have been on the receiving end of, and have given plenty of offence as a result of, garlic intake which could have knocked over a buffalo by my breathing at it, so I *sort* of understood. But have you ever tried cooking for people who eat nothing but veg, do not use salt, and will not allow the use of anything from the allium family? Only their Gods knew what it tasted like. By the way, these people had no problem with alcohol. Drank like the fish they were not allowed anywhere near. Bottle after bottle. Vegan-pure, sanctimonious, sweet of breath, but rat-arsed on best organic vegan red (no products used in the wine-making that came from any animal, please).

I am an evolutionist. I believe that mankind evolved to eat anything that moves, and that includes plants of course. I have no desire to grab a gun and go out hunting for my supper, but denying my evolutionary dietary preferences altogether would be the equivalent of taking a vow of silence and pretending that I did not develop a larynx. Yes, I know that there are monks who do this. Barmy as bats.

But, no, thinking about it, I can't really dump on vegans. I think they are several nuts short of a muesli, but that's far enough.

Hang on, though. Have you had a look at the range of vegan foods offered by various band-wagon-climbing manufacturers? No, of course you haven't. You were at the other end of the shop with the good stuff like lamb, beef and pork while I was doing research. So let me explain. One manufacturer I happened to come across in my five-minute research offers seven different variations on the vegan theme (which means that it is all made of strange fungi or peculiar Japanese curds, or beans, or something) and what are they called? Hot dogs, Sausages (two flavours), Nuggets, Burgers, Schnitzels, Cutlets. So there you have it. The poor vegans will not eat anything that comes from an animal. But boy, do they wish they could.

Hang on a bit longer. The reason for the above packaging disguise is to attract more meaters to veganism, or at least to vegetarianism, I am told. They see familiar looking stuff (which is, by the way, flavoured with meat-ish tasting chemicals of one kind or another), they try it, like it, and bingo, vegans. Nice try, but I don't buy it. If people want to become vegans or vegetarians, they just have to *do* it. By buying barrow-loads of spinach and alfalfa and getting on with it.

VIRAGOS
No balls at all, but growing several

Virago: Concise Oxford dictionary definition *"a fierce or abusive woman ... a woman of masculine strength or spirit."* Masculine, *please note.*

Several cheers for Michael Buerk, I say. And anyone else who stands up and says that women in positions of power are worse bullies and manipulators than men. I have always suspected that evolution played a part in so ordering things for billennia that (a) the male of the human species was put in charge and (b) the genetic and the psycho-social make-up of the female was just not suited to captaincy. I don't know. What I do know is that its all change, now.

It has been my miserable lot to have worked on several occasions with women who have burst through the glass ceiling like The Alien at birth, and their first task upon seizing power was to put the balls of any male within reach into a vice, and tighten it daily after lunch.

I once talked over the phenomenon with a female Managing Director, who actually revelled in her ability to make strong men weep, and she asked me why I was apparently able to accept abuse and unfair treatment from men-in-suits, but not from their female counterparts. Was it, she wanted to know, because I more than halfway expected the man-boss to behave that way, while I definitely expected more gentle treatment from woman-boss, and if so, why ? Yes, I said. No, I said. I don't know, I said. I tried to explain that there just *is* an edge to womanpower that cuts deeper and leaves a bigger scar, whereas chaps seem able to get over the wounds inflicted by other chaps more easily and more quickly.

But can I get away with this kind of massive generalisation? Probably not, because there must be thousands of high-flying women execs who behave with balance and decency, and I know perfectly well that there are equal thousands of men in similar positions who behave like male viragos.

So where does this leave me? Still uneasy – but grateful that my life no longer depends on taking orders from anyone, and especially not from any she-who-must-be-obeyed. Aside from my beloved, of course. But, interestingly, *she* feels about viragos much the way I do and on the basis of similar experiences. So it is not exclusively about excessive woman-on-man mental cruelty. Woman-on-woman too. So make what you will of that.

VIVISECTION
Several pigs short of a guinea

People who believe in a cause sufficiently fanatically to steal bodies from graves in order to make their protests ought to be force-fed very large quantities of both emetics and laxatives, left in a dungeon for a week, then cut up slowly for shark-food. No punishment is cruel or unusual enough for them. They are in jail now, and I sincerely hope they are being buggered rigid by very large men.

But loathing those extremists does not mean that I have much better feelings for those who experiment on animals for the "benefit" of the human species. Who insist that the only way to test a drug is to do unspeakable things to monkeys, rats, guinea pigs, dogs, mice and other innocents. The truth is that the only way to test a drug or a medical procedure for their effectiveness on humans is to *test them on humans.*

And if that is a test too far, then drop the whole idea. What arrogance we display as a species that in the third *Christian* millennium, we still assume that animals are there to be subjected to things to which we would never dream of subjecting ourselves. "But then", moans the pharmaceutical industry, "we would never have developed, oh, lots of medicines which have been saving lives ever since." Sorry, but I still don't buy it. Don't do tests on animals who can't give you their consent. Just don't, OK? If the pharm industry had been barred, totally, from tests on animals, you can bet every penny you own that they would, in time, have come up with exactly the same products which they had developed by torturing mice.

I have a niggling concern about awarding "rights" to animals. Rights and responsibilities are twin concepts, and you can't have one without the other. Several philosophers have come to this conclusion. In their view and mine, rights only have meaning if the putative right-holder knows that the right exists and can measure the extent to which it has either been respected or infringed. Animals do not have the cerebral wherewithal to take responsibility for the duties which come with our awarding them rights. This poses a question, though: if animals do not have rights according to my definition, what about humans who are seriously mentally impaired, or new-born babies that have no more cognitive capacity than a goat? They have no rights either? No, not in the way I define rights – but read on.

I feel much the same way about "rights" awarded to the dead. They are dead, and have no rights. A problem? Not a problem if we take the view that such unfortunates, along with animals, enjoy a very special status which it pleases me to describe as *"defendenda"*. From the Latin – deserving of complete protection. By those of us who are sentient, cognitive, human and alive. This is a much, *much* higher moral duty than merely awarding rights.

It means that those of us who ought to know good from evil do not have moral permission to do anything we like to, or with, animals, children, the impaired or the deceased. On the contrary, we have a *massive* moral obligation to see that they are not tortured, experimented upon, indiscriminately culled or have their lives or dignity attacked or affronted in any way.

But do we behave like that? No. When it comes to animals, not only do we subject them to awful torture – we eat them. So some of them eat us, given half a chance and a leg sticking out of a tent. Who can blame them?

VULGARITY (as in "schlock", previously)
Six kitches and a talking loo roll.

Complaining about vulgarity scoots me awfully close to being a snob. So, I may as well be hanged for a prancing mauve-green dragon as for a nodding dog. As I have had cause to remark, one man's vulgarity is another's cute memento. (See "Schlock") It's a class thing, and if you think that Britain has become a classless society, you have been living in a far distant part of the galaxy for too long. Welcome back.

The same applies in the US of A, where Americans get their boxer shorts into the most awful tangle if you even *suggest* that their country is every bit as class-riddled as Britain. The schlock/vulgarity-co-efficient is as good a measure there, as it is here.

The more you see of plastic madonnas which sing "Jesus wants you for a sunbeam", framed prints of Tretchikov's green Chinese woman, shoes covered in spangles, or knitted samplers of "Home Sweet Home" over the mantelpiece, the more sure you can be that you are looking at the lower end of the social scale. In the "classless" US, those who live in Manhattan's upper-crust areas, in Santa Monica, LA., or Nob Hill in San Francisco, would rather commit suicide than come within a hundred yards of a coffee-mug which claims that the owner plays with the biggest organ in the state (picture of church-organ on reverse side, hur, hur).

Sea-side resorts worldwide have endless table-top temples to vulgarity, with shops selling the most fantastically awful garbage to swirling, swilling and willing hordes of holiday-makers who just love to take home with them bagsful of Made-in-China genuine plasticette

Tony Blair masks, statuettes of mismatched copulating dogs (Made-in-China) and those gee-gad horrible little spheres which create a snowstorm over a church when you shake them (Made-in-China). Why does bad taste go so comfortably hand in hand with what some people describe as the lower social orders? Why does good taste become the preserve of the so-called higher social orders? I have no idea.

It has *nothing* to do with money. Some of the most shocking schlock costs a bomb, and can be see in pride of place in the homes of those for whom a bomb is small change. Have you seen the stuff Michael Jackson used to buy? Is still buying? Or footballers? They make the case for me, perfectly.

WAGNER
Five headaches and instant depression

I really have tried over the years to like Wagner's music. Wagner was a prolific genius, but O, welle, wolle and woe, did he ever make a meal of everything. An undiluted diet of Wagner is about as pleasant as an undiluted diet of Christmas pudding. In either case, great in very small helpings and not to be attempted again for another year. Clearly, no-one mentioned this to the BBC Radio Three nerds who decided (what a wizard jape, har, har!) to broadcast the entire Ring Cycle, (all fourteen hours of it) in one hit recently. The wards of several psychiatric hospitals are overflowing now with too-brave idiots who thought it would be a good idea to listen to the whole thing.

If ever you wanted proof of the fact that Wagnerian stuff is hard to take, just listen to the music broadcast by Classic FM, the monopoly commercial classical music station, now badly in need of competition. The only Wagner they play is the Ride of the Valkyries and that piece from Lohengrin. And they do not play *those* more than once in very blue moons, because they understand only too well that the sound of radio sets being turned off or retuned would be deafening and very bad for business.

As for Wagner operas, actually going to, and sitting through – leave me out, please. I did so once because I thought I was in love with a delightful creature at University, and she was an indiscriminate fan of opera in all its forms. If it had a plot as thick as borscht or as thin as gruel (incomprehensible either way) a cast of thousands and very loud music, she was there, loving it. So, to Die (or is it Das or even Der?) Reingold from the Ring Cycle we went. Or more truthfully, to part of the Reingold. A Ringlet. I left at the intermission, pleading in total truth both nausea and a headache and came away with my eyeballs revolving

THE HORROR.

THE HORROR.

in opposite directions, my ears thrumming with the vibrato of the soprano, my very innards twanging with the incredible noise made by the bass, who sang "**BAW!**" quite a lot. To be an operatic bass you have to have very big baws.

Mozart and Beethoven – even Mahler – did lighten up from time to time, and produced lively tuneful stuff which even an opera-avoider like me can get to love. But Wagner? No. He mined a deep seam in the Germanic soul and found what everyone finds there – dark solemnity and great skeins of brooding black mythology. Siegfried was not a barrel of laughs. You *like* Wagner? Gotterdämmerung!

WEATHER, BRITISH
A hundred millimetres thick with isobars

I have never had the slightest problem understanding why the British

I can't take any more crap

Empah was the greatest the world had ever seen. Thousands upon thousands of soggy Brits could not wait to get the hell out of here and go to some place where they could reliably dry their socks and stay warm without having to put their feet into a coal fire.

As I write this, the roof of my tiny office resounds to the tinkle-plink of raindrops falling quite close to my head. This has been happening for several days, so if global heating-up means that Britain will become a bit hotter and drier, then roll on, I say. (By the way, you note that I call the weather-thing by a name which says what is happening – global heating-up. I have had it up to here with the politicians and others who started with "global warming" and then realised that even this euphemism has a doomsday-feel to it, so they now refer, the lying hypocritical pussies, to "climate change").

There will always be enough rain in Britain (it's in the Magna Carta) and provided that we as a nation can wrestle our water-management out of the hands of the incompetent accountants who run the water companies, and actually find a way to capture and conserve our water rather than let it dribble away into the ground or the sea, then we will be fine. We would be no more likely to dry up than Tony Blair. My dearly beloved moans about not being to dry the washing, and being forced either to use an expensive tumble drier or festoon every room in the house with dripping sheets. She is forever rushing inside and back out again, watching the horizon, consulting the barometer/oracle/vestal virgins. Watching the weather forecasts and saying "oh, yeah?" or something equally scathing, because the forecasts for our micro-weather area are usually wrong.

I think umbrellas are crap, as you know. But I acknowledge that they are useful if you are walking somewhere in a wet dead calm. But what about cycling, which we are begged to do by every environ-mental and the Government? I love cycling, but it is truly crappy to arrive at my destination (fifty yards away is enough) soaked to the skin despite layer upon layer of sweat-making and useless rain-gear which not only does not work, but reduces the clothing underneath to creased and stained social disaster. And umbrellas do not mix with cycling. Just try it.

I am not a fanatical gardener, but when I have to watch as the lawn turns into a lake, the beds into baths and the walkways into the Wye then I get seriously bogged off, and down. Especially when I am sent pictures by well-meaning but sadistic friends in warm dry places where the sun shines, visibly, as opposed to lurking behind several layers of cloud until late in the day, showing its face long enough to say "Good afterno…" and then disappearing behind yet more grey sludge. My friends write from places where they have huge reservoirs of underground water – *underground*, where it belongs – and where it stays without leaking away. Where they have intelligent irrigation systems, and where the palm trees grow like weeds. And when it rains it does so in just sufficient amounts, politely, apologetically, occasionally, and quickly.

We try, we poor Brits, in full mid-summer, to organise fetes, fairs, weddings and sports fixtures despite certain knowledge that it is going to come down stair-rods on the day and the whole thing will be a wash-out. And have you ever sat in a bus, anywhere in the UK, or on the London Underworld or anywhere for that matter, among people whose clothes are steaming, whose shoes are soaked and whose temper is just a smidgeon short of murder? Of course you have. You, and they, grim and bear it.

So why don't I take my wellies, my brolly and my mac to the dump, and myself and my family to somewhere south of Lyon and north of Antarctica? Because it would mean moving house again, and that is something I cannot face, even in prolonged bright sunshine.

WEATHER-GIRLS
High pressure and low brow

It's an American thing, of course. It appears that no-one in America is able to believe, or even watch, a weather forecast unless it is delivered either by a capering goon in a gorilla suit, or a mini-skirted blonde bimbette with a really big mouth and a great many teeth, all of which are permanently fixed in what they imagine is a smile, but looks like a death-mask.

Barring the BBC, where TV weather-forecasters are (mostly) normal men and women, the rest of the 956 channels have American-type bimbos delivering the weather news, and I get so angry that I end up not knowing whether tomorrow will bring a Saharan heat-wave or whether it will be snowing poodles, because I have stopped listening. If I happen to be watching the news on a channel which employs one of these gurning numbskulls, I can hit the off-button on my remote faster than you could say "Rockall". She was about to tell me that I could expect Hurricane Norma to hit me tonight? I'll take my chances.

No matter what the forecast, the bimbos say everything with a fixed smile. Gales, snowdrifts, torrential rain, clear and fine – all the same to them, and always with an ever-widening grin. Especially at the end of the forecast, as they sign off with a cute little wiggle and a wave and a simper. "It's going to be tropical rain in your area tomorrow, with floods! Have a nice day!!"

It can't be that they all do this naturally. Someone is training these mindless juvenile cheerleaders to smile, smile, smile whatever the coming weather. He, the trainer (or is it she?) tells them, "That's what the great dumb public want, don't you see? They have just watched news from all over the world, delivered by a solemn autocue-reader in a suit, with murder piled upon mass mayhem followed by disaster and topped off by rape and a bit of genocide, so let's leave them with a cheerful smile, shall we, whatever the hell the weather is going to do."

WIND
Ten backing twelve and dis-gusting

The day I left the city where I had spent the first twenty or so years of my life, I rejoiced. Because I was free of hide-bound family and other tradition which was stifling me? Just a bit. Because I could not wait to spread my amazing talents all over the unsuspecting world? Silly.

Because I was pining for some fragrant creature who lived elsewhere?
Nyet.

I rejoiced because I was finally free of the non-stop howling gales
that blew 363 days of the year. The other two? Change-over days when
the wind moved from South to North, and six months later, back again.
In Spring-Summer it blew sand into every nook, cranny, crack and
orifice. In Autumn-Winter it picked up the rain and stuffed it
horizontally into everything else. It howled down the mountain,
through the city centre and, on one occasion, having blown a bus onto
its side, grabbed a terrified woman of a certain age and bowled her
several hundred yards into an ornamental fountain. Have you ever seen

the expression on the face of people on the upper deck of a bus as it teeters, totters, and tips over? Some smart photographer snapped it, and it appeared in the local newspaper. Made Munch's "Scream" look like mild surprise, multiplied manyfold. No-one hurt, miraculously.

The noise of a furious wind is like no other. You can hear it hours after it has slowed down to a mere gale. It makes my teeth and ears ache, brings tears to my sand-blasted eyes and makes it impossible to pee into a hedge. I will put up with quite a lot of rain, tolerate a certain amount of fog, large amounts of snow and as much sunshine as you like. But wind I cannot stand. And guess where I live now? Right in the teeth. But I have a sea-view, and that comes at a price. In Britain, sea view = sea breeze on a good day, banshee on a bad one.

WINE-BULL
Five amusing loads of cheeky rubbish, three corked

There is not a lot I can add to this subject – wine writers have been deservedly lampooned for decades by everyone who can get near a keyboard, but I have to get it off my chest my way.

There are Ozzes and Jillies and Jancises and many others who make a living out of writing about wine. They get to drink (*taste*, sorry, *taste*) a lot, too, which can't be bad.

The English language has 640,000 words, and writers-about-wine use them all. The problem these poor lambs have is that no-one has ever come up with a way to describe the taste or aroma of wine without comparing it to something else. Raspberries, strawberries, bacon, lemons (oh, lemons, lots and *lots* of lemon-imagery) guavas, pineapple, toffee, new mown grass, pine needles, vanilla, apple, pear, tropical fruit, toast, walnuts, the wood of every tree known to man, boot polish, plastic, rubber. Just have a look at the back-label of a bottle extolling the virtues of this or that estate-wine if you don't believe me. So, the bibber-scribblers strive, mouths a-pucker and brows a-furrow, to dream up ever more geeky ways to explain that the wine currently in their gobs tastes like … wine.

No-one tries this with steak, fish, vegetables or fruit. They describe the flavours of these other things, using simple adjectives which do the job. Brewers do not wallow in vocabu-hell and there are enough anoraks in the real-ale industry to give wine a serious run for its money when it comes to pretentious bullshit, if they were to put their minds to it. With wine, however, it is as though none of us have ever tasted any of it before. So we have to have it explained by reference to things we probably *have* tasted.

And then comes an attempt to pin down its "character". Delicate, robust, earthy, strong, gentle, sublime, crisp. Language for something between a lettuce and a weightlifter, all used to disguise what is really going on, viz.,

Delicate = tasteless
Gentle = *really* tasteless
Robust = crocodile's armpit, rough, mouth-puckering
Earthy = muddy
Dry = wet and stomach-churning
Rich = liver-destroying
Sublime = peculiar; what the hell is this made from?
Crisp = acid/sour/mmmmmmnnnnghhh
Light = might as well drink water

Some years ago, a deeply crooked but successful businessman in South Africa bought a huge wine farm with thousands of vines consisting of cultivars that had gone out of fashion decades earlier, and where the grapes were really manky and prone to every vineyard disease possible. He had an idea. Harvest the lot, juice the lot, chuck it all together (weeds and all) and then, using an accelerated process, ferment every gramme of sugar out of the resulting brew until it was dry enough to pucker a camel's hump. Was it crisp? See above. Did it taste of anything? See "delicate". But he called it "Premier Grand Cru" which gave every proper winemaker an instant stroke, because such a description was not only without meaning, but a cynical use of primary-school French designed to impart the cachet which anything apparently

French seems able to acquire even if it is *dernki piece* (See Wine, French, below).

He marketed this stuff as "the lunchtime wine" because, having so little sugar, it was OK, thought loon-brained executives, to drink it without feeling any guilt. The wine was so dry that they believed that it would not put more fat onto their already burgeoning spare tyres.

The puff on the back-label was the usual arse-clenchingly embarrassing whallocks of course, and completely skated round the fact that wine's ability to make drinkers fat comes from the amount of *alcohol* it contains. But that did not stop the lads who lunch. They drank this "PGC" like lemonade. They still do. Idiots.

WINE, FRENCH, TO BRITAIN, EXPORTED
Several mondieus and an alors

What? I can't be serious. Wine from the very country with which wine is synonymous? It's crap? What *am* I on about?

It is not a coincidence that "chauvinism" is a French word. It denotes precisely the kind of inward-looking arrogance for which the French are world-notorious. France as part of Europe? The world? *Mais oui, geographiquement.* But culturally, fraternally, *definitivement pas.* And wine is the perfect exemplar. Yes, the French produce some of the world's truly great wines, but the greatness is for the most part confined to the mighty Loire, Bordeaux and Burgundy vineyards and estates. However, a second mortgage is required in order to buy something of any true exception. When it comes to anything below that standard, the French keep everything worth drinking right there in *la belle France*, and export stuff they would not touch, to England.

So, when it comes to reasonably-priced French wine available in the UK, we get the most acid, tasteless, characterless liquids – and this is *years* of experimentation talking. I am a serious wine drinker. Meaning that I drink serious amounts of it over time, and I have always been willing to try anything once.

So, when the Aussies in particular, New Zealanders and South Africans (with a nod in the direction of Chile, Argentina and California) got busy making wine which did not cause the throat to constrict and the stomach to rebel, I was saved. I could enjoy really easy-drinking reds and whites, at prices which even my modest budget could stand. And the saddest part of all this? I go to France as often as I can. I love the country (and there is nothing wrong with Paris in particular that a cull of the population would not cure). When I get there, usually to a self-catering *gite*, I buy litres and litres of *ordinaire*, frequently in plastic bottles, and provided they are not left overnight, they are pleasant, immediately drinkable and immediately drunk. Maybe they don't travel well. Maximum ten kilometres from wine-factory (come on, we are not talking vineyard here) and they are fine.

And here's the funniest wine-joke of all. Each year, thousands of cases of something called Beaujolais Nouveau are shipped to England to be foisted upon the ignorant and snobby English, of the sip-and-bray class. There is even a race to get the first bottle of the stuff across the Channel. As its transport thunders across the coast of France, thousands of hysterical French can be seen lining the cliffs and beaches, falling about, crying, hooting with laughter at the great wine joke being played out yet again. Off it goes to do its annual job of taking the Michel out of the asinine Anglais and reducing their upper digestive tracts to acid-scarred wastelands.

Not long ago, I spent a delightful weekend with a friend and his family, on the Normandy coast. My liver is still recovering. From the food. It happened to be Beaujolais-Nouveau time. He had a bottle which he diffidently displayed. I could hardly believe it, until he explained the reason for doing this. He knew we were coming to stay, so he wanted to see how we reacted to this particular variety of *vinaigre francais*. We gagged, of course.

"Ho, ho", he chortled, zis is dernki piece, non?"

Dernki piece? We were flummoxed. Some very chi-chi but hopeless small boutique vineyard only Jean-Pierre knew about?

"Sorry, Jean-Pierre", I said, "what would that be in French? I'm afraid I don't ....."

"Dernki piece, dernki piece. *Pisse d'âne*".

Donkey piss. Well, there you have it, from the, from the, er, horse's, er, mouth. French horse, of course.

WITNESSES, JEHOVAH'S
Three damnations and a fizzling fireball

There is one thing about these very scary people that really impresses me. They are prepared to go out in all weathers and knock on doors, to be greeted with anything ranging from semi-polite turn-aways, to having the dog set on them. I suppose they calculate that if they manage to sucker one in every hundred into listening to their nonsense, they are doing well. Like every other organisation which employs modern marketing techniques, they will have quotas, hit- and conversion-rates and all the rest of the marketing gloppocks. And they *are* marketing a brand, oh yes they are.

I knew almost nothing about the inner workings of the JW's – none of their salespeople had ever got past my explanation that I was a committed Satanist and worshipped crocodiles on the side – until a member of my extended family found it necessary to join this organisation, and what it did to his immediate family was almost on a par with the sort of stuff which resulted in the murder and suicides of the wacko's in Waco. He had to attend services which left his family without him for hours and hours at a time. Given that his job took him away for most of the week anyway, he rapidly became a stranger to his wife and daughters. He was forbidden from celebrating any birthdays and as for Christmas, *that* was a major no-no. No tree, no turkey, no cake, and *definitely* no presents. Christ, no. All in all, he became a misery-guts, and his family came as close to splitting apart as makes no difference. The whole thing was a trial beyond anything his wife could be expected to bear, and all this in the name of a Jehovah of mercy and love, eh?

I have always thought that people who join dippy religious sects are several candles short of a 'labra, or that they are so desperately unable to cope with life that escape into a nest of nutters seems like a better option. JW churchies will tell me that I am wrong to describe the JW's as a sect at all, and they may be right. But the effect they had on the one person I am qualified to talk about was sufficiently devastating to make me unrepentant about the way I see them.

After about four years, the person in question left the JW's, but not without a great deal of trouble and quite nasty stuff from the church. But the choice was simple enough — lose the church or lose his wife and family. No contest.

WOMEN, OLD
One, but pressure rising, sorry mother

A very mild dislike. More a deep unease. Not rational, not remotely, and not PC either. But oh, how the patience is tried. Tired. There must be some genetic reason for the fact that old men, while they can cantank like mad, are on the whole less infuriating than old women. Some prehistorical instinct turned the permanently running hunters into utterly exhausted old-ish waiters-for-death, while the gatherers, still crammed with energy after a lifetime of sitting and rooting, with some gentle strolling, became sour scolds, gossips and harridans whose purpose in life was to make everyone else's life a trial by vile bile. Do you think that mother-in-law jokes came about by accident? Have you heard any father-in-law jokes recently?

Every family has a harridan. All right, almost every family. Or one in waiting. They are experts in disapproval, captains of criticism, perfectionists in the art of pissing people off. In my personal experience, one or other of the crones of my own family has ...

• Persuaded her husband to buy a seaside house at great expense, and then demanded to move out the very day they moved in because she did not like the sound made by the sea.

Seaside house. Sound of the sea? Hello?

- Took against a blameless daughter-in-law because the hapless girl produced a girl grandchild when only a boy would do.
- Informed one of *her* sons that one of *his* sons was not fathered by him, on the grounds that the little chap never developed his father's nose.
- Demanded a pet dog, filled it to the gunwales with Woofy-Biks and then consigned it to kennels as she tripped about the world using up her late husband's fortune. Never saw the dog again.
- Told the most inventively outrageous lies to anyone within earshot about someone who thought they had a long-standing friendship with her.
- Decided one day that she could drink nothing but champagne, and expected everyone to have it available at all times, with hell to pay if it was not.
- Approaching the bad end of macular degeneration, insisted on driving, drove up the bum of a parked car full of children, caused whiplash in three of them, and had to be forcibly restrained from driving away after she had rounded upon the driver of the (stationary) car and accused the poor man of reversing into her radiator.

And more. You too? I thought as much. Plenty of older women, of course, are delightful wisps of lavender, lace and love, and some are actually very attractive in every way, right into their eighties. Many are even outrageously energetic barrels of laughs who are growing old disgracefully, and we love them for it. Proper grannies or great-aunts, or just friends who behave impeccably and a mile from being goody-goody. But too many of their sisters-in-age give them a bad name.

XAVIER

At least one letter short of a name

I am scraping the barrel a bit here. Not too many words in English start with "X", and even fewer things I can bring myself to dislike. So stay with me, OK?

Like Xenophobe, or Xenon or Xylophone, there is a Greek root to this piece of pretension, but for heaven's sake, why the X when it is pronounced "Zavier, Zenon and Zylophone"? We have taken lots of Greek words and incorporated them into other Euro-languages, but we don't even attempt the "gch" throat-clearing sound to be found in lots of Greek. So why do we persist with that "X"? Did the Greeks pronounce "X" as though it were "Z", or was there more of a "ks" sound to it? I am investigating

I have known two Xxzzaviers in my time, and you know what? Pretentiousness oozes from every pore. They are given to wearing extravagant neckwear and OTT hats, one of them speaking in that almost-Brian Sewell über-English way which sets the teeth on edge. The other is French, talks the same way, and to make French sound Sewell-like is a real talent. Neither is gay. Just victims of their own Xxavierity. Xxzzavierness.

XENOPHOBIA

Three foreign imports and a jingo

Unreasoned hatred of people of a race other than your own. Virtually cornered by the English who talk tolerance and practise xenophobia, following the Cecil John Rhodes approach to life which held that being born

I can't take any more crap

"Stand back Evadne. I swear I can smell garlic on his bread. The swine."

273

English was to win life's First Prize. Arrogant Victorian prat. And wrong, too.

Fear or suspicion of foreigners is as old as man, who scowled askance right from the off at anyone not from the immediately next hovel. Strangers represented danger, weird eating habits, competition for food and the possibility that they might try to copulate with one's significant-other. Civilisation has not done a lot to change hard-wired pre-Neanderthal attitudes, and no matter how lightly you scratch the skin of a person of one race, you will find distrust of all others.

The English are permanently suspicious of the French who despise the Italians who dislike the Germans who detest the Dutch who cannot bear the Spanish who ridicule the Portuguese who simply do not understand the Irish, who know that Poland is a member of the EU now but can't see why, while the Poles laugh at the Hungarians who loathe the Germans who, etc,. And everyone utterly loathes the Turks. It is all done in a terribly civilised way these days, of course, and we at the civilised end of Europe leave the Africans, South and Central Americans, and Asians to demonstrate their xenophobia with extreme prejudice at the end of AK47's.

But what inanity lies at the root of xenophobic insanity. There are individuals I cannot abide, even if I haven't actually met them. Piers Morgan for example. The Reverend Ballsache. (Miserable old sod, retired C of E Vicar who lives up the road from me and whom I *have* met.) But disliking Piers Morgan does not make me hate the Anglo-Welsh.

I remember being told by a bigot-fogey who shopped in the same high street as I did that "he hated the ****ing Jews, and he did not blame the Nazis for wanting to … etc." I asked him if he knew the name of the butcher from whom he had been buying his chops for a decade. No. So I told him. Bloomberg.

XITROEN
Xhree x's and a xhy?

I don't know when this started or why, but in recent years the Citroen-

Peugeot car company has decreed that almost every Xitroen xas to xave a xame xtarting wth "X". Xsara, Xantia, and xo on. Xhich ix xery xilly. Oh, well. One out of xwo is xot bad, for the X-ing French.

Of course, the names are actually pronounced Zsara, Zantia and so on. (See above; X(Z)avier, X(Z)ylophone *et al*.) But then they have managed to go from the merely xilly to the utterly infantile with their Twingo (See Names, Car). Why not Xwingo? Pronounced Zwingo. Xho Xnows?

XMAS
Ten credit card heart-failures and twenty indigestion pills

OK, this should have come up under "C" but I have been saving it up to fill out the "X's" a bit. It actually irritates me when people write "Xmas" instead of "Christmas". I have slapped my wrist.

This year, I wish I could spend the period from 20th to 30th December in a Muslim country. I considered Israel, where I thought I would be safe, but I have learned that most Israelis have adopted Christmas as a festival to go with Hanukah; what the hell – Jesus was a Jew. So, not Israel. Why not just bahumbug myself into a state of anti-social hibernation right here at home and ignore it? Can't, that's why. No escape from the Xmaschlock which comes at us from every quarter starting in mid-August, and builds into a frenzy of disgusting over-indulgence around December 15th.

I don't want presents from anyone any more and I don't want to give presents either. I've done that for enough decades. I once worked out what I had spent over those years on Christmas presents, and it came to thousands of pounds, and I can't remember the figure any more because I had to blot it out before I had hysterics. And I don't think I still own one single item received as a present from well-meaning but misguided members of the family and/or friends. Certainly nothing I use even on an occasional basis. Of course this could partly be explained by the fact that close family and friends, knowing how depressed I get

around oh, no, ho-ho time, give me bottles of alcoholic things which alleviate the mood by causing me to be well lubricated through most of the gift season. By the way; "gift" in German means "poison". Hmmm.

I spent many years in southern-hemisphere places where Christmas was about barbeques in the hot sun, with a beach or a pool nearby, a great deal of well-chilled beer or wine and the bare minimum of Christmas bull. Not always though; in some places, barking ex-Brit colonials in Australia and South Africa for example still serve the full Christmas schtick from turkey to pudding with the temperatures approaching 100ºF. In non-Anglo hot countries, one is spared the torture of foul badly cooked fowl, gut-blocking puddings and horizontal freezing rain. It is still Christmas with all its awful over-indulgence, but very nearly good enough, and one hell of an improvement over the miserable British turkey-and-cash-fest in a blizzard. They do shell-fish, salads, glorious soups and so on.

Oh, but it's all about the kiddiewinkles. It's *their* time, isn't it? Is it hell. If we all got ourselves a few additional brain cells as presents this year, next year we would agree to do stuff which really *is* aimed *only* at children below the age of twelve. After that, spectators only. And that would include the food. No-one would be force-fed Brussels sprouts, because no-one under the age of twenty-five will come within a mile of them, given the choice. No more prison-raised Norfolk turkey, because it's norfolk'n good at all. No more dumb presents for Dad from daft Nana, bought by Mum and paid for by Dad.

X-wise, that's it. Unless you want me to go into XXXX's denoting kisses, which are so irritating. The XX's, not the kisses. No. Let's leave it there.

Y

YACHTS
Three sheets in the jib scuppers

There are two kinds of people: those who love yachting, and those who don't. Within the latter category there is me, because not only do I not love it, I think it's a crap activity, and it terrifies me.

I am not talking *all* boats here – I am talking sailing, because there is something about a really large gin-palace with whale-sized engines that I rather like. It's the huge-masted, billowing fabric, ropes-all-over-the-place things that I cannot handle, both literally and figuratively. Oh, I *have* tried. I went sailing with a family friend who bought a boat and then warbled for weeks about the wind and the silence and the peace and the joy of scudding over the sea powered only by the farts of the gods. On and on he went, until I thought, OK, I have to see what this is about, so I leaped athletically on board, and stood for three seconds on deck while the boat swayed this way and that. Then continued on my course toward the non-tied-up side and gave my lunch to the fish. In the harbour. Before we had sailed an inch in any direction.

Not good, observed my friend. Here's a motion-sickness pill. Go back on shore and let it work, then come back on board, OK? So I did. It worked and so did the side effects, which in my case caused light-headed disconnection and slightly crossed eyes. These notwithstanding, after a suitable hiatus away we went, amid a great deal of incomprehensible and foul-mouthed yelling from my friend who instantly became Captain Horrible and reduced me to a rope-tangled nervous wreck.

We left the harbour, where the water was dead calm, and immediately entered the Roaring Forties, in the English Channel. The boat leaned over until its mast was horizontal, the noise and anger of the heaving sea and the shrieking wind were everything I had imagined that they might be, and I was soaked to the bone in seconds. The motion-sickness pill stopped working, having been designed for moderate motion sickness, not for a stomach going twenty feet vertically and ten horizontally at the same time and then back again.

I was tied down in a cabin somewhere, semi-comatose. Finally taken back home in the back of a van, prostrate. Never to sail again. So, I had a bad experience. I should have done the thrown-off-a-horse thing, and gone sailing again as soon as possible afterwards.

Then I asked myself – why?

YAH'S
Three rahlys and a ... air, hellair!

There aren't many of these outside of London, and London gets what it deserves.

Yah's are usually couples, sometimes married, with the male being a Something Shitty in The City, earning a choking salary and bonus, yah, while the female Pee-ar'ses about in the fashion world, yah, also paid grossly too much for the little her small brain can do. He could well be American or Australian, she is English of the *really* middle middle class, but with pretensions *and* upwardly mobile aspirations.

They probably have two children, one or more, possibly, from previous marriage/s but that's enough, yah, and they were packed orf to boarding school as soon as possible to allow mummeigh and daddeigh/step-daddeigh the time they need to get into the nose-candy and booze, big-time, and go to lorts of parties, yah.

They have at least one Weimariner called something like Walpole, yah. If they could have thought of something beginning with "A" they would have done (they are A-list fixated), but one of their now-ex friends suggested Arsehole. Nort vey funneigh, yah.

They are terminally full of crap. They are devoid of principle, decency, modesty and honesty. But not short of money, the possession of which means that *tout est permis*.

Robert MacGregor

YOBS

Nine ASBOs and a slap on the wrist

Also see "yoof", below, for part of the story.

All yoofs are yobs. But not all yobs are yoofs. It's perfectly possible for yobs to be well past the first flush. Ageing rebels who have forgotten what they were rebelling against, but still like to push their bulging middles against the bar and throw back fourteen shots and twenty pints, then stagger outside, kick in a car door or two, and totter towards the nearest Indian. Restaurant, that its. Unless there happens to be an actual Indian within reach, in which case GBH is a distinct possibility. In the restaurant, the staff steel themselves for the coming terror of flying nan and lobbed gobs of dal, to the accompaniment of a torrent of Anglo-Saxon xenophobic abuse. The staff get their own back by over-charging and, I hope, pissing in the pilsner ordered by these louts.

It has all reached a point where telling them they are yobs is a waste of time. It's like trying to insult lawyers, as I have already explained. Yobs? *Yobs?* Is that the best you can do? "ASBO? Shagging ASBO? Don't make me larf. Me 'n me mates'll drop bricks through your 'ed and the lor'll just larf, narmean?"

Look around any town and you will see the cringe-making absurdity of well-wrinkled faces adorned with ear-studs, eye-rings, nose-bits. The body below the sagging neck is wearing a tank-top (what we used to call a vest) to expose unnecessarily hairy arms on which are tattoos of such blush-making explicitness as to frighten children – and filthy jeans above stained trainers.

I have heard them snarling and shouting at children (often their own). I have seen them peeing copiously against the wall of a local hospice. They have already reached the nadir of human existence, but they are capable of going even lower. Defies the laws of physics, that does, but it's true.

280

YOGA

Two dancing swans, and a camel on a cat

I complained that my back was getting tetchy and stiff. I should have shut my stupid mouth. Before I could say Ayurvedra I had been enrolled in a weekly yoga class, and I suffered all the tortures of the East for two sessions before I gave up and had my back, now in terminal spasm, treated by a physio.

No, I mean, really. It's all very well for lithe young things who can get into these positions by dint of lots of practice while love-making and think it's a wonderfully super turn-on to see the world upside-down

through the amusing little "V" made by the intersection between one's scrotum and one's beloved's left breast, but for mere mortals who do not seek beatific bodily balance, yoga is hell.

Especially when the class is being given by an irrepressible woman of uncertain age, wearing the kind of infuriating smile you would like to wipe from her face if only you could disentangle your knee from your ear and get close enough.

You try for the position she insists on your trying, but you are not built to keep up that kind of balance, so you fall over in an embarrassed heap, your elbow striking the (hard, wooden) floor with a musical "thwock" and your embarrassment deepens as you hear yourself say ★★★★★★★ and ★★★★★★★★★★★ into the kind of breathy silence which only a yoga class can produce.

The overweight man on the mat next to you grunts, grinds his teeth, cracks several joints and then farts with the effort of making himself into the crawling buffalo. Quite tension-relieving, really. Everyone else in the class would have fallen about if we had been able to. But we were coming out of the three-humped snake and into the creeping dragon at the time, and we were stuck.

YOOF
Nine zits and a backwards cap

Been and done some of this, earlier. I am not suggesting that all young people are yoofs. Far from it. There are plenty of attractive, decent, bright, cultured young people if you know where to look, but you have to know. Otherwise, here's what you get:

Male yoof (probably male, hard to tell sometimes) with arse-cleft showing and trouser crotch at knee level, oversized trainers (training to do what?) without laces or socks, beanie crammed over eyes, filthy finger nails, all to the accompaniment of the stink of stale cigarette smoke and beer-sick, walking the Cro-Magnon walk and talking the Cro-Magnon talk.

Female yoof? Lank hair, skirt up to here to show off fat wobbling thighs, just below exposed fat wobbling gut with silverette belly-stud. Cigarette clapped between pierced and curtain-ringed lips, which are mouthing an obscenity to a similar loveliness across the street.

There is a massive problem with teenage pregnancy in Britain. How, I don't understand.

YO-YO'S
Five twisted fingers and a walking dog

Invention of the devil himself. Designed to drive crazy those like me who simply cannot do it, no matter how hard we practice. And who, aside from a very bored and sick adult, wants to practice getting it right with a *yo-yo*, for heaven's sake? Three wobbling drops, four hopeless upwards lunges of the arm to get it to go back up again, but there it dangles, uselessly. Sad image, that, and Freudian to boot. I have watched impossibly small children master the thing, doing tricks – *tricks*, if you please – while I hide my embarrassment by explaining that I suffer from a rare disease. Dehootenholler's Syndrome. Inability to co-ordinate anti-gravitational forces.

I worked once with a company which staged an annual yo-yo competition, complete with logo'd yo-yo's, media campaigns, stage shows, the lot. As I had been responsible for writing some of the radio and TV commercials, I was expected to cram myself into the corporate jacket and have my picture taken along with half a dozen other poltroons, all of us looking like, and supposedly working, yo-yo's. I'm the one second from the left. I am trying to wind the damned thing up again, while everyone else is bouncing theirs around like billy-ho. (Billy Ho is on the far right, if I remember correctly). My tongue is protruding, my face is puce and I am clearly wishing I was dead.

I am reasonably well co-ordinated in just about every other sphere of human activity, and that includes several kinds of sport. But in the

children's game area, there really is something wrong with me. Would that my un-yo-yo-ness were the only problem. I was never able to hoola-hoop either. I cannot use a skipping rope. I cannot whistle. I am an embarrassment to my entire family.

Z

ZEALOTS, RELIGIOUS
Three tries and a conversion

Nothing wrong with good clean wholesome zeal. Shows enthusiasm, energy, commitment, all that. Good stuff. But when zeal is taken as their special preserve by the unhinged and the intolerant, then sprouts, I say. Also okra and snakes.

Odd, isn't it, that zeal is most often coupled with "religious"? Maybe not that odd. There are soldiers of Islam whose zeal takes them to extremes of action including wearing bombs and walking them into crowds of innocents. Equally, history is littered with Christian warriors who were equally indifferent to innocence and whose intolerance, even in the twenty-first century, has become synonymous with their own special brand of terror. I worry about Christianity and Islam which seem more muscular and steely in their zeal and evangelism than all other religions put together. They are the two religions which are bent on recruitment and conversion on a large scale, believing as many of their zealots do that they have not fulfilled their earthly tasks unless they have turned everyone else into Christians or Muslims. Those are mutually exclusive and self-defeating objectives, but they don't seem to notice that. Of course, there are plenty of zealous Jews and Buddhists, plenty of Hindus and Sikhs and Shintoists, all convinced that theirs is the One True Path, but they are by comparison with Christianity and Islam relatively tolerant of other religions.

If there is a God, or if there are Gods, I have to wonder what He, She or They make of all this. For Muslims, Jews and Christians, God is *roughly* the same deity, and He must wonder what to do with Himself on Monday through Thursday, given that He is most *frightfully* busy on Friday, Saturday and Sunday. But that aside, He must quite regularly want to put those zealots who over-egg the spiritual pudding over the celestial knee and give them the most unforgettably cosmic spanking. That might cool their zeal a bit.

ZODIAC, SIGNS OF, THE
Three piles of bull and a nebulous crab

Look about you, next time you are in or near a crowd. Within fifty yards, there are scores of people who were born under the same Zodiac sign as yourself, and the logical extension of that is simple enough. About one twelfth of the entire population of the planet shares your star-sign. Isn't that nice? Sharing is good, and global-villagey. But it's the cornerstone of an edifice built on crap.

Which does not stop people from reading their stars every day and seeing what they, and about half a billion others can expect, *today*, by way of love, money, anger from pissed-off partners, rollocking from the boss, etc., etc., because there is some atavistic comfort in believing that they are connected in a way beyond mystery with the stars and all that is in the heavens. It's entry-level astrology. But it can be taken a lot further.

First, you have to know the exact minute of your birth. (Was that when your head started to emerge, or when the midwife finally extracted your reluctant feet from your mother's grateful body? – this can cover a period of several minutes. Some say it is when you took your first breath, which seems a bit late, birth-wise. Whatever). Then you consult a proper astrologer and get a handle on what stellar and planetary influences came to bear when you were born, and how they would have affected you as you moved through life. Or that's the theory.

In order to do a little research into this, I decided to have a proper astrological chart drawn up, and I came a cropper at the first hurdle. My mother never told me exactly when I was born (feet first for all I know) so I had to *pretend* I knew. But the thing about these chart-wallahs is that, however ridiculous the nonsense they peddle, they are masters of the arts of observation, reading body-language and picking up signs of truthlessness. The astrologer I consulted knew damned well I was chancing my arm and saw me off the premises with the help of his goat and a strange fish-tailed person with a bow and arrow.

But who *does* actually know the moment of their birth? I suppose that babies born in our technologically advantaged new world would have had the moment of birth recorded by a computer, so no problem. But for the rest of us, born before such miracles or born in the bush, no such luck. Therefore the only people who could give an astrologer something to work with constitute a very small percentage of us. And even if I *did* know the exact moment of my birth, the whole thing is back where I started. Millions of babies are born at exactly the same time.

My belief in all this celestial mumbo-jumbo ranks alongside my faith in politicians and my respect for lawyers. And you know where I stand on those.

ZOOS
A thousand caged souls and counting

Animals don't have souls, huh? That's what you think. You are wrong. If humanity is prepared to accept that Stalin, Pol Pot, Saddam and Mugabe have souls, then I am more than content to believe that animals, most of them blameless and pure, have souls too.

No, I do not digress. And this bit is serious. I have a deep loathing for the arrogance of Man who finds nothing wrong in capturing wild animals and condemning them to life imprisonment without any possibility of parole or remission of sentence for good behaviour. For an animal sentenced to zoo, life means life. A murdering shite of a paedophile or a serial rapist can be out and free in twenty years, and usually a lot less.

I have stood before the miserable, dank, dark cell occupied by a

demented leopard, crying my eyes out as I watched this wonderful creature, imprisoned for the delectation of children and adults alike, pace back and forth in a repetitive pattern of insanity born of desperation. Bears, elephants, antelope, apes, every species known to the Earth, subjected to cruel and unusual punishment by mankind. It is almost more than I can write about.

I have had conversations with zoo-keepers and zoo-owners who justify what they do on the basis that almost every zoo these days does behind-the-scenes work in preserving species which are endangered and on the verge of extinction.

I don't care. I would rather see an animal species disappear altogether than have to capture and incarcerate even *one* of them in the interests of saving that species. That, in the immortal phrase, is exactly like fighting for peace or fucking for virginity. Countless thousands have gone naturally into extinction over the Earth's millennia, and in the absence of any assistance by man. And now, given that most of those presently in danger of disappearing are endangered as a direct result of the monstrous mess made by man, we compound the crime by striving officiously to keep them alive in conditions which are little better than a living death. To salve our consciences.

On the epitaph of the human species centuries from now when the Earth has finally had enough of its tormentors and has given itself back to insects and animals, will be written the greatest and most complete condemnation of *homo sapiens*. Not that we invented the H-Bomb, or caused global meltdown, or over-populated every inch of the planet. We created zoos (and circuses) to amuse ourselves.

EPILOGUE

Having said all of the above, I happen to believe that life is not about being consumed by the endless venting of spleen or the examination of endless piles of crap. That would make me a full-time curmudgeon, and I am not. Milk of kindness, sweetness and light, that's me, most of the time. Ask anyone. There is a great deal which sits on the other side of the balance and which I love a very great deal. Same with you, of course. So, here's a leavening of my bread:

- My patient, clever, insightful and beautiful other half (and better half by far) – the inspiration for the good things I do, the hammer of my idiocies and indiscretions and my sharp-eyed critic.
- My three sons – strapping, bright as day, full of love, super-achievers who set the family balance right against my own dilettantism and the focus-free fun-zone in which I seem to have spent so much of my life.
- My car – my elderly, creaking, rusting Mercedes-Benz, which cost me next to nothing and is making up for lost opportunities to devastate my bank-balance by dropping expensive bits all over the place – but when she is behaving she does so in style, at speed, cosseting me in comfort and safety. Say what you like – riding behind a three-pointed star, no matter how old, gives the modest-pocketed motorist a feeling of well-being which no other car can quite manage.
- Cricket, about which I am simply obsessive. I love *everything* about the game, and especially I love the fact that if you missed out on a British up-bringing you cannot *possibly*

291

understand it. OK, English up-bringing. I love watching apoplectic Germans, astonished French and, especially, I love trying to explain it to Americans who absolutely *hate* not understanding things, and whose frustration gets more entertaining with every hopeless explanatory sentence I offer.

- Golf, which I play sporadically and either badly or abysmally badly. That stuff about golf spoiling a pleasant walk in the country? Phooey. Hit something stationary, about the size of a quail's egg, with a long club to which is loosely attached a head equal in size to the bottom three inches of a cricket bat, the whole travelling at over 100 mph and you are a genius. Hit the egg in a straight line, and $E=MC^2$. Make it curve around corners and land where you want it to land, you are Ernie Els or Tiger Woods. Do any of this only occasionally, and the sense of satisfaction beats any other human activity.

- Except, maybe, flying a small plane, and going solo for the first time. Now that's the zenith of sensual experience, beating the best sex you ever had or ever wished you had had, say, on a golf course after having scored a hole in one, as it were. "If God had meant us to fly, he'd have given us wings"? Oh, but He did, He did, whoever He is.

- I love Namibia, which is the best-kept secret on the planet, and no matter how much I rave about it, those on the receiving end still say, "W-e-e-e-e-ll, yeah, but ...", and then make noises about how dangerous Africa is. I'm glad they think so. Namibia's economy depends heavily on tourism and I want it to succeed as a country but not to the extent that I have to meet you and yours wherever I go. It is simply a paradise on earth, and everything costs next to nothing. Until you show up.

- Snow, of which I do not get enough. I live in a corner of the UK where snow falls once in several years, and then disappears like, well, snow off Offa's dike. Snow is the cleanest, most satisfyingly pure substance in the universe. Angels' breast-feathers. Dry white rain, and how good is that?

It makes even the dreariest landscape look beautiful, and turns *any* landscape into heaven, wall-to-wall. And then you can slide about on it or chuck it gently at people you love (with venom at people you don't, sorry, sorry, ha-ha-ha-ha-ha, wasn't aiming at you, are you OK? snigger) while wearing the coolest warm clothes.

- Tessa. Our family mutt. She claims to be part Staffordshire bull-terrier and part whippet but one look and you know that several other mutt-genes got in there too. We rescued her from a family member who, sadly, has Alzheimers, and would feed Tessa, forget she had fed her, feed her *again*, forget that she had fed her, etc., etc., etc. Tessa was a sumo-dog, a McDog, a canine zeppelin on legs. Causing a little girl on a beach near us to say to her father, "Daddy, Daddy, look, a square dog!". Starvation diet, obesity biscuits, a lot more exercise, and now? Slim-line whippet-staffie-person, sleek and fit and lovin' it. And much loved.

I also love cashew nuts, some single malts, crispy bacon and eggs, proper coffee in France and only in France, my resolutely non-Apple PC. Grape Nuts, South African biltong, under-done fresh wild tuna steaks, good curry and rice, plain chocolate. *Any* chocolate. I love *my* mobile phone while I *hate* everyone else's. A good massage, followed by a really hot shower under a properly massive over-head shower rose. Roses, too

Have I been inspired by anyone whose opinions or general approach to life gave me the shove I needed to turn my thoughts into a book? You bet. Michael Bywater (if I could *half-think* like him, I would settle. A quarter. Can't do that either. No-one can). Alan Coren, still the drollest man in Britain with a sense of the absurd so fine it could curl the skin off an egg at a hundred yards – and he makes us laugh through both eye and ear. Bill Bryson. Jeremy Hardy. Sandy Toksvig. Marcus Brigstocke. Clive James when he is not being a super-pretentious *über-kultur-meister.* P J O'Rourke. Life-lighteners, all of them. Did I find any inspiration in Grumpy Old Men (quite entertaining and the best voice-over commentary of all time delivered by Geoffrey Palmer) and G. O. Women (rubbish) on TV? No.

That's it? Far from it. No sooner had I completed the "Z's" than a new list started to present itself at every stop along the alphabetical way. It, and I, could go on and on. Life breeds irritations and annoyances, and it breeds them with enthusiasm and fecundity. But this will have to do for now. A taster for next time round?

- Centralised, Whitehall, everything, our lives controlled by
- Farmers, whingeing, subsidised, chaotic
- French road-signs, impossibility of
- Ross, Jonathan; McGrath, Rory; Carr, Jimmy; Forsyth, Bruce, Clarkson, Jeremy and overexposed Lots Of Others.
- Labels, fruit, glued-on, also on clothing, anything
- Plumbers and electricians, expense of, disorganised, surly
- Political correctness, incorrectness of
- Printing, computer, madness-inducing
- Sunday supplements, pretentious London-centric crapulousness of
- Passport Office, the, comically exact requirements for photographs required by.
- Blair, Tony. Also Cameron, Dave. Also Campbell, Minging; Paisley, Ian; Salmon, Wild; Pyesley, Ian, etc ad nauseam.
- Heads, shaven, to make otherwise ordinary people look like convicts

See? Endless.